Delhi's Education Rev

Delhi's Education Revolution

Teachers, agency and inclusion

Kusha Anand and Marie Lall

First published in 2022 by
UCL Press
University College London
Gower Street
London WC1E 6BT

Available to download free: www.uclpress.co.uk

ISBN: 978-1-80008-140-6 (Hbk.)
ISBN: 978-1-80008-139-0 (Pbk.)
ISBN: 978-1-80008-138-3 (PDF)
ISBN: 978-1-80008-141-3 (ePub)
DOI: https://doi.org/10.14324/111.9781800081383

Contents

Acknowledgements

In 2019 I was asked to lead an Indian research team to look at what works in classrooms across India. Dr Kusha Anand joined me to put together and train this team of young researchers. I am very grateful for her unwavering support throughout the project.

Just before we were to start the fieldwork in March 2020, the pandemic struck, schools shut and borders closed. The data collection had to be moved online and completely reconfigured. My thanks go to the research team – Dr Megha Bali, Dr Aditi Banerji, Dr Samta Jain, Dr Feroz Khan and Dr Anviti Singh, who with Kusha's help interviewed the teachers. I am grateful for the funding received from the Board of Trustees, Modern School, which made this project possible.

While those who collect data are important, this book would not have been possible without the cooperation of 110 teachers from 15 Delhi schools. They shared their experience of the massive changes to education undertaken by the AAP government, their thoughts on what had improved and what was still 'work in progress'. It would have been impossible to understand the reach and importance of the AAP reforms without their contribution. I hope this book gives an accurate reflection of their voices.

Thanks also go to my friends and colleagues Prof. Geetha Nambissan, Prof. Saumen Chattopadhyay, Prof. Nandini Manjrekar and Dr. Shivani Nag, for advice and support during the data collection and writing-up phases. While the pandemic has kept me away from India, I cannot wait to see you all again.

As always, I am grateful for my husband's support. This book is dedicated to our silver wedding anniversary this year.

Marie Lall, January 2022

Organising and collecting data, in the pandemic, from over 100 participants is a huge task that could not have been shouldered by a few. Consequently, there are many people to thank.

Firstly, I would like to thank Professor Marie Lall for daily online meetings, where countless issues on literature review, research training, ethics and online fieldwork were discussed and decisions were reached. This book would not have been possible without the support of Professor Lall, with whom the journey has been shared.

I am also grateful to the research team who specifically supported my decisions in the online fieldwork. Thank you for your advice, ideas, collegiality, and laughs over many months. It was a pleasure to work and learn with you.

I would also like to thank all the participants for bringing intellectual richness to the interviews. Finally, I wish to thank my family in Delhi and my husband for their tireless support and encouragement.

Kusha Anand, January 2022

Dedication

"For my son Kian" (KA)
&
"For our silver anniversary" (ML)

List of figures, table and box

Figures

Table

Box

List of abbreviations

AAP	Aam Aadmi Party
ASER	Annual Status of Education Report
BEd	Bachelor of Education
BEEd	Bachelor of Elementary Education
BJP	Bharatiya Janata Party
CPD	Continuing Professional Development
DElEd	Diploma of Elementary Education
DIET	District Institute of Education and Training
DIU	Data Intelligence Unit
DoE	Directorate of Education
EFA	Education for All
EMC	Entrepreneurship Mindset Curriculum
EWS	Economically Weaker Sections
FT	Female Teacher (used in unique identifiers for interviewees)
GER	Gross Enrolment Ratio
HC	Happiness Curriculum
HoS	Head of School
ICT	Information and communication technology
INC	Indian National Congress
JJC	Jhuggi Jhopri Cluster
JNV	Jawahar Navodaya Vidyalaya
KV	Kendriya Vidyalaya
LCE	Learner-Centred Education

MCD	Municipal Corporation of Delhi
MHRD	Ministry of Human Resource Development
MT	Male Teacher (used in unique identifiers for interviewees)
MTP	Mentor Teacher Programme
NAS	National Achievement Survey
NCERT	National Council of Educational Research and Training
NCFTE	National Curriculum Framework for Teacher Education
NCT	National Capital Territory
NCTE	National Council of Teacher Education
NDP	No Detention Policy
NEP	National Education Policy
NGOs	Non-Governmental Organisations
NIEPA	National Institute of Educational Planning and Administration
NISHTHA	National Initiative for School Heads' and Teachers' Holistic Advancement
NUEPA	National University of Educational Planning and Administration
PTR	Pupil–teacher ratio
RPVV	Rajkiya Pratibha Vikas Vidyalaya
RTE	Right to Education Act
SCERT	State Council for Education Research and Training
SDG	Sustainable Development Goal (UN)
SEQI	School Education Quality Index
SMC	School Management Committee
SSA	Sarva Shiksha Abhiyan
SV	Sarvodaya Vidyalaya
TDCP	Teacher Development Coordinator Programme
TGTs	Trained Graduate Teachers
UDISE	Unified District Information System for Education
UT	Union Territory

1
Setting the scene

Figure 1.1 Map of Delhi

(Source: https://www.shutterstock.com/image-vector/administrative-political-street-map-national-capital-783694765)

This book reviews education policy and practice in Delhi government schools, focusing on six years during which Delhi schools experienced major reforms led by the Aam Aadmi Party (AAP) government. AAP, a party that emerged in India's capital and was at the time of writing only in power in Delhi, was elected in 2015 and reelected in 2020 based on improved public[1] service provision. They had promised to make government schools as good as private provision – a promise they seem to have largely delivered on, according to the media and the wider electorate.

Teachers are at the heart of any changes in education and this is an account of what teachers experienced as part of the reforms affecting their profession and practice, and how far such changes have improved education for all children, no matter from what background. It is based on 110 interviews with government school teachers from 15 high-performing Delhi government schools, in the summer of 2020 (during the Covid-19 pandemic). Interviews were conducted online and resulted in over 700 pages of data. The teachers reviewed the new programmes rolled out by AAP, discussed issues of inclusion and the pressures of achievement and examinations when working in classrooms with often more than 50 students. Apart from a brief account written by Delhi's Education Minister Manish Sisodia, this is the the only narrative that focuses on what happened in Delhi government schools as a result of the education reforms spearheaded by the AAP. The book critically evaluates the AAP government's education policy through the eyes of those most affected by the changes – the teachers. Since their role is critical in delivering quality education, it is pertinent to listen to teachers' voices when discussing education reforms.

The book has two aims. First, to review the education reform process and draw out the lessons learnt for Delhi's government and citizens. The account presented aims to be policy-relevant. Second, to give voice to those most implicated in and affected by the changing landscape of Delhi's education and wider public service reform process. This is important because the voices of teachers are rarely heard. If policymakers (and others) are to understand what has been successful or not, and why, we must look at the effects of reforms on the ground and in the classroom, and how practice has responded.

The voices of participating teachers show that listening to stakeholders is critical for the continued success of Delhi's reform processes. This supports the argument that the AAP reforms have largely been successful in delivering higher-quality and more appropriate education to a broad section of society. However, there have been costs to teachers' lives and practice, and children from the poorest

Table 1.1 Timeline and key events in Delhi politics between 2012 and 2020.

2012	The birth of AAP on 2 October 2012 AAP emerged out of an anticorruption civil society movement – 'India Against Corruption' (IAC)–which was led by social activist Anna Hazare and his associates.
2013	Bijli Paani Andolan It was launched by Arvind Kejriwal in 2012 to protest against inflated power ands water bills. AAP launched an agitation against the ruling Congress government, against its collusion with power distribution companies and the water tanker 'mafia'.
2013	Delhi Assembly Elections: 28/70 In December 2013, just over one year after its formation, AAP contested its first election, for the Delhi Assembly. It performed very well, winning 28 of the 70 seats and emerging as the second-largest party after the Bharatiya Janata Party (BJP) which won 31 seats. Congress, which had been running the Delhi state government for the last 15 years, was pushed down to third place, winning only 8 seats.
2014	Lok Sabha[a] Elections: 4/543 After failing to pass the Jan Lokpal Bill due to a lack of numbers in the Delhi Assembly, the AAP government resigned in February 2014 to seek a fresh and full mandate.
2015	Delhi Assembly Elections a Landslide Victory in Delhi: 67/70 Arvind Kejriwal's second term as Delhi chief minister.
2017	Punjab Assembly Elections: 20/117 AAP emerged as the second-largest party, winning 20 seats in 117-member Punjab Legislative Assembly.
2018	AAP enters into the Rajya Sabha (upper house) with three members. The three AAP MPs raised slogans against the BJP government over the farmers' protests, following which they were asked to withdraw from the house.
2019	Lok Sabha Elections: 1/543
2020	Delhi Assembly Elections: 62/70 Arvind Kejriwal starts third term as Delhi chief minister

[a]The Lok Sabha (or House of the People) is the lower house of parliament.

Note: This table is a summation from data sources and adapted from AAP,[2] Diwakar (2016), Forbes India (2020).

The Aam Aadmi Party and the 2020 Delhi Elections

AAP was born from an anticorruption social movement and politics of activism that started in 2010 (see Box 1.1 below for the main characters of the organisation). At base was the India Against Corruption (IAC) movement, led by Anna Hazare but including known personalities such as Arvind Kejriwal, Manish Sisodia and Kiran Bedi. In 2012 Kejriwal decided to found a political party[3] – although other leaders of the anticorruption movement such as Hazare and Bedi were against that move.

Box 1.1 Main characters in the Aam Aadmi Party

Anna Hazare is a social activist who headed movements to encourage rural development, increase government transparency and inspect and punish official corruption (Britannica, n.d.). The birth of AAP as a political entity is rooted in the legacy of IAC, a people's movement started by Hazare and a 'rainbow' coalition of activists demanding the passage of the Jan Lokpal Bill through parliament to work towards ending corruption (Siddarth et al., 2021). A splinter group from the movement jointly headed by Arvind Kejriwal, Yogendra Yadav, Anand Jha, Prashant Bhushan and Shanti Bhushan decided to form a political party in 2012, naming it after the common man. Hazare opposed the move and stayed away from advocating IAC's entry into direct politics, as he feared that 'elections require huge funds, which will be tough for activists to organise without compromising on their values and it would be difficult to ensure that candidates are not corrupted once elected' (NDTV, 2012 cited in Siddarth et al., 2021).

Arvind Kejriwal formed AAP along with several prominent leaders, most of whom were well known to the public during the IAC movement (Sengupta, 2012). Kejriwal, himself a charismatic figure and author of *Swaraj*, a best-selling book on self-rule, slowly consolidated power and support within AAP. This process came to a head in 2015, when several of the other prominent leaders and party officials were ousted for 'anti-party activities' (Sriram, 2015). This left Kejriwal as the sole remaining public figure associated with the party's IAC origins and as the single head of AAP, 'crystallising' AAP as a personalistic party centred around his leadership (Subrahmaniam, 2015).

Manish Sisodia, deputy chief minister and education minister of Delhi, is a senior leader of AAP and a member of the Political

Affairs Committee. In the past he was a journalist with Zee News and All India Radio, after which he became active in the struggle to get the Right to Information Act passed in parliament and played a key role in founding the Jan Lokpal Movement (Raghunath, 2020). His significant contribution to reforming the education system in Delhi has gained him a reputation as one of the best administrators and educationists in the country. The infrastructural transformation of Delhi government schools, launching curricula such as the Happiness Curriculum, the Entrepreneurship Mindset Curriculum and, more recently, the Deshbhakti Curriculum, the introduction of 'Mission Buniyaad' to improve children's learning in state- and municipal-run schools, sending teachers and principals abroad for training, all were initiatives taken by Sisodia (PTI, 2020).

Atishi Marlena worked as an adviser to Manish Sisodia during the period 2015–18. In her interviews and speeches at seminars in Delhi, Marlena has recounted how at the beginning of the term the problem in Delhi's government schools was even greater than shown by the miserable data in government reports (Sandhu, 2021). With regard to overhauling teacher education, more than the struggle for resources she found the main difficulty was to get the system functional. According to Marlena, the issue with the system is the inertia that comes with being a teacher in a government school (Sandhu, 2021; Dwivedi, 2018). This inertia described by Marlena was found in all government departments across the country and reflects a bureaucratic culture where little work gets done. Marlena also describes facing resistance from teachers regarding training. Therefore, the aim was to change the work culture and environment. In April 2018, Marlena was removed from the post of adviser and the team of volunteers working with her lost their momentum (Dwivedi, 2018).

The Aam Aadmi (common man) Party aimed to attract a wide range of people, not focusing on religion or class. AAP claimed that the common people of India had been unheard and unseen and promised to reverse government accountability, focusing on the Indian Constitution and the Gandhian tenet of *swaraj*. The main source of the party's ideology is Kejriwal's book *Swaraj* [Self-Governance], written in 2012, which stated:

Sixty years ago, India's founding forefathers had a dream for all of us – a dream of an equal and just society where every man, woman and child has the right and privilege to lead a fulfilling and nurturing life, free from all kinds of oppression. This was a dream and a hope over 60 years ago. The Constitution of India and specifically the Preamble to the Constitution of India, define a clear roadmap for the future of our country wherein the common man and woman hold the power to decide their destiny.

Today nobody can say that India has achieved this dream. Before independence the common man was a slave to foreign powers; today he has become a slave of the political system of our country. There is a new master in our country today – the political Neta. This Neta, who asks for our votes during elections, and then forgets us after he wins, this political entity decides the common man's destiny. ... This national demand for a change in the way our political system works has forced our anti-corruption drive to enter the political arena to clean it from the inside. ... The biggest problem facing our democracy today is that no one in government can or wants to hear the common man's basic needs (AAP, n.d.[4]).

AAP made a spectacular entry into politics in 2013 when the party won 28 seats at the Delhi Legislative Assembly elections and went into a short-lived coalition with the Indian National Congress (INC) with Arvind Kejriwal as chief minister. From 1998 until 2013, the city had been governed by the INC's Sheila Dikshit. Burakowski and Iwanek (2017) argue that AAP was victorious because it targeted and often successfully took over the Congress electorate(s). They explain that 'AAP was the first regional party to focus on Delhi-centered issues' (530). However, AAP was originally meant to be an all-India national party. After unsuccessfully contesting national elections in 2014, it refocused its efforts on Delhi and in 2015 won the Delhi Legislative Assembly elections by a landslide, with 67 out of 70 seats. AAP's 2015 manifesto had been presented as a '70-point action plan' and focused almost exclusively on Delhi issues.

AAP has developed an image as a more transparent party, accessible to the people. It has used social media successfully to communicate with ordinary citizens, taking note of their grievances and issues. This has fuelled the party's popularity. Countering the largely communal rhetoric of the Bharatiya Janata Party (BJP)[5] was easy for AAP, which defines itself as secular and left-leaning. It was harder for AAP to set itself apart from the INC, also a secular, left-leaning party. AAP's success has been based on the anticorruption drive as well as its accessibility and focuses on delivering the services citizens want, such as better education and healthcare.

The 2020 elections

The AAP government focused its 2020 election campaign on public services. Arvind Kejriwal, the national convenor of AAP, had promised to construct schools, hospitals and *mohalla* (community) clinics for the people of Delhi, to deliver cheap electricity 'round-the-clock' and water to every household, and build roads (India TV News Desk, 2020). AAP provided subsidised electricity and a free water supply, up to 20,000 litres per household per month. In 2019 the party announced free rides on Delhi Transport Corporation buses, which benefitted women passengers in particular. In addition, AAP developed a network of 1,000 *mohalla* clinics under the neighbourhood health-facility scheme. While dispensing free medicines and check-ups, it also allows for lab tests. The Mohalla Clinic project was complimented by former UN Secretary-General Kofi Annan and former WHO Director-General Dr Gro Harlem Brundtland (India TV News Desk, 2020).

Education, and in particular school fees, was an important part of AAP's campaign. The AAP government has not allowed private unaided schools to arbitrarily hike fees for the last five years (India TV News Desk, 2020). For the development of government schools, AAP worked to improve everything from infrastructure to teacher training and paying more attention to interaction with parents. In its 2020 election manifesto AAP claimed to have added 20,000 new classrooms in over 200 Delhi government schools.

AAP created history a second time, securing a majority of 62 seats in the 2020 Delhi Legislative Assembly elections, soundly defeating Congress and leaving the BJP with only eight seats. Rather than mudslinging, AAP chose to focus on its own 'report card', the work it had done in the last five years. Arvind Kejriwal proclaimed: 'Vote for us if you believe we have worked.'

In its campaign for the Delhi Assembly elections 2020, AAP stressed the development achieved in the previous five years. Its manifesto (AAP, n.d.) reminded voters:

Aam Aadmi Party is perhaps the only political party in independent India that fulfilled a large majority of its election promises made in the last Assembly elections. Some of the prominent promises fulfilled were – world class education system, mohalla clinics, providing free water and subsidised electricity, WiFi, CCTVs and marshals for women['s] safety in public buses.

Given AAP's focus on education reforms, this book aims to describe what those reforms looked like on the ground.

Methodological approach, positionalities and appreciative inquiry

This section outlines how the methodological approach that scaffolds the rest of the chapters in this volume was conceived. It starts with an explanation of the original research study that set out to explore what teachers felt worked in their classrooms. It includes a consideration of the participants and setting, the embedded nature of appreciative inquiry in the data-gathering methods and the use of thematic analysis as a data analysis lens. Both authors are former teachers and have been researching education (over two decades for Marie Lall and over a decade for Kusha Anand) through intense engagement with teachers, as part of fieldwork in India and other South Asian countries. As such, both authors were aware of the generalised critical stance taken by society with regard to teaching and teachers' responsibilities. In general, teachers are blamed for bad results but underappreciated when students do well. Society at large and parents in particular have little understanding of the classroom context and what helps or hinders learning, although some of this has changed due to the Covid-19 crisis in 2020–1, with students having to study from home and parents realising the daily job teachers perform. The authors therefore felt the need for a different approach towards education research and turned to appreciative inquiry as a way of for-mulating their work. Appreciative inquiry has the potential to enrich the body of knowledge in the field by providing new lines of inquiry around change. It occurs as a 'tool for recalibrating the lenses through which we experience a phenomenon' and to generate opportunities for future change constructed on historical and contemporary strengths (Harrison and Hasan, 2013, 67).

Appreciative inquiry, research questions and data-gathering methodology

The original study was aimed at exploring what worked, and why, in Delhi government schools. Previous research has highlighted the defi-ciencies, dysfunctions, issues, requirements and limitations of education in India. Instead of focusing on problems and what is not working and why, this study used appreciative inquiry to discover what worked particularly well and asked teachers to envision what it might be like if the best of what worked occurred more frequently (Preskill and Tzavaras Catsambas, 2006). The appreciative inquiry reflects recognition in the field for strengths-based approaches, which are able to inform research agendas that 'move beyond a deficit, or "fix-it" perspective' (McCuaig and Quennerstedt, 2018, 1). The aim was to 'put under the spotlight' the factors that work for government schools in Delhi, with dialogue being regarded as an important facet of changing organisational culture and bringing about positive change (London et al., 2019). In light of discussions and debates surrounding deficit discourses for decades, this research wanted to explore positive discourses in order to advance understanding in the educational field in challenging circumstances. As Scott and Armstrong (2019) argued, using the appreciative inquiry perspective can be a strategy to disrupt a deficit discourse, replacing it with growth and self-determined change.

The research was conducted with teachers in high-performing schools in Delhi to capture the rich grounded educational experience of the teachers and engage with their positive experiences in practice. In terms of rapport building and engagement in online interviews, the interview questions allowed teachers to open up to possibilities, consider problems and discuss concepts. Given the importance of interviewing in appreciative inquiry (Enright et al., 2014; Hill et al., 2016; Michael, 2005), the research and interview questions were underpinned by the desire to support teachers in their exploration of what worked in their classrooms. Due to the limited literature exploring what works and why in government schools in Delhi (and elsewhere), the application of appreciative inquiry focused mainly on the discovery phase. It allowed for a reflection and discussion on past and/or current success, initiated dialogue to act as a springboard for change and identified future aspirations for practice. The chosen approach allowed participants to reflect and discuss past or current successes.

A common concern with appreciative inquiry is that the approach may ignore the negative experiences of participants (Bushe, 2010; Egan and Lancaster, 2005). While the focus was on appreciating each teacher's practice in line with the aims of the research, the research also attempted to include the 'negative stuff' by asking questions about barriers to successful teaching and learning (van der Haar and Hosking, 2004, 14). To guarantee that there was an emphasis on reflecting and debating past and present success, a mixture of both appreciative inquiry and critical theory was used (Enright et al., 2014; Sargent and Casey, 2021).

The book is based on 110 in-depth teacher interviews across 15 'high-performing' schools, conducted between July and September 2020. The chapter on Covid-19 also draws on data collected in a different survey during the Delhi lockdown (which began in March 2020) with 288 teachers in Delhi government and private schools. The methodological choice of the research was to access teachers in high-performing Delhi-government schools, where things were generally working well. Rather than focusing on a deficit model, the research aimed to start from the premise that good government schools were able to deliver quality education to their students, and that teachers would be able to explain what they felt had worked well, as well as any barriers and challenges faced in the AAP education reform process. In order to identify high-performing or 'positive outlier' ordinary government schools, the only publicly available learning outcome indicators are for achievement in classes V and VIII and dropout/retention rates in class IX across India. Given the objective of the study, achievement scores provided by the National Achievement Survey (NAS) constituted the most relevant data. However, the NAS only compiles achievement scores at the national and state levels, and not at school level.[6] The nonavailability of achievement scores at a granular level is one of the limitations of datasets on school education in India, in general, and of the NAS, in particular. India's other main education dataset is the Unified District Information System for Education (U-DISE). It is the only dataset that provides school-level data. U-DISE aims to reduce 'data gaps', inform district planning and monitor and assess the performance of the school system (NIEPA, 2016). The ambition is to interest a range of stakeholders to engage with these data to increase accountability and improve outcomes. It is but one example of the rapid rise of datafication in education. With the rise of digital data platforms and infrastructures, the politics of digital datafication and their 'heralding' of new forms of governance and surveillance, and new modes of generating knowledge on education, has also elicited critical attention (Piattoeva, 2015; Sellar, 2015; Williamson and Piattoeva, 2019). One of the main ideas behind data platforms like U-DISE is that they encourage transparency and more democratic access to information. They are presented as contributing to reducing hierarchies (Gorur and Dey, 2021, 12). Indeed, decentralisation is one of the key stated principles of India's education system. However, such platforms also end up reinforcing new hierarchies. People at the bottom of the ladder end up mindlessly filling forms, struggling to balance their priorities and doing their best to comply with the data demands of the higher-ups (Aiyar and Bhattacharya, 2015).

picture of the Delhi govt. We depicted schools, and it's working. It was wonderful for us to work with you for the common cause of the betterment of education. Thanks a lot for your cooperation and flexibility (FT14 Hindi SV11).

It was indeed a good feeling to share with you our experiences with students. Thanks so much for giving me a chance to share my feelings (FT7 Mathematics SV1).

The teachers' comments above show that teachers are not routinely asked how they manage the teaching and learning experience in sometimes challenging circumstances. For policymakers and other education stakeholders to understand what is happening in schools, it is imperative to listen to these voices. After all, teachers seem very happy to share what they do and how they live the education experience.

Content

With this chapter having set the scene, Chapter 2 reviews Indian education policy, culminating in the new National Education Policy (NEP) 2020. The RTE Act 2009 has ensured a quantitative expansion of India's education system. However, the key problems in government schools are high-dropout and low-retention rates, as well as issues of poor quality (Bhattacharjee, 2019; Kundu, 2019; Khatua and Chaudhury, 2019). This is underlined by an exodus of the middle and lower-middle classes to private provision (Lall, 2013). Policy changes across governments since the economic reforms in 1991 have culminated in the 2020 NEP. However, to date, national education policies have not successfully improved the quality of Indian government schools. The success of the Delhi government is looked at in light of the national policy priorities.

The chapter then reviews AAP education policies and the improvements they have achieved at the school level. After the landslide victory of AAP in 2015, the party seems to have visibly transformed the ailing school education system of Delhi (Sahoo, 2020). The government allotted new funds to education,[11] introduced new teacher training courses and student learning programmes such as Mission Buniyaad and improved schooling infrastructure and cleaning (Sahoo, 2020; Praja Foundation Report, 2019).

The chapter also introduces Delhi National Capital Region (NCR) – India's capital of over 18 million residents that faces some of the country's biggest economic and educational challenges.

Chapter 3 reviews what teachers want from training. Training is an essential component of Continuing Professional Development (CPD) and has emerged as a critical contributor towards improving the performance of teachers as well as students in Delhi government schools. In light of the wider literature on teacher training in developing countries and as part of reform processes, Chapter 3 first provides an overview of teachers' responses to in-service and preservice training. Without undermining the importance of preservice training, which teaches introductory psychology and lesson planning and provides scope to experience and practise teaching at school, almost all the teachers were critical of its short duration and its overly theoretical approach. Teachers also have diverse opinions regarding preservice and in-service training, with more importance given to in-service training, as it is related to subject-specific and policy-specific issues and is often need-based. More than half of the teachers interviewed were positive about in-service training. This section will then provide insights into their training needs. The chapter will then highlight the impact of a few capacity-building programmes such as the Mentor Teacher Programme (MTP) and Teacher Development Coordinator Programme (TDCP) as well as the teacher-training programme in Singapore, initiated by the AAP government.

Chapter 4 starts by defining teacher agency – a concept that has emerged in recent literature as an alternative means of understanding how teachers might enact practice and engage with policy (Priestley and Biesta, 2013; Priestley et al., 2015). In India, Poonam Batra has written extensively about teacher agency (2005; 2006; 2011; 2014), which she recognises as the most unaddressed issue in Indian education reform. Batra's work sets the framework for the rest of the chapter.

From the interviews it emerged that teachers' professional agency is nurtured by the relationship with headteachers, which helps to build creative, curious and participative learning environments. The data also demonstrated that the quality of dyadic relationships between headteachers and teachers influences teacher agency. This helped teachers design and practise innovative teaching methods and transform theoretical knowledge into classroom teaching practices, school enhancement and self-development. The autonomy and discretion of teachers, for using innovative techniques, are also negotiated in the classrooms to facilitate a conducive learning environment for students.

the EFA 2014 report, one of the key challenges facing the Indian education system is the quality-related deficiencies at each stage, resulting in an unsatisfactory level of student learning. The phenomenon of underachievement among pupils depicts the quality-related deficiencies of the education system (Jain and Prasad, 2018, 12). Research shows that children do not have school-ready competencies in cognition and language, revealing the poor quality of the curriculum, deficiencies of the teaching-learning process and lack of quality teachers. If the foundation for children at school is weak, the possibilities for later educational interventions are reduced. Therefore, importantly, 'appropriate interventions need to be formulated and implemented to remove quality-related deficiencies at school-level' (Jain and Prasad, 2018, 12) and the education facilities should be equal for all, as quality education is the right of every student (Jain and Prasad, 2018).

This chapter gives the education policy and political background for the whole volume. While the book focuses on Delhi, it is important to understand Indian education policy as a broader context for what happened in the Indian capital and how education policy has been affected by wider national political priorities. The chapter therefore broadly reviews Indian education policy priorities including the politicisation of textbooks that have in effect contributed to the education crisis the country is facing. This is underpinned by an exodus of the middle and lower-middle classes to private provision (Lall, 2013). Policy changes across governments since the economic reforms in 1991 have culminated in the NEP of 2020. However, to date, national education policies have not successfully improved the quality of Indian government schools. Certain states, mostly in the south, have done better than those in the north. Recent reforms in Delhi have proved a notable exception. The chapter will also introduce Delhi NCR – India's capital of over 18 million residents which faces some of India's biggest economic and educational challenges.

The success of the Delhi education system run by the AAP government is examined in light of the national policy priorities. After the landslide victory of AAP in 2015, AAP seems to have visibly transformed Delhi's ailing school education system (Sahoo, 2020). The government allotted new funds to education, introduced new teacher-training courses and student learning programmes such as Mission Buniyaad and improved schooling infrastructure and cleaning (Sahoo, 2020; Praja Foundation Report, 2019; Lall et al., 2020). Online survey results from 2020 revealed that due to an improvement in the standard of education of Delhi government schools, 61 per cent of the respondents from

70 constituencies of Delhi prefer sending their children to government schools rather than private ones. Further, 82 per cent of respondents said that the quality of education and related facilities has been enhanced (Hindustan Times, 2020). There are also critical voices. According to the India DIU, which scanned the reports relating to the 70 promises made by the AAP manifesto in 2015, AAP fulfilled three out of a total of seven education-sector-related promises made in the manifesto.[1]

Indian education policy from Nehru to today

Following independence in 1947, Indian school curricula were imbued with inclusiveness and emphasis on the fact that India's different communities could live peacefully side-by-side as one nation. Drawing from Nehru's vision, and articulating most of his key themes, the Kothari Commission (1964–6) was set up to formulate a coherent education policy for India. According to the Commission, Education was intended to increase productivity, develop social and national unity, consolidate democracy, modernise the country and develop social, moral and spiritual values (Sharma, 2002). To achieve this, the main pillar of Indian education policy was to be free and compulsory education for all children up to the age of 14. The commission stated: 'One of the important social objectives of education is to equalize opportunities, enabling the backward or underprivileged classes and individuals to use education as a lever for the improvement of their condition' (Kothari Commission, 1964, 66, cited in Thamarasseri, 2008). Other features included the development of languages (Hindi, Sanskrit, regional languages and the three-language formula), equality of educational opportunities (regional, tribal and gender imbalances to be addressed) and the development and prioritisation of scientific education and research. India's curriculum had historically prioritised the study of mathematics and science rather than social sciences or arts. This was subsequently actively promoted, since the Kothari Commission argued that India's developmental needs were better met by engineers and scientists than historians.

Subsequent Indian governments regarded education policy as a crucial part of their development agenda. Emphasis has traditionally been placed on universality, pluralism and secularism rather than quality and excellence. Education has been a prime focus in India's development plans ever since independence. It is included as a part of the Directive Principles of State Policy in the Constitution, which states that 'the State shall endeavour to provide within a period of ten years from the commencement of this Constitution, for free and compulsory education for all children until they complete the age of fourteen years' (Article 21A, Constitution of India).[2] India's education infrastructure has developed some of the best higher-education institutions in the world (such as the Indian Institutes of Technology and Indian Institutes of Management[3]), but at the other end of the scale severe problems have persisted with basic education provision in rural and tribal areas (Nambissan, 2006).

In 1986 Rajiv Gandhi announced the New Education Policy (NEP) intended to prepare India for the twenty-first century. The policy emphasised the need for change: 'Education in India stands at the crossroads today. Neither normal linear expansion nor the existing pace and nature of improvement can meet the needs of the situation' (paragraph 1.9, NEP, cited in Shukla, 1988, 2). According to the NEP, the goals set out by the Kothari Commission in the 1960s had largely been achieved: more than 90 per cent of the country's rural population were within a kilometre of schooling facilities and a common education structure had been adopted by most states. How far these objectives had actually been met is up for discussion, as the Kothari Commission had aimed at universal primary education, which India had not achieved. The prioritisation of science and mathematics had also been effective. However, change was required to increase financial and organisational support for the education system, to tackle problems of access and quality. The problem with literacy levels also remained, as, despite the increased number of schools, literacy levels differed widely from state to state. The NEP was intended to raise education standards and increase access to education. At the same time, it would safeguard the values of secularism, socialism and equality that had been promoted since independence. To this end, the NEP stated that the government would seek financial support from the private sector to complement government funds. The central government also declared that it would accept a wider responsibility to enforce 'the national and integrative character of education, to maintain quality and standards' (Shukla, 1988, 6). The states, however, retained a significant role, particularly in relation to the curriculum. The key legacy of the 1986 policy was the start of overt privatisation. While private schools already existed, government education was seen as the main provision (Kingdon, 2017).

Economic reforms and post-reform education

In 1991 India embarked on major nation- and sector-wide economic reforms.[4] Early in 1992, when education policy was reexamined, the NEP was regarded as a sound way forward for India's education system, although some targets were recast and some reformulations were undertaken in relation to adult and elementary education (Ram and Sharma, 1995). The new emphasis in 1992 was on the expansion of secondary education, while the focus on education for minorities and women continued. According to Corbridge et al. (2005, 80), India had 'failed lamentably' to meet its performance targets, and the reforms made this all too visible. Sound policy goals (regarding access and literacy) and the effect on the ground of these policies were not congruent in many Indian states.[5] In the 1990s, government education provision needed to be expanded, resulting in quality being traded off for quantity, as new institutions were opened with declining allocations being spread thinly. Equity was also sacrificed, as the budget allocations for scholarships and welfare programmes 'waned' quickly (Tilak, 2018). The revised NEP (1992) suggested an expansion of the scope of Operation Blackboard to provide three reasonably large rooms and three teachers in every primary school and to extend the scheme to the upper-primary level (Tilak, 2018). However, in 1993, when the All-India Educational Survey (NCERT, 1997–8) was conducted, more than 20,000 primary schools in rural India, 17.1 per cent of the schools, were still found to be running in open space, nearly 2,000 in tents, 16,000 in 'thatched' huts and another 48,000 in *kutcha* (makeshift) buildings (NCERT, 2009; Tilak, 2018, 122). Most of these schools remained closed during rainy days as well as on severe winter and summer days (Tilak, 2018). With respect to the provision of ancillary facilities, the overall situation was unsatisfactory – for example, more than 60 per cent of the primary schools and 40 per cent of the upper-primary schools did not have drinking-water facilities (Tilak, 2018, 123).

The new education agenda looked at private provision to remedy the learning deficit. The required budget cuts, agreed to as part of the structural adjustment programme, did not allow the government to increase public spending on education to the level required to radically reform the system (Tilak, 2018).[6] It was argued that the expansion of education through the private and not-for-profit sectors would in turn allow for parental choice, congruent with the neoliberal reform policies on which the government had embarked. Private provision was not new, as the NEP agreed under Rajiv Gandhi had already started to encourage the growth of that sector. However, the post-1991 government shifted its focus from the allocation of public resources to mobilising non-governmental resources, then to alternative methods of cost recovery and the privatisation of education. Private institutions began to increase in number, at the cost of the growth of public institutions. This was broadly in line with the new economic policies, adopted by the government from the beginning of the 1990s, that favour privatisation and 'down-sizing' of the public system (Tilak, 2018).

Field surveys in the 1990s also began to report a surge in parental demand for private education, and this was accompanied by a new phenomenon: small fee-charging private schools (often referred to as 'low cost') emerged for the less privileged (De et al., 2005, 131–3). With the dwindling quality of government provision, it appeared that low-income groups were not only desiring education but were willing to pay for it (Tooley et al., 2010).[7] The new phenomenon was welcomed by education bureaucrats, since the government system was struggling with both access and retention issues, and many felt that the new private schools could be allies in achieving the universalisation of elementary education (De et al., 2005). Enrolment in private unaided schools thus rose most sharply following the economic liberalisation that raised incomes in the early nineties (Venkatanarayanan, 2015). In 1993–4 enrolment in the private upper-primary schools increased in proportion from 11 to 22 per cent (Tilak, 2018, 527).[8] Between 1999 and 2003, studies (PROBE Team, 1999; Tooley and Dixon, 2003) reported a 'burgeoning' sector of low-cost private schools. At the same time, the rise of private schools led to inequalities in differentiated schools (which use a variety of techniques to meet the needs if students with a wide range of abilities) and stratified schools (whose student bases vary in terms of social and economic standing) (Mehendale and Mukhopadhyay, 2020).

Béteille (2001) has argued that the middle classes have long supported differentiated schooling,[9] which would equip their children with better credentials, thereby giving them an edge when seeking employment. Middle-class parents had previously supplemented public schooling with tuition and made sure their children accessed higher education. One could argue that before the emergence of so many private schools, the main differentiating factor between the social classes was the length of schooling and whether or not a person went to university.[10] With the middle classes choosing to buy out, the poorer sections of society had no option but to take whatever the state provided. This led to a trend in deteriorating public education institutions at the school level, which meant that more and more aspired to leave the system, creating a vicious circle (Nambissan, 2006; Nambissan and Ball, cited in Lall and Nambissan, 2011, p.207).

The idea of 'quality' of education being related to learning outcomes, which found a place in Indian policy documents as early as 1986 (Sarangapani, 2010). The explicit operationalisation of 'quality' as measurable learning outcomes came to occupy the centre stage of policy and public concern with the publication of the Annual Status of Education Survey and the corresponding Annual Status of Education Reports (ASER), which started in 2005. Student academic learning scores as the 'outcomes' or indicators of quality, and ASER gathers information on other variables, providing hypotheses on their relationships to quality (Kumar and Sarangapani, 2004; Sarangapani, 2010; Mukhopadhyay and Sarangapani, 2018). Overall, the idea of 'outcomes as quality' and the concepts of efficiency and accountability have formed the basis of a new discursive regime, which is most significantly visible in the policy discourses that have veered towards the efficacy of the private (or the market) over the state in the provisioning of – and gradually even the financing of – school education (Mukhopadhyay and Sarangapani, 2018).

A related concept that has been influential in shaping the new discursive regime of quality is that of 'accountability', which comes to the foreground of educational discourse through a number of approaches, most of which engages with education in the Global North.[11] In India one strand of research has emphasised the strong interlinkages between the education system, especially teachers, and the political system in different Indian states (Béteille, 2009; Bhattacharya, 2001; Kingdon and Muzammil, 2013). The discursive framing of 'accountability' here has come to be one that stresses the need for policy solutions to address the problem of 'unaccountable' government school teachers who have been responsible for the poor quality of learning in the government schools, especially when compared to the private schools (Mukhopadhyay and Sarangapani, 2018). Besides accountability, the concept of 'efficiency' underlying the 'outcomes as quality' idea has received prominence, with this approach to quality being used to compare the provisioning and outcomes of state schools versus private schools in a number of studies. These studies claim that private schools, even unrecognised low-fee private schools, provide better inputs in terms of both basic infrastructure facilities such as toilets and desks and teaching-learning processes such as teachers' presence and time-on-task (Goyal, 2009; Kingdon and Teal, 2007; Muralidharan and Kremer, 2006; Tooley and Dixon, 2006). The concepts of 'efficiency' and 'accountability' underline the importance of 'value-for-money' in the delivery of public services such as education and are reflected in a number of India-wide and Delhi government policy texts. The centrality of the efficiency of the 'private' over 'public' (government) is evident in the policy solutions being proposed – not least with the Delhi government promising to make its government schools as good as private ones (Mukhopadhyay and Sarangapani, 2018). However, education 'quality' is not the only issue tackled by India's central and state governments. Much of what has been written about India's education reforms centres on the school textbooks – as discussed below.

Background to textbook revisions in India

A key issue in Indian education policy has been the politics of textbook content. In India, education is a responsibility of both central and regional government, meaning that different types of textbooks can coexist across different states, depending on which political party is in power and regardless of the government in Delhi. At the centre, the National Council of Educational Research and Training (NCERT) is a key institution, as it defines the official guidelines for curricular development and develops model textbooks within different school subjects (Flåten, 2017). The NCERT also develops curriculum frameworks which are used in schools across India, affiliated to the Central Board of Secondary Education (CBSE) (Naseem and Stöber, 2014). It is thus in charge of determining curriculum standards for the whole of India. Over the past few decades, the NCERT textbooks have been revised as successive political parties have come to power at the centre (Lall, 2008; Lall and Anand, forthcoming 2022).

The textbooks that had been conceived in the 1960s and 1970s were political instruments to help construct a united India in the Nehruvian tradition; the elites accepted that for India to be united, it needed to be secular (Guichard, 2013). In the late 1990s, the NCERT textbooks published in the early 1980s were criticised as 'Marxist', and between 2002 and 2004 they were replaced by new textbooks under the Hindu nationalist BJP-led NDA government (Lall, 2008; Guichard, 2010). The rise of the BJP to political power at the centre as part of the NDA coalition in 1998–9 meant an end to the separation of religion and education in government schools.[12] Under the BJP's logic of majoritarianism, the Indian nation had to be reconceptualised as Hindu (Lall, 2008; Lall and Anand, forthcoming 2022).

In 2000 the NCERT published the National Curriculum Framework (NCF) for school education based on the Hindutva ideological agenda under the slogan 'Indianise, nationalise and spiritualise'. The policy engendered a massive textbook revision that justified an anti-minority outlook. The BJP appointed scholars to rewrite the history textbooks because the old textbooks were secular (as well as out of date) and did not focus on Hindu achievements (Guichard, 2010). The main product of history, as a part of education, was highlighted as the development of the 'national spirit' and 'national consciousness' by instigating pride among the youngest generations regarding India's past or distinctive religio-philosophical ethos, presented as Hindu (Lall, 2008, 176).

The textbook revisions were contested by a petition to the Supreme Court, brought by three activists who argued that the NCERT had not followed the correct procedures of consultation with the states and that it was attempting to introduce religious teaching, which is forbidden by the Constitution. However, the petition was rejected by the Supreme Court.[13] The Congress-led United Progressive Alliance (UPA)[14] government that came to power in 2004 had to deal with the inherent problems in the education system as well as needing to reverse the Hindutva-inspired changes introduced by the NDA. Only a few weeks after the elections, on 12 June, the new government ordered a panel of historians to be constituted to advise on the issues of communalisation and inadequacies of the history textbooks of the NCERT. The panel acknowledged that though there are different interpretations with regard to historical facts, at a school level, history teaching should reflect the current scholarly consensus. New post-2004 NCERT textbooks were produced, but not adopted universally. Delhi, for example, developed its own textbooks under the Congress leadership of Chief Minister Sheila Dikshit.[15] Then, when the Congress-led coalition introduced the third set of textbooks, ministers of the states where the BJP was in power refused to accept the new curriculum and the change of textbooks. Notwithstanding these cases of resistance, the NCERT textbooks have symbolic importance, as material coming from a central institution: they constitute the official discourse and enjoy greater visibility and credibility than textbooks produced by the State Textbook Boards (Guichard, 2010).

In 2014 the BJP came back to power, with Prime Minister Narendra Modi winning an absolute majority. Between 2014 and 2016 the Ministry of Human Resource Development (MHRD) was occupied by officials who routinely consulted influential members of the Rashtriya Swayamsevak

Sangh (RSS, a Hindu nationalist organisation). Due to these connections right at the top of the MHRD, the Sangh Parivar[16] ('RSS family') was able to push for significant changes to the school textbooks that had been drafted during the Congress period after 2004 to return to a pro-Hindutva agenda in the name of cultural nationalism (Sharma, 2016). Textbooks in Delhi, however, were set by the AAP-led government and did not follow the Hindutva agenda. AAP claims to be secular and inclusive, and as such the curricular and textbook revisions in Delhi have to be seen as an opposing act to the BJP's national Hindutva agenda.

The section above has shown how education is politicised, as curricula and the content of textbooks have been redrafted across India. Delhi became a notable exception, replacing the Hindutva-inspired books just four years after they were rolled out. This book engages less with the politics of curricular and textbook content (covered in Lall and Anand, forthcoming 2022) and more with the reforms pertaining to access, quality and equality across Delhi schools.

Key education reforms – access and quality across India

Sarva Shiksha Abhiyan and the Right of Children to Free and Compulsory Education Act 2009

In the last two decades India has put in place policies and legislation to improve the quality of elementary education and access to it. SSA[17] has been operational since 2000 and aims to universalise elementary education in India. The SSA Framework 'provides a broad outline of approaches and implementation strategies, within which States can frame more detailed guidelines keeping in view their specific social, economic and institutional contexts' (Government of India, 2012, 7). In 2009 the Rashtriya Madhyamik Shiksha Abhiyan scheme was launched to enhance access to secondary education and improve its quality (Government of India, 2012).

India passed the RTE Act into law in 2009. The legislation was made to achieve the vision of Article 21A, which was inserted into the Constitution of India by the Constitution (Eighty-Sixth Amendment) Act 2002, which stated, 'The State shall provide free and compulsory education to all children of the age six to 14 years in such a manner as the state may, by law, determine' (Government of India, 2012, 7). For the first time, there was now a constitutional right to education that included regulations for pupil–teacher ratios (PTRs), public school infrastructure, education funding and private school enrolment (Tilak, 2016). It also imposed the reservation of 25 per cent of seats in private schools for the economically weaker sector.

SSA and the RTE Act have successfully managed to increase enrolment in the upper-primary level (classes VI–VIII), but not achievement (Bhattacharjee, 2019). Nationally, between 2009 and 2016, the number of students in the upper-primary level increased by 19.4 per cent. According to U-DISE data, the Gross Enrolment Ratio (GER) in 2016–17 for classes I–V was at 95.1 per cent (Government of India, 2019, 63). However, the data for later classes indicates some serious issues in retaining children in the schooling system. The GER for classes VI–VIII was 90.7 per cent, while for classes XI–XII it was only 79.3 per cent and 51.3 per cent, respectively, indicating that a significant proportion of enrolled students begin to drop out after class V and especially after class VIII. In absolute numbers, an estimated 6.2 crore (62 million) children of school age (between six and 18 years) were out of school in 2015. According to U-DISE, in 2018–19 the GER in elementary and secondary were 91.64 per cent and 79.55 per cent, respectively (Government of India, 2020[18]). There are also massive discrepancies between states. For instance, in the age group of six to 10 years the enrolment was more than 97 per cent in Odisha but less than 80 per cent in Andhra Pradesh (Kundu, 2019). While the states of Bihar, Uttar Pradesh and Rajasthan have seen a steady increase in their enrolment numbers in the upper-primary section, Madhya Pradesh, Assam and West Bengal saw a significant decrease in the same period, due to a lack of access to basic sanitation facilities (Bhattacharjee, 2019).

One of the most important contributors to higher enrolment is sanitation; there is a positive correlation between access to basic sanitation facilities and higher enrolment rates. This has led to an increase in female student enrolment as well as female teacher retention (Kundu, 2019). As sanitation and hygiene improved there was a decrease in sick days and therefore students and teachers stayed in school. Female teachers are also more likely to be present in schools with clean toilets (Kundu, 2019). In this regard, government programmes such as 'Clean India: Clean Schools', which focus on adequate water, sanitation facilities and the overall hygiene of a school, have contributed to better implementation of the RTE (Kundu, 2019).

While SSA and RTE had a positive effect on state-school infrastructure and teacher absence rates, they did not improve literacy and numeracy skills for students in government schools due to teaching quality, curricula or pedagogical methods, as shown in ASER surveys in 2013 (Bhat, 2017; Muralidharan and Sundararaman, 2013; Mukerji and Walton, 2016) – issues that will be discussed further below. The issue of education quality was picked up again in India's 12th Five-Year Plan (2012–17), which promised to 'place the greatest emphasis on improving learning outcomes at all levels' (Government of India, 2013, 21). The MHRD also backed the drive to raise the standards of learning, as seen in the emphasis given in its Joint Review Mission report of July 2012 to measuring learning and to ensuring good learning outcomes. While the solutions typically sought for remedying low achievement and for achieving quality involve increasing the physical resources of schools, raising teacher–pupil ratio, improving teacher certification and increasing teacher salaries, the failure of such input-based approaches is well documented internationally (Altinok and Kingdon, 2012; Glewwe, 2002; Hanushek and Woessmann, 2011).

Problems in and with government schools – focusing the blame on teachers

There is a significant variance in the quality of public education across institutions and states. The main issues with public education are clustered at community and school levels, as detailed below. It is because of this India-wide backdrop that AAP engendered the Delhi education reforms, focusing its message on how government schools can be made to deliver the same quality education as private schools.

Parental abandonment of government schools has played a key part in the reduction of quality in such schools. As mentioned above, increased private schooling has followed the 1991 economic reforms. Parents perceive the quality of private education as better than public education (Kingdon, 2007). Although private education is mostly preferred in urban regions, public education remains the more affordable option for most. The proportion of students in private schools in the urban areas of many states in India is higher than in any developed country (Shah and Veetil, 2006, 3). Studies conducted in Delhi (Ohara, 2012), Haryana, Uttar Pradesh, a Rajasthan, Calcutta (Nambissan, 2003) and Andhra Pradesh (Woodhead et al. 2013) report that low-fee private schools are growing at an exponential rate. The official data presented shows a steep growth of private schooling and a corresponding rapid shrinkage in public schooling in Uttar Pradesh, suggesting parental abandonment of government schools (Lall, 2013; Kingdon, 2017). While this used to be a middle-class phenomenon, today all classes and sections of society look for private alternatives. Research shows that the parental choice of private schools is mainly due to perceived quality and an inadequate provision of government schools (Alderman et al., 2001; Heyneman and Stern, 2014; Kingdon, 2007; Tooley and Dixon, 2006). A particular aspect of the rise of private education is the growing demand for English-medium schools. In India it has been suggested that 'the English educated form a caste by themselves' (Dakin et al., 1968, 24). There is a great desire among disadvantaged and marginalised communities to learn English, and they are acutely aware of its economic importance (Markee, 2002). There is also increasing evidence to show that it is the medium of instruction and its implications for children's future roles in society that dominate the schooling choices of parents, rather than information about the quality of a school (Munshi and Rosenzweig, 2006). Miller (2005), in the context of Delhi, notes that over the last decade there has been a growth of private schools, often referred to as 'teaching shops', aimed at the urban poor. A key selling point is that they are English medium. One of the ways in which the English-medium nature of the school is conveyed is by using 'public school' in their name. Jeffery et al. (2007, 54) describe how in Bijnor city some schools, including a Catholic convent school, appeal to a 'modern constituency' by including 'public school' in their names.

Higher teacher absenteeism in government schools (Kingdon, 2007; Kremer and Muralidharan, 2008) than in private schools (Mehrotra and Panchamukhi, 2006) and other factors, such as better teaching activity (Härmä, 2009; Singh and Sarkar, 2012; Tooley and Dixon, 2006), lower pupil–teacher ratio (Goyal and Pandey, 2009; Mehrotra and Panchamukhi, 2006) and higher pupil test scores (Goyal and Pandey, 2009). The abandonment of government schools has led to a decline in quality. Those who use government provision generally do so because they cannot afford the private alternative.

However, the private alternative is still costly to the government. More than one-fifth of the government expenditure on elementary education goes on subsidies to private schools at the elementary level (Tilak, 2018). This proportion is nearly 50 per cent at the secondary level. Huge subsidies of this kind to private schools are considered to be affordable for government education institutions, and so private schools prosper, to the detriment of government schools (Tilak, 2004). Government workers can enrol their children in private schools and have fees reimbursed in the same way as the 25 per cent of pupils who are from Economically Weaker Sections (EWS).[19] So unaided private schools are heavily subsidised by the state, at the expense of government schools (Tilak, 2018).

Teacher absenteeism is frequently seen as the most critical issue plaguing the government school system. It is now widely used as a governance indicator for education in India, as it is also directly associated with students' learning outcomes (ASER, 2018). Studies of teacher absenteeism and of teachers' time-on-task have attempted to measure teacher effort in India (Kremer et al., 2005; Sankar, 2007), and studies of teacher pay and professional development have considered ways to improve that effort, for instance through performance-related pay (Duflo et al., 2012; Muralidharan and Kremer, 2006; Kingdon and Muzammil, 2013) and performance-related promotion (Kingdon and Muzammil, 2013). Muralidharan and Sundararaman (2013) emphasise that government school teachers tend to spend significantly more time on administrative work than private school teachers. Other factors that impact teacher absenteeism and accountability include poorly developed systems of teacher preparation, recruitment and deployment; inadequate institutional mechanisms for teacher mentoring and support; and inadequate working conditions for teachers in terms of alignment to essential teaching-learning tasks (Azim Premji Foundation, 2017).

Béteille (2009) explains the relationship between politicians and teachers – and its impact on teacher absenteeism – as one of political exchange. Politicians have used discretionary powers, given in transfer rules for teachers, as a patronage opportunity for granting the latter their desired postings; in return, teachers have provided politicians with electoral support. Béteille's analysis displays a richness and complexity, especially in the understanding of strategic links between teachers and politicians, mediated through informal offices of the middleman (known as a *dalal*) and power hierarchies, and is based on sources that include interviews and newspaper reports (Béteille, 2009, 83–5). Using the concepts of formal political economy and rational choice, a series of dilemmas mark the working of existing policies: teacher accountability that cannot be enforced due to teacher–politician linkages, patronage opportunities and the political power of unions. Educational decentralisation, teacher absenteeism and the appointing of para-teachers are seen as ways of breaking the centralised power of teachers (Priyam, 2015).

However, teachers are key to the success of any education reform process, and while they might not receive the necessary structural support to do their jobs well, they are often blamed when achievement levels drop. Over the last decade, the role of Indian government school teachers has been questioned because of the deteriorating levels in children's learning (Kundu, 2019). The PISA (Programme for International Student Assessment) results for 2009–10[20] put India in 72nd position out of the 73 countries that participated in student assessments in mathematics, reading and science (Singh and Sarkar, 2012). Public debates on the quality of education have invariably led to how teachers can be made accountable and what the government should do to ensure that teachers attend school and teach children (Ramachandran, 2005; Singh and Sarkar, 2012).

In order to cope with the shortage of teachers in government schools there has been a nationwide practice of recruiting para-teachers with lower academic and no professional qualifications to serve in the formal public para-school classrooms on a contract basis (Dey and Bandyopadhyay, 2019). The practice of recruiting untrained and academically underqualified teachers – referred to either as 'para-teachers' or 'contract teachers' – to serve in the formal elementary schools of the country has been widespread since the 1990s as part of the Universal Primary Education Programme of the Government of India (Dey and Bandyopadhyay, 2019). The rationale for the appointment of contract teachers ranges from cost-effectiveness (Kingdon and Sipahimalani-Rao, 2010) to increasing access to education in remote, underserved areas (Govinda and Josephine, 2004; Robinson and Gauri, 2010). Though the role of contract teachers is not restricted to remote villages, most of them are assigned to remote location: the NUEPA 2007–8 report shows that 92 per cent of all contract teachers are appointed in rural areas (NUEPA, 2010). Their appointment has also been actively supported by international agencies, primarily the World Bank, as a key reform intended to make teachers more 'accountable to performance' (Bruns et al., 2011, 10). Researchers have raised serious concerns about para or contract teachers' capability to teach in the country's elementary schools and warned against the deprofessionalisation of the teaching cadre (Dey and Bandyopadhyay, 2019).

One key issue that is bound to hinder teachers' performance is their lack of autonomy. In today's education system, much of what a teacher does in the classroom is controlled and micromanaged from above (by the headteachers and the state). The syllabus is prescribed down to what has to be taught every week. Instructions are issued about what has to be tested and when, what kind of notebooks must be maintained by students, what kind of assignments are to be given to students, as well as what kind of questions may be asked in the class (Gupta and Ahmad, 2016). When teachers with some initiative try out something different, they are more likely to be ignored or penalised than commended. If they continue, they are 'derided' by the authorities. Accountability is confused with the idea of surveillance. In the absence of any positive or creative endeavour to create a meaningful and enriching work culture that would support and encourage teachers to give their best, there are moves towards greater control. Monitoring and surveillance of teachers have taken many forms, from the use of technology in biometrics and CCTV to the often unwarranted intervention by supervisory agencies in classroom practices (Gupta and Ahmad, 2016). The NEP discussion document, circulated in April 2015, posed the question: 'How can technology be used to ensure the punctuality of teachers?' The Delhi government has already initiated its 'plans to install CCTV cameras in all classrooms at all government schools' (The Hindu, 2015, cited in Gupta and Ahmad, 2016). These orders fetishise technology, criminalise all teachers and create a milieu far removed from one that upholds the ethics of freedom of expression and fearlessness. With these interventions, teachers experience shrinking academic authority and autonomy and face growing scepticism at all levels – on the part of the authorities and the larger public, as well as self-doubt – over their role in the school (Gupta and Ahmad, 2016). Despite the prevalent discourse that paints a bleak picture of the qualities and motivations of teachers in the state-school system, conversations with the teachers reveal that many are committed to the ideals of education and want to do their best for the students under their care (Gupta and Ahmad, 2016). For more on this, see Chapter 4.

Beyond teachers, classroom practices are also key in improving the quality of teaching and learning. For over two decades India's government has been attempting to shift its classrooms towards Learner-Centred Education (LCE), which is seen as a model for potentially addressing the challenges it continues to face in rote-based pedagogy, low learning levels and discriminatory practices in many government schools (Ramachandran and Naorem, 2013; ASER, 2015). However, the attempts to implement LCE have been fraught with challenges, including practical constraints in the school environment of many government schools: overcrowded classrooms, multigrade situations, inadequate infrastructure and limited resources. This is coupled with a lack of systemic alignment around LCE, since curricula, textbooks, examinations and teacher supervision systems are often at odds with the LCE's vision. Moreover, both in-service and preservice teacher education programmes have remained of low quality, meaning that even teachers who have been trained in learner-centred approaches are poorly equipped with the understanding or skills needed for implementing LCE (Dyer et al., 2004; Ramachandran, 2005). Teachers are also often faced with students who are unable to engage with the curriculum prescribed for a certain class (World Bank, 2018), which makes practising LCE more complex. This happens when students lack the prior knowledge or experience assumed by curriculum writers. Basic language and numeracy skills are often missing in upper-primary classes. In such a situation teachers, quite naturally, blame the students and their background, teachers of previous classes and the education system, which has allowed students to move up the classes without acquiring the necessary skills. The problem is further exacerbated for students who are absent for long periods due to seasonal migration or for health reasons. Ten years of ASER surveys (2005 to 2014) have repeatedly pointed out that over 50 per cent of children in class V are not able to read a class II text or do simple arithmetic (ASER, 2005–14).

The 2019 national elections and the National Education Policy 2020

After the 2019 elections, when the BJP won an even greater majority of seats than in 2014, national education reform returned to the agenda, with the new NEP being published.

The NEP 2020 was released in the summer of 2020. Key features of the new policy are the restructuring of the education pathway into 5+3+3+4 years, the freedom for children to mix-and-match subjects across the science, arts and social science divide, increased vocational training and greater use of Indian languages, with an emphasis on mother-tongue education. Teachers interviewed in Delhi as part of a wider project on classroom practices (Lall, Anand et al., 2020) mostly viewed the new policy as positive, although some had reservations on how it would eventually be implemented. How the NEP 2020 was inspired by the Delhi Education Revolution is discussed further in the Epilogue.

Numeracy and literacy skills

Economist Lant Pritchett estimates that four out of five schoolgoing children in India who start the school year unable to read will make no significant progress on reading. For these children the classroom, as Pritchett describes, is where they 'serve time', more than learn. They move from class to class but fail to attain even basic literacy and numeracy. This matters a great deal because, as the ASER surveys show, most schoolgoing children are well below grade-level expectations. Crucially, they fall behind at the start of their learning trajectory – from class II onwards (Aiyar, 2020).

The NEP 2020 document recognises the twin tragedies of a large proportion of children in elementary schools failing to attain foundational literacy and numeracy, and an assessment system that tests 'rote memorisation skills' and 'requires months of coaching' to master (Aiyar, 2020). It proposes two solutions. First, an emphasis on early childhood care and education, the need to build a curricular and pedagogical framework for early education, linking the Anganwadi (childcare centre) to the primary school and introducing a preparatory class in the government-school system before class I. Second, addressing the challenge of foundational literacy and numeracy through a national campaign with a clear deadline of 2025. Crucially, the document articulates a framework for shifting the focus away from the syllabus to what children learn, by mandating schools to define learning goals, linking assessments to these goals, using innovative pedagogy and reaching beyond the teacher to involve the community in achieving this mission (Aiyar, 2020).

However, the challenge in higher classes is more complex, and this is where the proposed policy pathway is unclear. NEP correctly argues for the need to shift the assessment structure away from rote memorisation to learning, but how this will be done remains open to question.

Public and private provision – teaching practices

The NEP 2020 emphasises experiential learning and asks for a pedagogy which 'must evolve to make education more experiential, holistic, integrated, inquiry-driven, discovery-oriented, learner-centred, discussion-based, flexible and, of course, enjoyable' (3). It elaborates: 'In all stages, experiential learning will be adopted, including hands-on learning, arts-integrated and sports-integrated education, story-telling-based pedagogy, among others, as standard pedagogy within each subject, and with explorations of relations among different subjects' (12). This means that it is expected that teachers will use more child-centred approaches and move away from rote learning. The policy, however, is silent on how impediments will be removed. The child-centric nature of education is underscored by the promise that foundational literacy will be developed through a play, activity and workbook based 'school preparation module' (9) for all class I students. To minimise the gap in achievement and learning outcomes, the NEP 2020 proposes to shift classroom transactions 'towards competency-based learning and education' (12). To create joyful classrooms, it intends to embed integrated art education in classroom transactions, reflecting the success of the Delhi DoE's HC. The NEP 2020 also focuses on smart classrooms as a part of digital pedagogy to enrich 'the teaching-learning process with online resources and collaborations' (20). It has proposed developing this in a phased manner.

Inclusion

Reflecting the 2005 National Curriculum Framework, the NEP 2020 also emphasises inclusion: 'The new education policy must provide all students, irrespective of their place of residence, a quality education system, with particular focus on historically marginalised, disadvantaged, and underrepresented groups' (4). The NEP 2020 reiterates the definition of inclusion as given in the Rights of Persons with Disabilities Act, a 'system of education wherein students with and without disabilities learn together and the system of teaching and learning is suitably adapted to meet the learning needs of different types of students with disabilities' (26), and endorses all its recommendations concerning school education.

Children with specific learning disabilities are mentioned specially, the policy emphasising the need to identify them at an early stage: 'the awareness and knowledge of how to teach children with specific disabilities (including learning disabilities) will be an integral part of all teacher education programs, along with gender sensitization and sensitization towards all underrepresented groups to reverse their underrepresentation' (27). The NEP 2020's view on inclusion expands the scope of school education to facilitate learning for all students, with emphasis on Socio-Economically Disadvantaged Groups (SEDGs). However, it seems that non-formal and vocational alternatives are being thought of as possible solutions for including SEDGs, which would have long-term consequences for the life chances of these children.

Teacher training

For preservice provision, the NEP declares:

> All B.Ed. programs will include training in time-tested and the most recent techniques in pedagogy, including pedagogy concerning foundational literacy and numeracy, multi-level teaching and evaluation, teaching children with disabilities, teaching children with special interests or talents, use of educational technology, and learner-centered and collaborative learning. All B.Ed. programs will include strong practicum training in the form of in-classroom teaching at local schools (23).

For CPD, teachers will be given self-improvement opportunities and learn about the latest innovations and advances in their professions. They will be offered in local, regional, state, national and international workshops and online teacher development modules. Online platforms will be developed so that teachers may share ideas and best practices. Each teacher will be expected to participate in at least 50 hours of CPD opportunities every year, driven by their interests. CPD opportunities will systematically cover the latest pedagogies regarding foundational literacy and numeracy, formative and adaptive assessment of learning outcomes, competency-based learning and related pedagogies, such as experiential learning and arts-integrated, sports-integrated and storytelling-based approaches.

> School principals and school complex leaders will have similar modular leadership/management workshops and online development opportunities and platforms to improve their leadership and management skills continuously so that they, too, may share best practices. Such leaders will also be expected to participate in 50 hours or more of CPD modules per year, covering leadership and management and content and pedagogy to prepare and implement pedagogical plans based on competency-based education (22).

The policy does little to address the endemic problems that plague India's education system. Most proposed interventions are based on a shallow understanding of the basic realities of education in an unequal society and could encounter serious problems in execution. Hence, underlying assumptions could take several of the innovations proposed by the NEP 2020 along an unintended path that might exacerbate existing educational challenges and perpetuate inequality (Batra, 2020).

This volume engages with how these issues were dealt with in Delhi prior to the NEP 2020, and how the NEP 2020 reflects some of the lessons learnt in Delhi government schools. The next section introduces Delhi, India's capital, where the research was conducted.

Introducing the Delhi National Capital Territory

This section describes the contextual background of Delhi, including an overview of the government schools landscape in Delhi, covering enrolment, teacher recruitment and parents' involvement in their children's education. This is followed by a review of the various educational policy initiatives by AAP, which has been ruling Delhi since 2015. The section concludes with a summary of non-governmental organisation (NGO) involvement in government schools.

Delhi, India's capital, was made a union territory (UT) in 1956 and was expanded from 9 to 11 districts with 33 'Tehsils' or subdivisions in July 2012. The districts are Central, East, New Delhi, North, North East, North West, Shahdara, South, South East, South West and West Delhi. Haryana surrounds Delhi except for on the eastern side, where the city borders Uttar Pradesh. Delhi National Capital Territory (NCT), an 'Urban Agglomeration',[21] covers 1,483 square kilometres, of which 369.35 square kilometres is designated as rural and 1,113.65 square kilometres as urban, making it the largest city area in the country (Economic Survey of Delhi, 2018, 1). Delhi's population in 2020 was estimated to be 30.29 million. As recorded in the census of 2011, Delhi had a population of 16.8 million, an increase from the figure of 13.9 million in 2001, making it the 18th most populated state in India, with a 21.21 per cent growth rate (higher than the national average of 17 per cent) (Economic Survey of Delhi, 2018, 24). This highlights the need to develop infrastructure (education, health, transport, housing) to support the growing population. The population density is relatively high, at 11,320 persons per square kilometre compared to the national average of 382 persons per square kilometre (Economic Survey of Delhi, 2018, 30). Delhi attracts the largest flow of migrants anywhere in urban India, mainly from Uttar Pradesh and Bihar (Risbud, 2016, 11). The increase in population could, in part, be attributed to the influx of people looking for the work, education, business and other avenues of growth and development available in a national capital.

According to the Economic Survey of Delhi Report (2018), Delhi is considered a prosperous state, with the second-highest per capita income in India. A significant share of income is from the service sector, which is treated as the growth engine for fast-developing states in India (Estimates of State Domestic Product of Delhi, 2018–19, 6). Despite the high per capita income of Delhi, nearly one-fifth (19 per cent) of Delhi's population lives in households with a monthly income of INR 5,000 (c.GB£50) or less, comprising the lowest income group. In contrast, only 4 per cent of Delhi's population live in families with a monthly income of more than INR 50,000, containing the highest income groups. The most significant section of Delhi's population (36 per cent) live in households with a monthly income of INR 5,000–10,000 (Risbud, 2016, 16).

Delhi's diversity and disparity are revealed through different settlement types, categorised by diverse degrees of formality, legality and tenure. These settlements are planned 'colonies' (informal settlements), slum designated areas, *jhuggi jhopri* clusters (JJCs),[22] *jhuggi jhopri* resettlement colonies, unauthorised colonies, regularised illegal colonies, rural villages and urban villages (Centre for Policy Research, 2015). This categorisation also indicates the inequality of access to essential services, which is, to some degree, a result of differences in income and social status (community, caste). Independent of the social criteria (class, caste and community), settlement types also impact service delivery, access to education, health, nutrition, sanitation and so on (Heller et al., 2015). Delhi's segregation is the combined effect of income differentials, socio-economic status and professional group, caste, religious affiliation and geographical origin (Risbud, 2016, 26).

Delhi also has a stark educational divide, with a severe lack of primary school education for poor children existing alongside India's best educational institutes (Bissoyi, 2018). The MHRD (2016) estimates that Delhi has a population of 1.7 million children in the age group of 6 to 10 years and 0.88 million in the age group of 11 to 13 years. This indicates that 8.52 per cent of the population requires primary education. According to the last census of 2011, the literacy rate in Delhi is 86.21 per cent, higher than the all-India average of 73 per cent (Economic Survey of Delhi, 2018, 17). However, it is still lower than the literacy rate of states like Kerala (94 per cent), Mizoram (91.3 per cent) and Tripura (87.2 per cent) (Economic Survey of Delhi, 2018, 17).

Government schools in Delhi

Government schools in India are run by either the central government, state governments or public sector bodies and are entirely financed by the government (British Council, 2019).[23] Delhi has 5,726 schools across the NCT (EduDel, 2020). The Delhi government has 1,227 government and government-aided schools, which is 21.3 per cent of the total schools operational in the NCT. The central government runs three categories of schools – the Kendriya Vidyalayas (KVs) (literally translated as central schools), the Jawahar Navodaya Vidyalayas (JNVs) and the Central Tibetan Schools for Tibetan refugees. KVs were created in 1965 as separate schools for the children of transferable central government employees (Juneja, 2010, 4). JNVs, residential schools, were set up to cater for rural children all over the country after the Education Policy of 1986 (Juneja, 2010, 5). As most good private schools were in urban areas, the National Policy on Education 1986 envisaged residential schools in rural areas. Thus, the JNV mandate was to provide quality education for those who lived in rural areas and otherwise had no access to it (Noronha, 2017). Delhi also has Patrachar Vidyalayas (PVs), providing correspondence education at the school level, established in January 1968. The PVs run under the administrative and fiscal control of the Directorate of Education (DoE), Delhi. These schools' primary aim is to support and prepare for board examinations students who failed in class VIII (onwards) and those who have been out of the formal education system and want to resume studies (Praja Foundation Report, 2019, 18).

In the 1970s and 1980s there were two types of government schools: municipal primary schools run by the Municipal Corporation of Delhi (MCD), the New Delhi Municipal Corporation (NDMC) and the Delhi Cantonment Board; and secondary schools run by the state government (Juneja, 2010, 20). Since the 1990s two new categories of schools have been set up by the Government of Delhi – the Sarvodaya Vidyalaya (SV) and the Rajkiya Pratibha Vikas Vidyalayas (RPVVs). SVs select their students through a lottery, while RPVVs hold admission tests. Further, quasi-government schools have increased in number, with new schools for children of defence officers, police officers and civil servants (Juneja, 2010, 20). According to Juneja there has been a diversification in the types of schools run by the Delhi government in the past decade, which promoted hierarchies in access to government schools. For instance, besides the MCD and NDMC schools, which add to Delhi government schools' hierarchical structure, there are 'model' schools. These are some of the primary and secondary schools which were better staffed, with better provision, and were expected to serve as 'models' for other schools (Juneja, 2010, 4). The MHRD Report defines a 'model' school as having infrastructure and facilities of at least the same standard as a KV, with stipulations on PTR, information and communication technology (ICT) usage, holistic educational environment, appropriate curriculum and emphasis on output and outcomes. Juneja's study further illustrates that admission to SVs is prized over admission to ordinary municipal schools and admission to an RPVV is prized over admission to a regular senior secondary school (Juneja, 2010, 20). After AAP came to power in Delhi, it added five more Schools of Excellence to its list of government schools in 2018, all of which are English-medium schools.

When the Congress government was in power in Delhi in 2009–10, government schools had a 2 per cent to 3 per cent lead over private counterparts. In 2009 private schools had a pass percentage of 86.42. In 2012 this got closer to 90 per cent and then became 92 per cent in 2014 (Tyagi, 2017). As far as learning and literacy levels were concerned, three out of four students in class VI were unable to read their textbooks (Bissoyi, 2018). In addition, parents were not actively involved.

School Management Committees (SMC) are mandated under the RTE Act 2009 but were not formed in most schools before 2015, since there was a chronic shortage of teachers and school infrastructure was poor (Bissoyi, 2018). There was no appropriate maintenance of the facilities and headteachers had to engage with different government departments for the maintenance of school buildings. All these factors incentivised parents to choose private schools.

The hierarchies of private and public schooling have led both a sharp stratification and a large number of unrecognised schools across Delhi (Menon, 2014, 125–8; Menon, 2017, 454; Mooij and Jalal, 2012, 144). As mentioned above, government schools dominate in terms of enrolment at the middle stages, but the share of the private sector increases at the secondary and higher secondary stages (Planning Commission, 2009, 257). The absence of adequate planning and provision for schools by the Delhi government, combined with control over land by the central government via the Delhi Development Authority, has led to a severe shortage of and overcrowding in government schools, especially at the secondary and senior secondary stages (Menon, 2017; Saxena, 2013). The state response has been to provide more schooling by running existing schools in two sex-segregated shifts and opening more schools within the existing school space. This has led to 'slumming and dilapidation', with government teachers complaining that they are no longer 'educators' but have been reduced to being 'herdsmen' (Menon, 2017, 454–6).

As far as enrolment is concerned, the State Report Card for Delhi (2016–17) by the National Institute of Educational Planning and Administration (NIEPA, 2016) noted an enrolment of 2.99 million children, out of which 1.63 million were in government schools, accounting for 54.7 per cent of total enrolments. Further, the School Education Quality Index (SEQI) 2019 report stated that Delhi had 100 per cent adjusted NER[24] at the elementary level (the highest among all UTs) while at the secondary level, it was 83.10 per cent in 2015–16, which increased to 85.90 per cent in 2016–17.

The pass out or the transition rate for primary to upper-primary level tracks the percentage of pupils enrolled in the highest class at the primary level (class V) who transition to the lowest class at the upper-primary level (class VI) in the next academic year. Delhi reported 94.60 per cent pass out in 2015–16 with not much increase and 94 per cent in 2016–17 (SEQI, 2019). Since 2010, for the first time, the pass percentage in Delhi government schools for class XI touched 80 per cent in 2019, having been 63 per cent in 2014–15 and around

72 per cent since then (The Logical Indian, 2019). Delhi government schools 'reached a record high' of 90.68 per cent pass rate for class XII in 2018, a 2.37 per cent increase from 2017, outperforming the private schools that stood at 88.35 per cent (The Logical Indian, 2018). The reason for this could be attributed to the fact that about half the students at Delhi government schools fail class VIII. This means that only the most capable students take the class XII board exams (Sharma, 2018). Due to this 'filtering' system, the number of students who pass class XII is equivalent to the number of students who pass class IX (Sharma, 2018). This is reflected in a report by Praja Foundation (2019), which stated that in 2017–18, 55 per cent of students did not pass from class IX to class X [AY 2016–17] (Praja Foundation Report, 2019, 14). Though no particular reason was mentioned in the report, this could be attributed to the government's No Detention Policy (NDP).[25] Students are promoted without failing till class VIII, whether or not they have acquired the basic literacy or numeracy skills. Hence, in the earlier classes, the retention rates remain comparatively higher. For instance, 97 per cent of students transitioned from class VI (in 2014–15) to class VIII (in 2015–16) (Praja Foundation Report, 2019, 15). However, the pass percentage increase indicates the effect of the Delhi government schools' policy initiatives like Mission Buniyaad and Chunauti (described below); such initiatives had been introduced by AAP since 2015, when it came to power, in an attempt to increase the pass out percentages.

Regarding Delhi teachers, the State Report Card (NIEPA, 2016) noted that out of 138,849 teachers in schools, 76,000 teachers (54.74 per cent) are employed in government schools.[26] There is a teaching staff crisis due to a centralised, long and complicated process that delays teachers' recruitment. Although Delhi is short of roughly 25,000 teachers, in 2017, for example, the Delhi government considered only 7,646 posts vacant, as nearly 15,402 guest teachers and 2,792 contract teachers were employed (Kalra, 2017).

The next subsection elaborates on the initiatives by AAP, which include changes to in-service teacher training, new programmes on the HC and EMC and the formation of SMCs to increase the involvement of parents in the schools and their children's education (Marlena, 2017).

Aam Aadmi Party education policy

As detailed in Chapter 1 of this volume, AAP was established in 2012 by Arvind Kejriwal, against the backdrop of a movement that started in

2011, fighting against corruption in India. After AAP's landslide victory in Delhi in 2015, the party visibly transformed Delhi's schools (Sahoo, 2020; Boston Consulting Group, 2020). Under the leadership of Arvind Kejriwal and Education Minister Manish Sisodia, the government allotted more funds to education,[27] introduced new teacher training courses and student learning programmes and made specific funds available to improve ailing schooling infrastructure (Sahoo, 2020; Praja Foundation Report, 2019). Other efforts made by AAP towards improving government schools include making education free up to class XII and increasing scholarships for students scoring 80 per cent and above (Bedi, 2019). AAP claimed that this 'government will be working on a plan to achieve 100% literacy in the national capital' (Hindustan Times, 2017). As shall be seen throughout the rest of this volume, these reforms mark a distinct break with previous education policy in Delhi and share a common framework with international education discourse. Some of AAP's major educational reform initiatives for improving the standards of government schools are summarised below.

Of the 500 new schools promised in the 2015 AAP manifesto, only around 30 have been built, due to land shortages. Nevertheless, the Delhi government has managed to build 8,000 new classrooms in existing schools. The student–classroom ratio improved from 1:66 to 1:45 (Bedi, 2019). By 2019, 21 new buildings were constructed with modern facilities. In addition to the extra 8,000 classrooms of the first phase of construction, the construction of 11,000 equivalent new classrooms was started in 2019, to expand the infrastructure of school facilities (Baruah, May 2021). In addition, the AAP government had invested significantly in infrastructure, providing green boards in all classrooms and installing 750,000 modular desks as well as providing improved sports facilities in the schools (The Hindu, 2020). Government schools were also provided with financial assistance to upgrade labs, equip SMART classrooms with digital learning facilities and develop e-modules to make learning attractive (DoE, n.d., 24–6). From an infrastructure point of view, all Delhi government schools now have functional drinking-water facilities, separate girls' and boys' toilets and electricity connections, and 88.82 per cent of schools have computer facilities (Sahoo, 2020). Another initiative includes installing CCTV cameras in classrooms and giving parents access to the live feed (Bedi, 2019). Improved infrastructural facilities have led to increased enrolment and attendance (Anwer, 2019).

But AAP has not only focused on infrastructure. Improving education quality was also seen as a function of curricular content and student engagement. The World Happiness Report 2019 ranked India 140th out of 156 countries. As a response, the Delhi government launched the Happiness Curriculum (discussed further in Chapter 4) in all 1,030 government schools, from nursery through to class VIII, in July 2018. Implementing the curriculum was seen as a first step in allowing a formal, public education system to focus on the holistic development of all learners, invest in their well-being and improve the overall quality of education in line with SDG4 (Kim et al., 2019). A study by Narula and Kalra (2019) exploring in-service teachers' beliefs about happiness and HC in Delhi government schools revealed that teachers perceived it as a positive and desirable endeavour to improve students' lives. Participating teachers, whose voices are included in this volume, spoke about how the happiness classes calmed and centred pupils at the start of the day.

In order to improve classroom practices, the Delhi government started a pioneering in-service teacher training exercise in 2017. The State Council for Education Research and Training (SCERT) undertook an extensive capacity-building exercise for more than 36,000 government school teachers – 26,000 TGTs and 10,000 post-graduate teachers (Sahoo, 2020).[28] The concept of group-based learning was introduced in teacher training so that the technique could percolate to Delhi classrooms. The new teacher training was designed to keep teachers abreast of contemporary knowledge in their subject (Marlena, 2017). In 2018, 200 teachers received training from the National Institute of Education (NIE) in Singapore and, after the completion of the course, were regarded as 'mentor teachers'. The trained teachers were assigned around five or six schools, which they visit regularly to observe classroom practices and provide on-site learning support to other teachers (Sahoo, 2020).

Beyond teacher training, a key element of the reforms included supporting weaker students. Given Delhi's population profile, government schools cater to the poorest sections of society, many of which are migrant populations from other states who have come to Delhi to find work. Some of these families do not speak Hindi adequately, and their children suffer in Hindi-medium schools. In response, 'Chunauti' was launched in June 2016 across Delhi government schools. Inspired by Nobel Laureate Dr Abhijit Banerjee, whose work has been used to reduce the dropout rates of students (The New India Express, 2019), it aims to bridge the learning gaps of classes VI to VIII and ensure zero dropouts in class IX. Students are divided based on their learning levels and provided with additional learning support. It is understood to impact 0.95 million students from classes V to X (Education Booklet, 2018). A subsequent version of the scheme, 'Chunauti 2018',[29] was also launched in 2018, under which students from classes VI to VIII were mapped, and their learning levels enhanced (The New India Express, 2019). Consequently, class XI results also showed noticeable improvements in pass percentage, from 71 per cent in 2017–18 to 80 per cent in 2018–19 (Sahoo, 2020). Despite its success, ability grouping is of course contested and problematic – as shall be discussed in Chapter 4.

In 2016–17 the AAP government experimented by convening a group of 62,277 students who had failed to pass the class IX exams. They named it 'Vishwas'. This group was coached separately and made to appear for class X through Patrachar Vidyalaya (a CBSE open school). However, when the results came, 98 per cent of the students in the Vishwas group failed, though the government claimed that it had improved the pass percentage of class IX from 52 per cent to 57 per cent between the sessions 2015–16 and 2017–18. However, critics said this had been achieved by pushing the weak students out of the school (Ahmad, 2019).

In another bid to help weaker students, the AAP government launched 'Buniyaad' in April 2018, a three-month summer campaign to ensure that all children of classes III to IX can read, write and do basic maths, designed along the lines of the 'Chunauti scheme' (Business Standard, 2018). Its purpose is to address the concerns raised after the NAS found that the majority of students between classes III and V in MCD schools did not perform well in science, mathematics and languages (Bhanj, 2018). Under this mission, the students were set into three groups; this means those who performed at par were taken into the 'Ujjawal' group, those who scored medium-level marks were placed in 'Utkarsh' and those who were behind their peers were placed in 'Udyam', receiving targeted help for their level (Hindustan Times, 2018). The mission has led to a 20 per cent increase in the number of students, between classes III and V, who can solve arithmetic division problems and a 12 per cent increase (between pre-test and post-test) in those who can read a story in Hindi. Additionally, there was a 15 per cent increase in the children of classes VI to IX who could read an 'advanced story' in Hindi (India Today, 2019).

Section 21 of the RTE Act 2009 mandates the formation of SMCs in all elementary government, government-aided and special category schools in the country. SMCs are primarily a model of decentralised governance with the active involvement of parents in the school's functioning, in cooperation with teachers, headmasters and local authorities' elected representatives (DoE, n.d., 21). SMCs monitor how their schools function, prepare and recommend the school development plan, oversee the utilisation of the grants received and perform other such roles as may be prescribed (Praja Foundation Report, 2019). AAP has made SMCs part of their core strategy, bringing families on board. Of the state-government-run schools in Delhi, 99.51 per cent had SMCs compared to 82.22 per cent of KVs in 2017–18 (Praja Foundation Report, 2019). The SMCs decide how the contingency fund is spent. This has empowered parents and kindled their interest in the schools, countering the myth that parents of government-school students are less concerned about their children's education than those who pay for private schools (Ahmad, 2019).

AAP has also been very proud of its Schools of Excellence. In 2017 Delhi Education Minister Manish Sisodia declared that five English-medium schools would join the Schools of Excellence scheme. These schools are coeducational from nursery to class XII and with outstanding government school teachers. 'There will be two special education teachers, one full-time nurse and one part-time nurse in these schools, and students will be admitted from a neighbourhood without any filter' (Hindustan Times, 2017). A delegation of teachers from the USA visited one of the Schools of Excellence in 2019 to learn about their best practices and government interventions (Outlook, 2019). This indicates that the Delhi government intends to showcase these schools as a model of quality education on a par with English-medium private schools. AAP has not been going it alone – as will be seen in Chapters 3 and 4, the Delhi government has benefitted from NGO support and involvement in Delhi schools.

Conclusion

AAP's multipronged approach, which includes infrastructure, training, new programmes, targeted interventions for children that need extra help and increased parental involvement, has borne fruit. Recent online survey results[30] have revealed that due to the improvement of standards in Delhi government schools, 61 per cent of the respondents from 70 con-stituencies across Delhi now prefer sending their children to government schools over private ones. Further, 76 per cent of respondents are satis-fied with the quality of education offered at Delhi government schools and 84 per cent also expressed their satisfaction with government school infrastructure (Hindustan Times, 2020). A staggering 82 per cent of respondents said that the quality of education and related facilities has been enhanced in the five years that AAP has been in power (Hindustan Times, 2020). There is a visible transformation in the government school system in Delhi. In fact, one of the key reasons for AAP's back-to-back landslide victory in the 2020 Assembly elections was its remarkable performance in improving the school system. With a catchy slogan of 'education first', the AAP-led government between 2015–2020 had put a lot of effort into a 'moribund' education system, particularly the government-run schools in Delhi (Sahoo, 2020). However, there are also critical voices – according to the India Today Data Intelligence Unit (DIU), which followed reports relating to the 70 promises made in the AAP manifesto in 2015, AAP fulfilled only three of its seven education-sector-related pledges. And the Boston Consultancy Report (2020) that sings the praises of the reforms indicates that 'currently only 57% students who enter the system in Class VI finish Class XII, primarily because of the low Class IX passing rates. This indicates that the learning in Class VI to VIII needs to be further strengthened as well' (13). This means there are still some challenges that need to be met.[31] The following chapters will engage with classroom practices, teacher training and the issue of inclusion, showcasing the voices of teachers who are living through AAP's education revolution.

Notes

1. AAP's 5-year report card: Did Kejriwal's govt fulfill its promises?' *India Today*, 7 February 2020, Retrieved from https://www.indiatoday.in/diu/story/aap-s-5-year-report-card-did-kejriwal-s-govt-fulfill-its-promises-1644302-2020-02-07 accessed 18 March 2022.
2. Something subsequent Indian governments did not achieve.
3. Indian Institutes of Technology and Indian Institutes of Management are renowned as world-class institutions. The majority of their graduates end up abroad, contributing to the phenomenon known as the brain drain in India.
4. For details on these reforms, see Lall 2001, and on how they affected Indian education and Indian politics, see Lall and Anand (forthcoming 2022).
5. A notable exception to this has been Kerala, which still boasts the country's highest literacy rates. It is interesting to note that with India's increased globalisation and integration into the world economy, public investment in education had increased to around 4 per cent of GDP by 2004 but was still well below the 6 per cent GDP level recommended in 1968 by the Kothari Commission.
6. In the financing of education, the trends in India correspond with the global trends – high rates of growth in public expenditure on education in the 1960s, negative rates of growth in the 1970s, steady but slow positive growth in the 1980s and declining growth in the 1990s that accompanied the adjustment policies (Tilak, 2018).
7. The issue of low-income groups preferring to pay for education is highly contested … (Srivastava, Tooley, etc.) However, since this book focuses on government schooling, the debates on the role of private education in Delhi are not discussed. For more on India's neo-liberal education policy, see Lall and Anand (forthcoming 2022).
8. Recent figures show that between 1993 and 2017 enrolment in private unaided schools grew rapidly by 25.6 percentage points (Central Square Foundation, 2020, 100).
9. The growth of a 'tiered' market in education, with over nine types of schools that cater to the 'varied purchasing powers of its clientele', has further led to a highly differentiated schooling system that is currently institutionalised in Indian society for children belonging to different sections of society. Each of these differential arrangements mirrors the hierarchical socio-economic divisions of stratified society (Vasavi, 2019, 2). Students of the most disadvantaged

social groups that face exclusions in education, namely the Scheduled castes (SCs) and Scheduled Tribes (STs), constitute nearly 30 per cent of all enrolments in elementary schools across all management types, with a majority of students from the poorest households attending government schools (Vasavi, 2019).

10. This is also why reservations for SCs and STs were limited to higher education and not seen as relevant at school levels.

11. See work by Stephen Ball, Anna Yeatman, Sharon Gewirtz, J. Broadbent and R. Laughlin.

12. By this time secularism in politics was long dead. The Congress Party at times has also sought to downplay its secularist roots and embrace pro-Hindu sentiments (Jaffrelot, 2019). However, until 2000 the Indian curriculum and textbooks had remained secular.

13. Judgement by Justices M.B. Shah, D.M. Dharmadhikari and H.K. Sema in Writ Petition (Civil) No. 98 of 2002, Ms Aruna Roy and others vs Union of India and others.

14. Member parties of UPA were the INC, Dravida Munnetra Kazhagam, Nationalist Congress Party, Rashtriya Janata Dal, Indian Union Muslim League, Jammu and Kashmir National Conference, Jharkhand Mukti Morcha, Kerala Congress, Marumalarchi Dravida Munnetra Kazhagam, Revolutionary Socialist Party and Viduthalai Chiruthaigal Katchi.

15. In a number of states the BJP textbooks remained, as state governments were ruled by the BJP.

16. The Sangh Parivar has always shown interest in the teaching of history, not only because it contributes to defining the national identity, but also because the Parivar believes the version of the past portrayed by secularists does not reflect reality. Its impression on the Modi government is also evident (Jaffrelot and Jairam, 2019).

17. 'Education for All Movement'.

18. http://dashboard.seshagun.gov.in/# accessed 18 March 2022.

19. Students belonging to EWS are those whose annual gross parental income is up to Rs.4.5 lakh [c.US$5,800] (MHRD, 2016).

20. India has not taken part since 2009–10.

21. An urban agglomeration is a continuous urban spread constituting a town and its adjoining outgrowths, or two or more physically contiguous towns together with or without outgrowths of such towns (Centre for Policy Research, 2015).

22. The JJC is one of the types of 'unplanned' settlements designated by the government of the NCT of Delhi. JJCs are located on 'public land' – land owned by agencies like the Delhi Development Authority, the railways or the Central Public Works Department – and have been constructed without permission, and as a result, JJCs are often described as 'encroachments' by governing agencies in Delhi and their residents have experienced repeated waves of eviction and resettlement since the 1960s (Centre for Policy Research, 2015).

23. Private schools in Delhi: the landscape of Delhi's school education cannot be completed without the mention of private schools, which have increased (both in number and enrolments) in the past decade. The schools run by non-state players in the Indian education system include low-cost private schools, schools run by NGOs, alternative schools and non-formal schools (Iyer, 2019, 15). An article reported that in this decade, 645 private schools were opened in Delhi, an increase of 31 per cent, showing maximum growth between 2011–12 and 2014–15; this means they increased from 2,026 to 2,656, respectively, and the number of students enrolled in private schools grew from 1.38 million (2011–12) to 1.67 million (2014–15) and 1.86 million (2018–19) (The Times of India, 2019; The New Indian Express, 2019). A study by Iyer (2019) reported that the low-cost private-sector schools have attempted to address the issues faced by government schools in terms of access and equity (Iyer, 2019). However, this book focuses on government schools, so more information on private schools is not provided.

24. SEQI (2019) defines Adjusted Net Enrolment Ratio as referring to the total number of pupils in a particular stage of school education, enrolled either in the corresponding stage or the next stage of school education, expressed as a percentage of the corresponding population.

25. The RTE Amendment Act 2019 amends the NDP by reintroducing examinations for classes V and VIII.

26. It was noted in the Praja Foundation Report (2019) that the PTR, at 29 for Delhi government schools in 2017–18, has been below the prescribed norm of 30 for primary and 35 for secondary levels. However, these numbers do not bear out in reality, and NIEPA has not published new report cards since 2016–17.

27. In the financial year 2018–19, the education sector continued to be the priority sector, with a maximum share of allocation of 27.36 per cent of the budget allocated for schemes and projects by the Delhi government, run by the AAP (Economic Survey of Delhi, 2018, 6). During 2017–18, Delhi was at the top, with 23.4 per cent of its budget estimates earmarked for the education sector, followed by Chhattisgarh (19 per cent), Maharashtra (18.6 per cent) and Assam (18.3 per cent) in comparison to the national average of 14.8 per cent (Economic Survey of Delhi, 2018, 17).

28. Observer Research Foundation (ORF). Retrieved from https://www.orfonline.org/expert-speak/how-did-aam-aadmi-party-fix-delhis-broken-government-schools-60961/ accessed 18 March 2022.

29. The students from classes VI to VIII were divided into three sections – Pratibha (for the best students), Nishtha (for the average ones) and Neo-Nishtha (for those who barely pass) – according to their learning levels and test results for arithmetic, reading in the language that was the medium of instruction and reading in English (Grewal, 2020). More on this in Chapter 5.

30. The survey was conducted by the Neta App Janata Barometer Survey, before the 8 February 2020 Assembly elections. The survey was based on the responses of over 40,000 citizens across all 70 Delhi constituencies between 20 and 27 January 2020 to gauge the public verdict on the performance of the AAP government in the key performance areas of education and health: https://www.hindustantimes.com/education/61-prefer-sending-kids-to-delhi-government-school-says-survey/story-2baF9nJo0uxunPLGfrK4yL.html accessed 18 March 2022.

31. 'AAP's 5-year report card: Did Kejriwal's govt fulfill its promises?', *India Today*, 7 February 2020. Retrieved from https://www.indiatoday.in/diu/story/aap-s-5-year-report-card-did-kejriwal-s-govt-fulfill-its-promises-1644302-2020-02-07 accessed 18 March 2022.

3
Teachers, training and capacity building: what do teachers want?

Our mentor teachers come from different places and urban regions; they hardly visit the schools located in rural areas, or they generally visit for a brief period. So, they train us as per different region and when we try this in our school *'bacche schote pata nahi sir kya sikh ke aae hain'* (children think we don't know what sir has learnt). So many times, it may not work. We want the mentor teachers to have to be from the same background as us (FT6 SV8 Social Science).

Introduction

Education reforms start with a change in practice, which in turn starts with training and professional development. AAP understood that in order to change teacher practice in schools, a new model of teacher training was required. This chapter addresses initiatives in teacher education[1] and professional development in Delhi. The chapter begins by situating the discussion in the broader debates in India as well as within the changing nature of teacher education in Delhi. It then provides an overview of teachers' responses to in-service and preservice training, detailing current innovative practices, challenges and trends regarding teacher training or education in Delhi. Teacher-training reform has been a key aspect of the AAP education reform programme, and clearly progress has been made. However, many of the changes are related to in-service training. Without undermining the importance of preservice training in Delhi, almost all the teachers were critical of its short duration and its overly theoretical approach – something that remains untouched by AAP. The chapter then highlights teachers' experiences of the new in-service training programmes. An overview of their responses regarding in-service training is provided, following a discussion on the capacity-building programmes by AAP, such as the MTP and the TDCP. The participants shared that they do enjoy in-service teacher-training seminars; however, overall, they are unable to implement everything due to cultural differences and the high PTR. Like preservice, the in-service teacher-training initiatives led by the Delhi government do not address teachers' local needs or support sustained change in teacher practices.[2] Participating teachers felt that they do not receive the needed academic stimulation at the preservice level and the 'expert' knowledge coming from in-service training institutes is not linked with their local context.

In order to frame this discussion, we should look at the overarching issues facing the teaching profession in India. The ASER quantified the monumental challenges in India related to teacher absenteeism and the number of untrained teachers. According to the Ministry of Education data (2018, cited in Khanna, 2020, 2) there were around 1,140,000 (11.4 lakh) untrained schoolteachers in 2017 (12.8 per cent of the total in India) and this number was projected to reach up to 2,540,000 (25.4 lakh) (28.5 per cent) in 2019–20.

It is further estimated that one out of every six of India's elementary teachers is untrained (ASER, 2015; 2016). Untrained teachers comprised more than 45 per cent of the total number of elementary teachers in some rural areas of India (UNESCO, 2008; 2010). In response to this, the Justice Verma Commission (JVC) (2012) identified problems that needed to be addressed, including stand-alone institutes of teacher education, the proliferation of private teacher-training institutes and the paucity of institutional capacity to prepare teachers and teacher educators (Batra, 2017). Many teacher education institutes face challenges, the most difficult being arranging the internship or practice teaching or school experience programme. The study by Chennat (2014) identifies a mismatch between the perspective of the student teacher, who is keen to initiate dialogue with the subject teacher on teaching practice, and that of the subject teacher, who is in a hurry to complete the syllabus according to plan in the school calendar. The mismatch between the pedagogue's understanding of teaching, which is subject-centred, and the understanding of the teacher educator, who is concerned with building an awareness of educational discourse, creates a dilemma among student teachers (Gupta, 2018).

The JVC report of 2012 clearly stated that a 'broken teacher education sector' is putting over '370 million children' at risk. The report revealed that on average 85 per cent of trained teachers failed to qualify for the post-qualification competency test – the Central Teacher Eligibility Test (C-TET). The report confirmed that the 'aged' curriculum and pedagogy, within which teachers are educated, has a mismatch between instruction and practice. The report gave specific recommendations including the restructuring of preservice and in-service teacher education.

With over one million teacher vacancies in India's schools and a large cadre of poorly qualified teachers, the NEP 2020 was expected to implement the recommendations of the Supreme Court's Justice Verma Commission (MHRD, 2012). This includes enhanced public investment in teacher education, strengthened institutional capacity in states and curriculum redesign to teach for diversity and inclusion. However, the NEP's proposed single model of teacher education disregards the specific needs and concerns of diverse states and of different levels of education. It imposes a homogenised and standardised system of preparing teachers and an over-centralised regulatory structure that is sure to exacerbate centre-state conflict (Batra, 2020, 597).

Teacher education, as an institution, is constructed in service to the larger community. Such service is embedded in teacher practice and often highlights participatory forms of agency. Indeed, educators are and can be responsible agents in producing knowledge to improve their practice (Britzman, 2012; Koirala-Azad and Fuentes, 2009; McTaggart, 1991). To quantify the impact of teacher practice and agency[3] both at the macrolevel and microlevel is challenging. In India, Naik (1979, 3) termed this challenge the 'elusive triangle' of providing equality within a high-quality education system which is accessible to a large number of learners. Probing the social context of teacher education also contributes to elusiveness. The challenge requires dissecting how teacher practice is embedded in the economic, political, sociocultural and sociohistorical milieu of a place (Byker, 2014; Byker and Banerjee, 2016; Freire, 1970; Iyengar et al., 2014; Kumar, 2005) and the contextual details of a place – including the historical legacies – and how these shape a school and a teacher's daily reality. Kumar commented that such context 'should sensitize teachers' and shape their practice and assessment of children (Kumar, 2005, 14). The contextual milieu encompasses learning as a social process, which becomes embedded within the culture, norms and practices of a community (Lave and Wenger, 1991). Framed as such, this chapter provides a critical representation of the challenges, innovations and outcomes of teacher education across the best-performing schools in Delhi.

Innovative teacher education interventions in Delhi

Many South Asian countries (such as India, Pakistan and Bangladesh) have attempted to reform teacher education by altering implementation practices to make it more efficient. Typically they combine different aspects, such as curriculum redesign, provision of textbooks and teacher guides, with teacher training and education[4] (Iyengar et al., 2014). The sections below show what is on offer in India and what the Delhi AAP government has put in place to improve education in the capital. Each section is followed by the comments of teachers who took part in the research study, giving an insider view of the Delhi programmes.

Preservice teaching training

Preservice training is essential to becoming a teacher and trainees leave with either a Bachelor of Education (BEd), a Diploma of Elementary Education (DElEd) or a Bachelor of Elementary Education (BElEd) (Iyengar et al., 2014; Lall, Anand et al., 2020). The BEd programme is run largely in teacher-training institutions and universities across India. These institutions are managed by government or private bodies. The standard of teacher education is regulated by the National Council of Teacher Education (NCTE)[5] based in New Delhi. The main objective of the NCTE is to achieve planned and coordinated development of the teacher education system throughout the country, with the regulation and proper maintenance of norms and standards (NCERT, 2006; NCTE, 2009; Yadav, 2012). Preservice teacher education faces several challenges, such as lack of uniformity in curriculum and teaching methods across states, substandard quality of teacher educators and the problem of supervision (Singh and Shakir, 2019). Teacher selection, duration of teaching, 'mushrooming' of teacher education institutes, poor infrastructure and insufficient time for practice teaching are other issues of preservice teacher education (Dayal, 2018). The existing preservice teacher education programmes have come under severe criticism for not addressing the contemporary issues of school education and not preparing teachers to meet the diverse needs of students (Gupta, 2018). Since the National Curriculum Framework for Teacher Education (NCFTE) 2009 came into being, many universities have revised their syllabus accordingly. Recent changes in the duration and design of teacher education, including the adoption of a two-year semester system, has paved the way for redesigning the curriculum. This is complicated by the multiplicity of organisations, such as NCTE and the NCERT, involved in issuing directives about the framing of the curriculum (Kauts and Kaur, 2019). The framework of teacher education in operation in India is incompatible with the contextual reality of schools and is not linked appropriately with the preparation process for teachers. Although the NCTE seems comprehensive and socially sensitive, the agencies of teacher education have not been able to completely translate this framework into practice by developing appropriate curricula and courses (such as the DEIEd and BEd) (Bawane, 2019). None of the courses on offer sufficiently emphasise the philosophical underpinnings of progressive education, alternative education and the significance of addressing the social and educational inequities embedded in a classroom (Bawane, 2019). Rather, the outlook of the teacher-training institutions towards teacher preparation has been based on two assumptions: first, that children are homogeneous and learn at the same pace and in the same way; and second, that teachers are homogeneous and need similar inputs regardless of who they are and where they are from (Ramachandran, 2018; Bawane, 2019).

Delhi also does not have a uniform preservice teacher education curriculum, despite it being a rather small UT. However, the four-year BElEd Programme offered by the University of Delhi has been 'hailed' as one of the most robust programmes of elementary teacher education in India (Nawani, 2013). It is perhaps for this reason that AAP has not included preservice teacher training in its education reform programme.

The next section provides an overview of teachers' voices on preservice teacher training in Delhi. It provides insights into the nature and status of preservice teacher training, reviewing how adequately teachers are prepared for the classroom. Following a brief discussion of teachers' attitudes towards preservice teacher training in Delhi, the section is structured around a number of thematic questions. First, the section engages with theory-to-practice and teacher agency, looking at insufficient practical training. Then the discussion moves to the relevance of preservice teacher training curricula in today's classrooms, looking at the real-life challenges teachers face. This section highlights the nature and status of the teaching practicum, a core component of learning how to teach. Finally, the section concludes by drawing these themes together, examining possible policy and practice implications.

The theory-to-practice binary and teacher agency

The implementation of preservice teacher education curriculum at the elementary stage in various states and UTs in India lacks a proper integration of theory and practice,[6] as well as the use of ICT[7] in the teaching-learning process (Yadav, 2012). Even in Delhi, preservice teacher-training programmes lack innovation and are insufficient in terms of theory-to-practice to provide the required quality education and methods of teaching. The scale of enrolment in preservice teacher education is often too large to allow for any meaningful instruction (Goel, 2019). Nevertheless, teachers in Delhi perceive preservice training as a gateway to the teaching profession (Lall, Anand et al., 2020) – something they have to go through or engage with if they want to become teachers.

While sharing experiences about their preservice training days in Delhi, the respondents described the process as 'theoretical' or 'theory-oriented' (Lall, Anand et al., 2020, 11). Although it is theoretical, a few participants said that the preservice teacher training imparts 'knowledge' and 'understanding' of classroom dynamics and student behaviour. A maths teacher shared an example: 'the conditioning theory teaches us about the behaviour of small kids. We apply these theories differently in the classroom. The way it is described in the book is different from the way we use it to apply it in the classroom' (FT10 Primary SV3). The participants explicitly commented that there is an overemphasis on educational theory and much of this theory lacks relevance to the practice of teaching. In addition to the lack of a joined-up, coherent approach between courses and teaching practice, there has been concern regarding dissonance and tensions between the different curricular areas, such as foundations of education, curriculum and pedagogy, in the school internship and practice teaching. The participants described the preservice teacher-training curriculum as an amalgamation of diverse theories of learning and education which many times do not align, creating confusion among prospective teachers (Gupta, 2018).

Since classroom experience is crucial for teachers' performance, the practice teaching or school experience programme – both parts of the DElEd and BEd – is particularly important. In Delhi, teachers reminiscing about their days in practice teaching found it helpful only in 'learning the ropes of teaching' (Lall, Anand et al., 2020, 11). Practice teaching emerged as the most crucial contributor towards enhancing student teachers' understanding of the school, as well as teaching techniques. Almost all participants expressed that practice teaching was fruitful for their agency and self-efficacy; however, they had concerns about the nature and extent of the practical sessions in the preservice teacher training in Delhi.

The participants reflected on what they had learnt in the practical sessions in Delhi: 'I learnt how to make lesson plans, how to stand in the class, how to use chalk, and how to position it. These are very important things for me. The activities I learnt in BEd are not in practice today' (FT3 English RPVV3). Another participant shared that 'We just learn how to maintain a register and diary. Only lesson planning[8] from the preservice training helps' (FT2 Primary SV4). Another teacher elaborated on her experiences of practice sessions: 'We took classroom training for one month. We just taught one or two chapters. We were not able to learn how to engage students and answer their questions. So, we learnt all theoretical things' (FT2 Primary SV8). Lastly, a maths teacher also shared his experience: 'The real experience we get from this training is the school experience programmes. There should be more' (FT10 Primary SV3). These interview excerpts suggest that teacher trainees should receive more practical sessions in the preservice teacher training. The participants explained that it provides greater scope for the development of sound knowledge in different areas such as content, teaching-learning methodologies and the pedagogy of teaching-learning among the teacher trainees.

When asked to elaborate on their experiences of practice sessions in the preservice teacher training in Delhi, a participant said, 'I came to know about the realities of students when I started teaching. I realise that we are not catering to the students who come from well-to-do families. It is important to learn this in trainings' (FT2 Primary SV11). In terms of self-efficacy, a participant expressed that practice sessions built her confidence in interacting with the students. She said that 'It [preservice] helped me get rid of my hesitations while going into the class. It [practice sessions] provided me with opportunities to interact with students, which helped me in becoming a teacher. It helped me in improving my communication skills related to children, but there should be more of these practical sessions, as I should've learnt more in my training' (FT3 Primary SV4). This implies that the teachers need to spend more time in practice teaching during preservice training, to gain more practical knowledge about the job. A participant shared that 'the preservice training was helpful but lacked transacting the desired amount of practical knowledge. My experience of being a guest teacher and then a permanent job of a government teacher provided much scope to have real classroom experiences' (FT2 Primary SV8). Overall, teachers reported dissatisfaction with the preservice teacher-training programme, due to its duration, rigid curriculum and method of practice teaching or school experience programme, which leaves little scope for trainee teachers to adopt reflective practices. This could be because the preservice teacher-training curriculum does not allocate enough time for practical aspects (Karunakaran and Bhatta, 2013). Teachers explicitly expressed that they need to strengthen and make links between theory and practice (Flores and Fernandes, 2014; Darling-Hammond, 2006; Peercy and Troyan, 2017).

the children of migrant workers or EWS, the respondents shared that their classrooms have a majority of students from EWS and mentioned that the background of students was not covered in their preservice teacher training. A participant stated:

> children who come to government schools are from different backgrounds; we cannot even imagine the things they experience in their lives. This should be added to the training. Cribbing about homework not being done won't suffice here. I need to find out why the child is ready to be reprimanded but not to do homework. No matter how good a lesson plan or teaching aid one is using. The background of children matters about which anything was not there in our preservice training; it was all theoretical hence not that useful.
>
> (FT3 Science SV12)

Only teachers teaching students with special needs are taught inclusion policies and methodologies in the preservice training programmes. One of the special educator participants also expressed concern over insufficient training sessions: 'I have done a SNAP[14] course or three months. In that course, we taught children with special needs … I learnt from my experience in preservice teacher training … Inclusion policy is very recent; we have learnt it in in-service teacher training' (FT4 Social Science RPVV1). These interview excerpts imply that teachers are not taught about inclusion or to work with students from diverse groups, something explored in more detail in Chapter 5. This also shows a lack of awareness of inclusion in preservice teacher education programmes (Flores and Fernandes, 2014).

The voices of teachers highlight the theory–practice gap in preservice training, the relevance of the preservice training curriculum today and the challenges they face in implementing what they have learnt, in the classroom. Teachers' voices imply that preservice teacher training is devoid of the realities that exist in government schools in Delhi, which teachers are exposed to only after becoming a teacher. All the quotes mentioned in the section above bring to the fore the experience of teachers as the most crucial dimension, which helps them devise methods to teach students based on their needs and requirements. The preservice training undoubtedly prepares student teachers for some parts of the job. Yet, it is in real classroom situations that teachers get the opportunity to flex their teaching and classroom management skills. It looks like the preservice teacher education as offered in Delhi lacks a clear framework regarding a teaching practice phase, and it is therefore surprising that this crucial dimension was left out of the AAP education reforms. The next section reflects on in-service teacher education within India and Delhi, before turning to the views of participating teachers.

Overview of in-service teacher training in India

At the national level, the NCERT prepares modules for various teacher training courses and also undertakes specific programmes for in-service training of teacher educators. Institutional support is also provided by the National University of Educational Planning and Administration (NUEPA)[15] (Kidwai et al., 2013). At the state level, the SCERTs prepare modules for teacher training and conduct specialised courses for teacher educators and schoolteachers. At the district level, in-service training is provided by the District Institute of Education and Training (DIET) (Kidwai et al., 2013). The Block Resource Centres and Cluster Resource Centres form the 'lowest rung' of institutions in the vertical hierarchy for providing in-service training to schoolteachers. The administration and organisation of all teacher-training activities are undertaken by Sarva Shiksha Abhiyan (SSA) (sometimes in partnership with a few NGOs) at the state and district levels. SSA finances the training and organises teaching materials and resources through district-level resources, primarily the DIETs. Figure 3.1 shows the structural flow of in-service teacher training in India (Kidwai et al., 2013, 20).

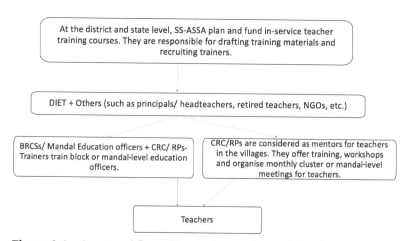

Figure 3.1   Structural flow of in-service teacher training for government primary school teachers.

(Adapted from Kidwai et al., 2013, 20)

A study carried out by the NCERT (2017)[16] to assess the quality of in-service training of teachers and its impact on classroom transactions found that the revised school curriculum and associated teaching practices were not being practised in the training. There was great variation across states in terms of the quality of resource persons and their behaviour towards teachers, from being respectful, to authoritative, to indifferent (NCERT, 2017). In another study, the NCERT (2017) reported that the multiplicity of agencies working to impart in-service teacher training focused on diverse themes such as leadership skills, subject matter expertise, or inclusive education, forcing teachers to be absent from classrooms for days, affecting their teaching (NCERT, 2017). In yet another study, Singh et al. (2020) revealed that in-service teacher-training programmes are fraught with issues at all levels, including policy, planning, implementation and follow-up. A major problem identified through the various studies is that the teacher educators, key resource persons or subject matter experts neglect the knowledge, attitude and beliefs of the teachers they train (Kidwai et al., 2013; Dyer et al., 2004; Batra, 2014). In 2018, the National Initiative for School Heads' and Teachers' Holistic Advancement (NISHTHA) was launched by the Department of School Education and Literacy, MHRD, to provide in-service teacher training. It is the first of its kind wherein standardised training modules are developed at the national level for the whole country. However, states and UTs can adapt it according to local demography and culture by adding their course material and 'recourse persons', as long as they fulfil NISHTHA's core motives, topics and expectations (NISHTHA, 2019). The programme strives to improve the digital infrastructure for knowledge sharing (using platforms such as the National Digital Infrastructure for Teachers, or DIKSHA) and enhancement of pedagogical and leadership skills of headteachers and teachers, thereby improving the learning outcome of students. Various government organisations (such as the NCERT, SCERTs, Kendriya Vidyalaya Sangathan) and others in partnership with different NGOs[17] working in the field of elementary education have developed teacher-training modules and are partnering with agencies to implement the programme across the country through NISHTHA (NISHTHA, 2019). Although NISHTHA was launched in August 2019 in a face-to-face mode, the Covid-19 pandemic forced stakeholders to launch the programme through the DIKSHA portal so that the learning continuum of teachers and students would not be restricted (Mir, 2020).

Overview of in-service teacher training in Delhi

As the two initial chapters have shown, before the AAP government the levels and quality of education in Delhi were poor – even in comparison to a number of Indian states (Iyengar et al., 2014). In order to improve the quality of education in Delhi government schools and enhance teachers' instructive capabilities, the AAP government introduced in-service teacher-training programmes with the aim of keeping teachers well informed and up-to-date in their knowledge of their subject (Marlena, 2017; Goel, 2019; Lall, Anand et al., 2020). A number of institutional schemes for improvement in teacher education already existed – there were initiatives such as the Learning Enhancement Programme under SSA for elementary teachers and the 'orientation of secondary school teachers' that were designed to offer professional development opportunities for classroom teachers in Delhi and elsewhere (Government of India, 2014). But despite these initiatives and the official discourse of child-centred learning, a series of government reviews including the aforementioned Justice Verma Review 2012 and Joint Review Missions for in-service teacher education, serious deficiencies and challenges within the system remained (Banks and Dheram, 2012; MHRD, 2016).

Endeavouring to be proactive in improving basic education, AAP launched a series of new programmes directly under the DoE to support teachers (such as the MTP, the TDCP and Jeevan Vidhya Shivir[18]) as well as the Principal Development Programme for principals and headteachers.[19] This included international exposure: 102 Heads of Schools (HoS), 7 DIET and SCERT faculties and 8 officials from the DoE attended the education leadership programme in Cambridge (UK). Also, 22 HoS, 27 DIET and SCERT faculties and 10 DoE officials visited Finland to observe the Finnish school system (DoE, n.d., 16). The following section reviews the status of in-service teacher training and teacher development, with a specific focus on CPD and capacity-building programmes in Delhi. CPD is a process of supporting teachers and their development and is inclusive of the range of approaches, modalities and institutional arrangements operating in Delhi (Singh et al., 2020).

Mentor Teacher Programme

The MTP was launched by the Education Minister in April 2016,[20] selecting 200 teachers, out of 1,100 applicants who adopted innovative pedagogies with proven results, to serve as mentor teachers (DoE, n.d., 13). After two rounds of training, the mentor teachers were each assigned five to six schools which they had to visit regularly (DoE, n.d.). Mentor teachers are also responsible for creating supplementary learning materials for children, in consultation with other teachers. They have been pivotal in supporting the implementation of several Delhi programmes such as Chunauti – a programme aimed at bridging learning gaps or deficits for students (from classes VII to IX).[21] They also facilitate workshops organised by SCERT and help to edit and develop content for the Pragati series. These books are supplementary materials for students of classes VI to VIII, in English, Hindi, maths, science and social science subjects, which are aligned with topics prescribed in the NCERT textbooks. Pragati works as a tool for child-centred pedagogic discourse in the classrooms of the DoE schools. It uses 'simple language, illustrations, instances from the context of children in Delhi, and worksheets to help children understand the concepts' (DoE, n.d., 4). The Pragati series subject books are simplified in language and the content is supported by visuals and diagrams. This helps children overcome the problems they face due to difficulties in reading. In sync with the latest innovation in classroom learning, the concept of group-based learning was introduced in teacher training so that the technique percolates to Delhi government schools' classrooms (Lall, Anand et al., 2020). In addition, mentor teachers have been given wide national- and international-level exposure to augment their observation, facilitation, content understanding and pedagogical skills. In 2018, about 200 mentor teachers attended a five-day course on mentoring at the NIE in Singapore. Teachers' experiences of these initiatives will be discussed in the section below.

The Teacher Development Coordinator Programme

Considering the challenges faced by teachers in the present-day school environment, the AAP government created a community of professionals possessing special mindsets and skills to work together to identify shared challenges that they face and to create solutions to these challenges in Delhi (Goel, 2019). This was launched 'to develop Education Leaders within each school in order to assist the Head of School (HoS) in creating a culture of collaborative learning in schools' (DoE, n.d., 14). It provided a platform for the DIETs to engage with the schools and transform the model of in-service training. In collaboration with mentor teachers, the teacher development coordinators (TDCs) have succeeded in strengthening the academic discourse in schools. The role of the TDC is broadly to facilitate sessions for teachers where they can share their learning and experiences of the classroom with each other, providing feedback to other teachers based on observations with a focus on improving teaching across schools. The role of a TDC is also to support teachers in developing schools as learning organisations by supporting a consistent and cohesive academic environment in which everyone can learn. Once every three months TDCs are required to attend capacity development sessions designed for them by SCERT (Goel, 2019). This programme has been developed in partnership with STiR Education[22] and focuses on teacher professional development through multiple platforms (DoE, n.d.).

The Delhi training paradigm follows a 'cascade' transmission of knowledge model in which key concepts and examples of 'quality' teaching are passed down to 'master trainers', then to trainers at regional levels and finally to government school teachers. In such models, 'knowledge' is assumed to be a given, independent of context or experience, and easily transferable. The following sections will present teachers' voices on in-service teacher-training programmes.

Teachers' voices on in-service teacher training and its relevance to teaching praxis in Delhi

This section highlights how the effectiveness of capacity development initiatives is perceived by teachers and mentor teachers. Teachers reflect on the challenges[23] of funding, quality, working at scale, absence of a coherent policy and emerging trends in the usage of ICT.

Mentor Teacher Programme – mentor teachers' views

As seen above, mentor teachers are a key part of the AAP governance framework – not only to change in-service teacher training but also to institutionalise a form of on-site support. Mentor teachers leverage their creative expertise to strengthen the academic and pedagogic capacities of other teachers at DoE schools. The old in-service teacher training in Delhi (and elsewhere in India) consisted of classroom instruction of new content or pedagogy by trained resource persons or faculty from DIETs or SCERTs, without any follow-up to assess whether the training was being translated into changed practice in schools and whether it was yielding any results in terms of improved student outcomes. The mentor teaching programme shows that AAP has been trying a new model, including learning from nations that have high student achievement levels. However, this was not necessarily successful, given the radically different contexts in play.

Reflecting on the five-day course on mentoring at NIE in Singapore, the participants shared that they observed the teaching procedures at Woodgrove Secondary School in Singapore, attended sessions with school mentors and learnt about new avenues of teaching that focus on student development rather than rote learning. Upon probing about the implementation of learnings from these training sessions, almost all reported concerns about the Singapore training sessions. Though they found training sessions in Singapore on child-centred teaching 'very useful', they face challenges in implementing them in their schools in Delhi. One participant shared, 'in Singapore, the population is four to five million; the culture is different there than in Delhi. In Delhi, there is diversity, students come from diverse backgrounds; they have their way of speaking. We are also trying our best to change the culture, trying to make teaching child-centred, use group learning; we are trying to adapt their pedagogies. But how much can one do?' (MT1 Science SV7). Mentor teachers also shared that sometimes they feel low self-efficacy due to the high PTR in the classroom and the low level of motivation among teachers in Delhi, discussed in detail in the following paragraphs. While critical of the Singapore-based training, mentor teachers were proud of their new role. They shared how the programme in Delhi has strengthened their understanding of innovative classroom practices. One of the mentor teacher participants said, 'I feel the Delhi education landscape has improved as a result of these programmes. But we have a long way to go to motivate teachers. I want to say that today the children who are studying in the schools their confidence has improved, their understanding has developed. I attribute this to the capacity-building programmes or training that teachers have received, which has been wonderful, and teachers' confidence has also improved' (MT6 Mathematics SV11). The MTP also aims at developing a culture of collaborative learning among teachers at school. One of the TDCs, who has also worked as a mentor teacher (and is now coordinating the meetings with teachers), discussed the vision of the programme and how this is meeting the needs of teachers in Delhi, saying,

we are trying to make the school sound by first making the teachers academically sound, which has increased over the 45 years because of the DIKSHA[24] portal, cybercrime app [software application-POSCO], and ChalkLit app.[25] However, it takes time to bring changes in teachers' actions, as it is a burden for us, first of all. But, when I attended the meetings and trained teachers, and received the feedback, all of us felt quite good about it. Now teachers are transforming; so are the students, but many teachers are not motivated (FT1 Science SV12).

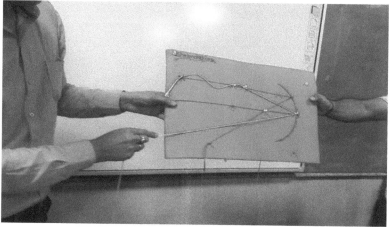

Figure 3.2 Training session by a mentor teacher.
(Source: authors).

Another mentor teacher also shared that there is a low level of motivation among teachers to learn new practices. She mentioned that 'Like when the TDC programme started, in the beginning, it was difficult to convince everyone to stay. Nobody wants to stay. They used to think we have better work to do' (FT1 Science RPVV1).

Almost all mentor teachers linked 'low motivation' among government school teachers in Delhi with 'resistance' and 'reluctance' to learn and implement innovative practices in the classroom. One mentor teacher mentioned that due to the diverse backgrounds of the children at the schools, it sometimes becomes a challenge for the teacher to accommodate everyone. So, they are resistant to change:

> there are a few teachers who don't want to evolve, to be very honest. They usually say that it is not possible with their students. They think that what they know is the best method, and they don't try to. They also don't even try to change their mindset so that you know they're closed mindset is a big barrier for us, a few teachers, not all, and that is also changing their tribe with the help of communication with the help of a lot of other activities. So, we are trying to mould those also (MT9 Science SV1).

The mentor teacher participants felt that 'teachers should be open to ideas, refine decision-making skills and become more effective at integrating theory and practice. In this context, one of the mentor teachers also explained her positionality, saying mentor teachers are co-learners. There is inertia in teachers to change; they are not willing to change. What we need is to have training in small groups. The big group of teachers never listen, and training happens with 50–100 teachers. Training should be like where everyone gets to learn something. The discussion should be between 15–20 teachers.

(FT2 Hindi RPVV1)

However, in some cases there are issues of power relations while working with other teachers:

we were a bit sceptical about the whole thing because the teachers themselves are mentors. When mentors reached schools, teachers thought the mentors were coming to do some kind of boss or something, give them commands and something. But gradually, as time went by, they realised we were like their friends and are helping them to solve their problems. But teachers don't listen to us.

(FT2 Science SV12)

To help establish them, in each school the mentor teachers receive support and guidance from a dedicated Academic Resource Team. It consists of a diverse group of secondary teachers with the intrinsic motivation to implement new classroom strategies and be role models for other schoolteachers (Goel, 2019). However, despite this, the results of the programme seemed to be quite mixed.

Teachers in Delhi are often divorced from the discussions and formation of educational policymaking. This means that when policymakers direct teachers to implement educational changes, such implementation often happens in a vacuum with little regard to the teacher as a leader and contextual decision-maker. Naturally, this leads to resentment and frustration. There were many similar statements from mentor teachers, which implies that teachers are sceptical of the mentoring programme in Delhi. It seemed that mentor teachers need more expertise in assessing the needs of fellow teachers, so as to customise their training accordingly.

Teachers' voices on the mentor teachers, MTP and TDCP

The new in-service teacher education programmes initiated by the Delhi government have generated mixed responses from participant teachers. Some teachers are happily incorporating the training in their classrooms. Some, however, are frustrated with not being able to implement the practices learnt – largely because of their classroom context. When it comes to implementing new classroom practices, in-service training (especially the MTP) appears to be the most useful. Both perspectives were explored in detail. The participants shared their views on the efficacy[26] of teaching using innovative practices that were improved by in-service training programmes, especially through learning about how to improve the relationship with students and teaching using child-centric approaches. Language teachers shared that they found the in-service sessions with mentor teachers extremely useful for learning about innovative practices to teach grammar (FT1 English SV3, FT1 English RPVV3). An English teacher elaborated

> they [mentor teachers] don't focus much upon theory. They teach us how to recite a poem, and how to teach poetry because these particular skills need polishing. Such skills are basically developed in us through seminars, and workshops for two to three days. Even the mentors are in my contacts even today because I take the number so that even if I'm facing any problem, later on, I can just communicate with them, and they can give me a way out (FT1 English RPVV3).

Mentor teachers also shared useful strategies for teaching controversial or difficult topics; a social science teacher participant explained how a mentor teacher during in-service teacher-training seminars helped him to teach the distinction between controversial topics such as nationalism and patriotism. He shared that 'nationalism and patriotism are important but very difficult topics. This is an important topic for exams. Students ask us the difference between both. I wasn't sure so I asked in the seminar [and] the mentor clarified; so we learn new things and we learn how to answer the questions' (FT6 Social Science SV8). Teachers also feel confident after attending in-service teacher education programmes, meeting mentor teachers and discussing new topics. Many participants expressed a high level of motivation and confidence in dealing with students' queries after attending in-service training seminars. Even those sceptical about in-service training said that mingling with other teachers during training and sharing ideas helps more than the methods taught by the mentor teachers and that these sessions help teachers find 'solutions to our problems and concerns in the classrooms' (FT6 Social Science SV8).

Despite the positive feedback, there are still issues. The situation in Delhi seems to be that training plans are largely conveyed through state circulars that reach schools directly in a top-down way, bypassing mid-level government apparatuses and ignoring the contextual variations of individual schools, not to mention consulting with individual teachers (Yan, 2019). Some participants reported that the MTP or mentor teachers do not understand local contexts and needs. A participant expressed concerns over the teaching strategy shared by the mentor teacher, with an example:

> our mentor teacher explains how to teach articles and adjectives. They teach us through activities. But the thing is that till the time you are not going to understand the problem of children at that particular place and then train the teachers, words are not going to work. They [mentor teachers] come from different places, and urban regions, they hardly visit the schools located in rural areas, or they generally visit for a brief period. So, they train us as per some different region, and when we try this in our school *'bacche schote pata nahi sir kya sikh ke a gae'* (children think we don't know what sir has learnt). The mentor teachers have to be from the same background.
>
> (FT1 English SV8)

The participants shared that some of these initiatives have had limited success in the classroom, as they ignore the local needs of teachers and thus remain unable to support sustained change in their classroom practices.

In certain cases there is a complete mismatch between teacher needs and mentor expectations. A Sanskrit teacher participant expressed complete dissatisfaction upon meeting with mentor teachers:

> Till now, they have conducted 2–3 seminars. But I did not get any benefit out of it. No, *'moh mat khulwao ye sab chije naam matr ke liye hoti hai'* (don't insist that I open my mouth, these things are for the namesake). There is nothing for Sanskrit … They explain everything from the book, and how to teach students. But if I start to follow their idea, then it will not work for me.
>
> (FT1 Sanskrit RPVV3)

This in-service mentoring model can be successful when there is participative project development, context sensitivity, formative re-educative models of training (like examining the effectiveness of existing teaching practices) classroom-centred training that helps teachers and students, collaboration at all system levels, responsiveness towards the teacher's needs and CPD (Iyengar et al., 2014).

Some participating teachers were scathing about the mentor-teacher arrangements but conceded that teachers could learn from each other:

> The in-service training, in reality, is a farce. The mentors use it as time pass, and we also use it as time pass. But we get to learn things from the other participants [teachers];[27] we share our experiences regarding classroom practices and learn many things from these discussions ... The mentor does not help us in this. He is there only for the thousand rupees that he gets as an honorarium for conducting sessions. The mentors are from among ourselves, so they are afraid of us and think that the trainees will pull their legs, so they take their thousand rupees, choose a normal topic, give sessions and go away (FT10 Science RPVV3).

Some participants reported that existing in-service training arrangements and mentor teachers are incentive-based and do not match their preferences and expectations; for example:

> In-service training *wo kuch khas nahi hai bas bat hoti hai in service mai concrete kuch nahi hota waha pe blank hai* (The in-service training is not so good. They only talk, which is far away from reality). In one training session, I raised the question, why can't you conduct one training session for the teachers who are going to evaluate board papers?[28] *Mera experience blank raha hai waha se kuch nahi sikha* (my experience is blank; I have not learnt anything from there). *Waha pe na methodology acche se discuss karte hai, na content acche se discuss karte hai na how to teach acche se to discuss karte hai* (they do not discuss methodology, content or how to teach properly), they just pass three days or five days.
>
> (FT5 English RPVV3)

These quotes imply that teachers' professional knowledge seems to be entirely overlooked, positioned as irrelevant, 'soft', or deficient, by policy and programme interventions.

Indeed, professional learning should offer various forms of reciprocal interaction between mentors and teachers (such as brainstorming, modelling, sharing ideas and conflict resolution), which acknowledge the complex theoretical base from which teachers draw (Putnam and Borko, 2000). Instead, the introduction of mentor teachers has created a managerial class within the ranks of teachers where everyone supervises everyone.

As discussed above, despite its strengths, the MTP shows signs of weakness. This is because the focus on classroom-teaching-based teacher education tightens the link between teacher professional development and teaching outcomes (Sandhu, 2021). Therefore, this model exists within a performative culture that emphasises examination scores and an instrumental view of education. The mentor teachers and headteachers behave like the managerial class and accept the necessity of imposing targets, indicators and evaluations as a means of making the school system accountable (Sandhu, 2021). The consequence for teachers' professional development is that the whole collaborative process of professional learning through peer discussion is directed towards improving learning outcomes. Teachers' voices in this section show that behind the technical and structural changes envisaged by the education reforms lies the reform of their subjectivity. This changed subjectivity is with reference to the alignment of the behaviour of teachers with the efficiency model (as described in Chapter 1). In this model, teachers feel they are good and successful if they produce good test results and help children move up the learning categories. Therefore, a 'good' teacher is one who is efficient in pedagogical skills and effective in producing high scores and volunteers for leadership roles, such as the mentor teachers (Sandhu, 2021).

The MTP is not the only new in-service programme that AAP has put in place. The section below looks at other programmes, including Jodo Gyan and online training.

Teachers' views on other in-service training

Jodo Gyan and online training – the ChalkLit app

For subject-specific training, most of the primary mathematics teachers found Jodo Gyan[29] training and activity-based training extremely useful in enacting the curriculum as well as improving student agency and engagement. The Delhi government recognised that the abstract nature of mathematics makes it difficult for children to learn the subject. By making mathematical concepts real, children could understand the subject better and relate it to real-life situations. Therefore, in 2015, the Department of Education started a pilot project with Jodo Gyan to develop and implement a primary school mathematics curriculum for classes I to V. The programme was then extended to all the 451 Sarvodaya schools.[30] Jodo Gyan is inspired by the Realistic Mathematics Education approach and has been working towards making mathematics more applicable in reality. It includes various toys for early learners: rangometry,[31] *ganitmala* (a string with sets of four coloured beads), *ganit* racks (two rods one below the other with 10 beads each), dienes blocks, fractions kit, *aakar-parivar* [story making and story telling on the basis of colours and shapes], triangles kit, tessellation kit, jodo blocks, jodo straws, geo board, place value cards, tangrams, sorting sets and books for children and teachers form the bulk of these resources (Sarangapani et al., 2017). When asked how they enact the curriculum using these training sessions, a maths teacher explained,

> Jodo Gyan training in maths teaching familiarises us with rangometry, 70 number line that helped me in teaching maths. In my classroom, children get excited to do the activities based on these learning materials; otherwise, they are too shy; they do not want to come to the blackboard. The activities break the monotony of regular teaching and increase engagement (FT2 Primary SV4).

Echoing that view, another participant shared in detail what she learnt from the Jodo Gyan training and how she enacts it in the classroom: 'there are shapes like triangles, circles, rectangles; we stick these shapes to the blackboard. You can also make pictures on your desk with it. You can create a number of pictures. Children then can identify the shapes used to create the hut' (FT3 Primary SV4). She enjoyed enacting the training on rangometry in her classroom and reported increased engagement and student agency as a result: 'rangometry was very good. Children enjoy playing and creating with it. First, we assign groups with rangometry and then ask students to create a hut, or anything, then ask them to count the number of shapes they have used to create that picture. In that training, we gave them "ginladi" (number line, counting), which was also good. Students really enjoyed and understood the concepts well' (FT3 Primary SV4). However, the lack of resources in many schools also impacts teachers' professional learning opportunities and students' experiences. A motivated teacher said, 'Jodo Gyan training in 2015 or 2016 provided us with new ideas to teach. The ideas we get are quite encouraging. The training was based on using the math kit. I was so excited to use it in my classroom. The issue was that we did not get the kit for one or two months, after the training' (FT1 Primary SV10). Besides teaching aids, participants also raised the issue of internet connectivity before the pandemic. The majority of the participants reported that this created an obstacle in using the audiovisual method of teaching. A participant reported an incidence from her school: 'many days I wish to show my students some videos but there is no internet. I do report this issue to the administration, but nothing is done so far. These issues do prevent us from implementing innovative ideas and affect students' engagement' (FT8 RPVV1 Hindi). On similar lines, another participant said that they needed time and resources to practise innovative child-centric approaches: 'if I am supposed to practise innovative child-centric teaching, then I need time and resources to teach. We do not have the resources. Sometimes the children do not take an interest in the technique [lecture method] we try to implement, because every child is different. If one or two children get interested, it won't help me. I need to teach all the children' (FT3 Mathematics SV2). This implies that schools are underresourced and teachers often have little access to books, computers and other teaching resources or aids. Other studies have also shown that this in turn leads to significantly low motivation among teachers (Kremer et al., 2005; Ramachandran and Pal, 2005).

In terms of online training, the Delhi SCERT provides topic- and lesson-specific training only for teachers of classes IX and X in mathematics, science and English via a mobile app called ChalkLit,[32] developed by an NGO – the Million Sparks Foundation – in 2016 (Jha, 2019). Sunita Kaushik, the SCERT director, asserted that efforts are now underway to provide similar training for class IV and V teachers in mathematics and subjects in classes XI and XII as well. Kaushik said[33] the push to train teachers online was prompted by limitations of time and space (Jha, 2019).

Historically, India's commitment to the development of Open Educational Resources (OER) started with the National Knowledge Commission recommendations in 2008 to create a national e-content and curriculum initiative (National Knowledge Commission, 2008, 109, cited in Perryman, 2013). Perryman's research[34] reveals that the potential benefits of the system include the contribution to ICT, which focuses on professional development for teachers by broadening the range of the curriculum, providing teachers with the flexibility to create lesson plans that cater to student needs and providing a platform to be reflective about teaching practices[35] (Perryman, 2013). Teachers at Delhi government schools have been 'ordered'[36] to join online training provided through the ChalkLit app. From the participants' narratives, it appears that ChalkLit is helping them in understanding policies such as POCSO,[37] corporal punishment and child and sexual abuse. Most of the teachers interviewed are using this software application for training and many have provided positive feedback about it – in particular how it is helping them to improve their teaching techniques, understand students and their backgrounds and gain knowledge of various government policies. Particularly, they found the collection of resources such as 'videos', 'illustrations' and 'descriptions' very useful for planning lessons (FT4 Primary SV1, FT3 Science SV12, FT3 Mathematics SV2). However, some participants also expressed criticism of using the ChalkLit app for developing teaching capacity and concerns over the lack of space for teachers to discuss things. A participant stated: 'using a single platform for teachers and students is not the right thing, especially for issues like child sexual abuse' (FT5 Hindi SV2). Lastly, some teachers do not like the way it has been imposed upon them – taking up more of their time outside of the already lengthy school and preparation hours.

According to the teachers interviewed, none of the in-service programmes incorporated strategies directly related to local needs, such as training teachers in how to work in highly constrained environments with high PTRs and working largely towards system-driven demands of completing the syllabus, administering exams and engaging in other mandatory administrative work (Chandran, 2021). In India, teachers perceive the administrative aspects of their work, such as documentation, testing and reporting, as taking precedence over pedagogic ones. The administrative duties and official control do not allow teachers to use their training experiences in pedagogic roles (Chandran, 2021). Even in Delhi, respondents are obliged to spend about a third of their time on administrative tasks. The everyday reality of bureaucracy is shaped by a 'paper tyranny' for respondents. The documentation has for a long time been a part of the teachers' daily routine, maintaining different types of registers of various activities at the school as required by the authorities. Respondents explained that there were circulars issued from the Block Education Officers (BEO), sometimes two or three a week, for which data had to be furnished on the same day. Teachers spend their time on this type of paperwork rather than planning lessons. Respondents said they felt like clerks, and this had become worse since the introduction of child-centred education. Teachers' nonacademic administrative tasks thus took precedence over academic ones, for which teachers blamed the BEO's failure to maintain proper records (Chandran, 2021; Aiyar et al., 2021). A core principle of child-centred education, teacher autonomy (Kumar, 2019; Nawani, 2013; Chandran, 2021) was conspicuously absent from the teacher discourse.

The above quotes show that in-service teacher-training programmes on classroom management did not necessarily meet the needs revealed by the participating teachers. In fact, the programmes were not infrequently found to 'not match expectations' or 'not solve real-world problems. The excerpts from the interviews also showcase the outcomes of capacity building on teacher agency (Brinkmann, 2019; Anand, 2019). The voices of teachers reflect that they are eager to adapt the training received for use in their classrooms (Lall and Anand et al., 2020). However, the obstacles mentioned above need to be resolved to enable teachers to apply all the practices learnt during the training.

NGOs and Delhi government schools

NGOs are increasingly involved in government schools to facilitate education and learning through various means such as teacher training, innovative educational methods, offering after-class support for weaker students in non-formal education centres, providing midday meals and more. A report on the NGOs' role in the education sector claimed that NGOs are working in the capacity beyond 'the gap-filling initiatives to step into innovation and capacity building' (Deloitte, 2013, 15). India has 4 NGOs for every 1,000 people in the urban areas, and 2.3 NGOs for every 1,000 people in rural areas (Swamy, 2021). In Delhi there are a large number of NGOs working in the education sector. Some of the prominent ones working in school education are Pratham Education Foundation, CHETNA, Room to Read, Smile Foundation, Teach for India, Akshay a Patra Foundation, Central Square Foundation, Deepalaya, Saajha, Oxfam India, Child Rights and You (CRY), STiR Education, Vidya Education, Hope Foundation, Katha, Save the Children, Simple Education Foundation, Goonj, ASPIRE – among others (Education World, 2016; Arya, 2018). The official website of the DoE has a list of NGOs[38] working with the Delhi government. According to the Delhi government, it partnered with 11 NGOs (unnamed) to train 764 special educators working in Delhi government schools. Besides this, a number of NGOs are involved in providing support through Special Training Centres (STCs)[39] for MCD and government-run schools[40] (DoE, n.d.). A study on Delhi NGOs working in the education sector reported that there are also NGOs carrying out education work without necessarily partnering with any government entities. For instance, there are NGOs operating in Delhi that have established themselves within a single neighbourhood, where they run one or multiple small learning centres. These centres provide additional tutoring in school materials, preparation for standardised tests and training in basic work skills to equip the students for the labour market (Kumar, 2018). NGOs have become 'a key ecosystem of support for poorly functioning government schools in different cities where the intervention is functioning' (Subramanian, 2018, 44). The Delhi government has taken full advantage of the NGO support on offer, with mixed results, and teachers are not convinced they are particularly useful or helpful.

A few teachers shared that they receive training and support from NGOs. A teacher expressed, 'they give training to selected teachers only. I don't get access to this. Anyways it is difficult to implement as the work is too much for us' (FT7 Science SV8). Even those who have received training from NGOs say they face several structural constraints: 'NGOs call the teachers and train them like the Ramakrishna Mission. They developed software and gave it to us, but it required a projector and a limited strength of students. But due to the paucity of time, we could not do it. I discussed this with them. They wanted a separate period for it, and a separate teacher should be engaged for this. But we could not have a separate period for this, and all the students couldn't fit in the computer lab at the same time. That was not feasible for us' (FT4 Mathematics SV7). When asked about pedagogical barriers, a few teachers shared that these NGOs are unaware of the realities on the ground, such as students' backgrounds. A teacher shared her experience:

'I don't remember the name of that NGO ... there. I have like there was IT. Like the person who works on a computer, he was assigned the job by an NGO. He has introduced software which helps us you don't have to a take book to teach students you can go to the software ... like they install that software into the computer because the computer he's other workers ... I was given an opportunity to teach from that software – they have given the full book – and you can also on its audio, either you can explain the chapter on your own, or you can go for the audio section where the software plays the chapter for children this helps them in pronunciation, plus they will get the change from the voice of their teacher to whom they listen daily ... for the activities ... But this is not suitable for my class, as my students need me.

(FT6 primary RPVV1)

In terms of classroom management, a teacher expressed: 'they [NGOs] train us at a different level; according to them, all the students are here to listen to us. But it does not happen like that – there are naughty students, and we have to keep them involved; otherwise, they get distracted easily. We have to use our strategies.' (FT3 Primary SV8).

In addition, teachers questioned the performance of NGOs and their impact on students' achievement. A teacher shared an example of pedagogical inequity:

> an NGO was working, and it has a separate section of children to teach. Once, the director from the education department visited our school and was impressed with the performance of students who were under the care of the NGO. Those students responded to the director's query quite confidently and shared their ambitions with her. The class was managed quite well. The director visited our classrooms and interacted with the students; they did not respond the way she expected them to. She was furious with us and told us to learn from the NGO. But during exams, the students who were under NGO asked us the answers, and it appeared that they did not know anything. Our children scored much better than those children. I am not criticising the NGO, but I want to tell you the reality of the NGO. They are only concerned with presenting the work they are doing; they are not worried about the quality of the work. Academically our children performed well. I do not think that they were wrong; their method was also suitable. But the academic level should also be taken care of (FT10 Science RPVV3).

The teacher's observations alluded to the NGO model's pedagogical limitation.

The teachers' voices show a degree of tension between them and NGOs. The procedures by NGOs at times establish parallel structures of governance, fragment the teaching-learning process and weaken the position of the government school teacher. Research on NGOs has underlined how their programmes challenge professional teacher education and promote school choice procedures because of the underresourced public-school systems across the world (Straubhaar and Friedrich, 2015). This reflects how the boundaries between state and non-state are becoming porous and the New Public Management (NPM)-led norms are reshaping both the public and the private (Ball, 2003; Gewirtz, 2002; Gewirtz and Ball, 2000). In the educational reform process, the teacher and the ways in which different conceptions around the work of teachers and the concept of teaching itself have been shaped according to ideas coming from the 'new discursive regime' that are found to be similar to those that come from the NPM discourse in education in other countries and the educational reforms centred around ideas of accountability, efficiency and cost-effectiveness (Jain and Prasad, 2018) (see Chapter 1). Neoliberal reforms led to the substantial devolution of state responsibility to a network of NGOs and individuals who were not traditionally a part of the formal state apparatus but became 'instruments through which strategies for governing populations and communities, and fashioning proper selves, are deployed and legitimized' (Sharma et al., 2016, 9). Public-private partnerships emerged as conduits of reform through which the Indian state attempted to restructure itself and transform its social relations of provision and service by subordinating them to the 'discipline of the market' (Kumar, 2018, 6). This new logic of reform that privileged the 'discipline of the market' intersected with a 'gamut' of NPM discourses that emphasised privatisation, competition and the outsourcing of services to the most cost-effective organisations, to improve the quality of performance in public sector institutions (Clarke et al., 2000). As seen in this chapter, public-private partnerships are increasingly becoming imbricated within larger transnational discourses on NPM which emphasise efficiency and quality (Jain and Prasad, 2018).

Conclusion

Innovations in education across the globe are changing everything from school culture to student assessment. Preservice and in-service teacher training has become crucial in this aspect. However, studies in the field of teacher education point towards various lacunas in preservice as well as in-service teacher education in India (Goel, 2019). Overall, the participants in this study unanimously expressed the view that preservice training needs to be more practical rather than theoretical. Most teachers valued preservice much less than in-service training, as the former was seen as not sufficiently relevant to their daily reality. A majority of teachers also expressed that they feel empowered to teach effectively and to improve the learning outcome of students in government schools from the in-service teacher-training initiatives in Delhi. However, teachers also expressed concerns about in-service training being conducted based on generic policies or practices and failing to resolve or touch on the problems teachers face in their classrooms. Teachers' experiences also imply that in-service teacher-training programmes are less effective in linking with teachers' needs and incorporating a participatory and collaborative approach.

This chapter shows that whether in preservice or in-service training, teachers learn new strategies. However, to implement these in the classroom, they have to modify them due to time constraints and adapt them to the specific requirements of students and the local context. The chapter also shows how teachers' official relations are regulated by a 'technocratic model' under which they lack the autonomy to formulate the means to achieve ends appropriate to their context (Chandran, 2021). Official insistence on a technocratic form of accountability and managerial instruments of compliance does not allow for flexible pedagogic conceptions, in direct contradiction with the goal of the reforms, which were intended to be child-centred, creating dissonance in the teachers' pedagogic narratives (Chandran, 2021).

The NEP of 2020 acknowledges the terrible state of teacher education institutions and the presence of poor-quality institutions that have mushroomed over the years in India (Kaur, 2019). The policy identifies bureaucracy and the need to unburden teachers of non-educational duties, which imperative to facilitate vibrant professional communities and give teachers more autonomy in the classroom. However, the proposed transformation as stated in the NEP 2020 will require changes in pedagogy and, consequently, the capacity development and training given to teachers will need to be adapted (Kaur, 2019). The AAP government has tried to transform Delhi's teacher-training systems by strengthening the capacities of the teacher. The next chapter presents teachers' narratives on what has actually changed in their classrooms and their commitment to pedagogic reform.

Notes

1. The terms 'teacher training' and 'teacher education' are used interchangeably in Indian education reforms, although there is an implicit difference between them (Brinkmann, 2016). As suggested by Peters (1967), training usually implies the acquisition of skill through some amount of drilling, without necessarily an understanding of the principles involved. In contrast, education involves also developing knowledge, understanding and a deeper cognitive perspective; this distinction is perhaps significant for teacher education in India (Brinkmann, 2016).
2. Clarke's (2003) empirical study of teacher-training mechanisms in the 1990s showed how the delivery of in-service training failed to work with teachers' existing and often competing frameworks for learning. It was thus difficult for new pedagogic ideals to gain traction in teachers' practices.
3. Teacher agency is defined as 'the capacity of teachers to act purposefully and constructively to direct their professional growth and contribute to the growth of their colleagues' (Calvert, 2016; Soundararaj, 2019, 29). In India, Poonam Batra has written significantly about teacher agency (2005; 2009; 2011; 2014), which she recognises as the most unaddressed issue in Indian education reform (Brinkmann, 2016). According to her, teacher agency encompasses empowering teachers as 'public transformative intellectuals' guided by critical social opinions and research-based learning theories, who can think and act unconventionally, resist state ideological pressures, actively engage with social change and adapt their teaching to local

needs to ensure that all children learn (Batra, 2005). Her main recommendation for elevating teacher agency is to restructure teacher education to make it a longer-duration, interdisciplinary programme grounded in broader critical academic discourses such as BElEd (Brinkmann, 2016).

4. Examples include India attempting to improve school infrastructure, provision and creation of teaching-learning materials and teacher training, and emphasising teacher empowerment through developing teacher-created assessment tools for classroom management in India (Nilsson, 2003).

5. A statutory body, passed by the Parliamentary Act in 1993.

6. Theory-to-practice activities are generally more prominent at preservice levels and practice-to-theory-to-practice activities are more prominent at in-service levels. These relations are not very explicit in preservice teacher training (INEE, 2012).

7. Jena (2015) found that in-service teacher education lacks an updated curriculum, lacks orientation or training in new teaching methods and places no importance on the application of ICT in learning.

8. Herbartian steps to lesson planning.

9. This asymmetrical power relation is discursively connected to other central modernist binaries, such as mind–body; thinking–acting/performing/experiencing; text–voice; seeing–listening; masculine–feminine and, ultimately, as are the sexed bodies that have performed science and pedagogical practice with children during the last century, men–women (compare the list of binaries in Davies, 2000, 51).

10. In the normal classrooms before the pandemic.

11. With 20 to 30 years of experience.

12. This is a technology-led academic support system.

13. For more details on teachers' views on inclusion and how they manage it daily in the classrooms, see the comprehensive chapter on inclusion in this volume (Chapter 5).

14. Special Needs and Parents.

15. Both the NCERT and NUEPA are national-level autonomous bodies.

16. This was an extensive study to assess: the adequacy of training inputs and the transactional modalities of the training programme of 2010–11; the capabilities of resource persons in terms of their training and experience and their preparedness and views on the input of training of teachers; and the perceptions of teachers about the efficacy and usefulness of in-service training.

17. Such as Kaivalya Education Foundation, Tata Trusts, Azim Premji Foundation, the Aurobindo Society and UNICEF.

18. This programme aims at 'consciousness development through value education. It is based on the co-existential philosophy propounded by A Nagraj' (DoE, n.d., 15). The programme has been attended by DIET faculties, DoE teachers, HoS and mentor teachers.

19. This programme was launched 'to provide wider learning experience to the Heads of Government schools [HoS] in order to strengthen their leadership abilities through in-house sessions and international exposure' (DoE, n.d., 12). The monthly sessions of the HoS to strengthen their leadership skills through peer learning are organised in collaboration with Creatnet Education. Each session involves a cluster of 10 HoS and is facilitiated by a senior HoS, trained as a core facilitator. It is reported that '500 principals have attended sessions at IIM [Indian Institute of Management] Ahmadabad and Lucknow on different aspects of school leadership'. Not only this, but 102 HoS have attended an educational programme at the University of Cambridge and 22 at schools in Finland to understand the school education model in these two countries and practices that can be implemented in Delhi (DoE, n.d., 12).

20. 'To support teachers from the Delhi Government to leverage creative expertise by providing on-site learning support to other teachers and organise workshops suited to the pedagogical needs of their fellow teachers' (DoE, n.d., 13).

21. More on this in Chapter 5. Chunauti 2018 was launched in June 2016 to bridge the learning gaps of students in classes VI, VII and VIII as well as to achieve a substantial improvement in the pass percentage of class IX. Students were grouped into three sections based on their foundational skills. In this programme, different kinds of pedagogy and content were used with the three groups, starting with bridging the learning deficit. In the first year, on average, there was an improvement of 20 percentage points across the three domains – ability to read Hindi, ability to read English and ability to solve basic maths. Even the pass percentage in class IX was improved from 52 per cent in 2015–16 to 57 per cent in 2017–18. For teachers,

this programme provided an opportunity and space to help children acquire foundational skills and then connect them to a class-appropriate syllabus (DoE, n.d., 2).

22. STiR Education is an NGO that supports education systems in India (Delhi, Karnataka and Tamil Nadu) and Uganda.

23. Freire (1970) defined praxis as the connection between 'reflection and action on the world in order to transform it' (28).

24. The DIKSHA platform offers teachers, students and parents engaging learning material relevant to the prescribed school curriculum.

25. ChalkLit is an app for teacher education and training. It provides tools, resources and training for teachers to help them teach better in their classrooms.

26. Teacher efficacy highlights teachers' attitudes towards their aptitude to influence the student results (Hoy and Woolfolk, 1993; Wheatley, 2002).

27. 'I faced difficulty while doing a practical, which I shared with one of the participants, and she shared her experiment, and I tried and learnt the thing from her. I learnt to use songs to teach science from one such participant' (FT10 Science RPVV3).

28. 'For some essays, one teacher gives six marks and another nine. There should be logical reasoning. Why can't we talk about the marks process?' (FT5 English RPVV3).

29. https://jodogyan.org accessed 18 March 2022.

30. Currently, Jodo Gyan is also working with the governments of Kerala and Sikkim.

31. Rangometry helps children to make creative designs through colourful foam shapes while learning about shape and geometry. This activity is aimed at enhancing curiosity and learning aptitude in children: https://jodogyan.org/activity-resources-primary-rangometry accessed 18 March 2022.

32. The ChalkLit app has specific modules. The modules are generally for around 10–15 working hours, and teachers are given 15–20 days to complete them. They are then tested on the app, and those clearing it with 40 per cent and above are given a certificate of completion.

33. 'Through the app's modules, we are able to reach out to 6,000–7,000 teachers at a time. We lack the space to train so many teachers face-to-face. Also, training in large numbers can dilute the content. Here, teachers can respond individually to the training, and there's also a "teachers' chaupal", where they can get queries cleared by their peers. Their routine work is also not disrupted, which is important, given a large number of teaching vacancies in government schools' (Jha, 2019).

34. On the contribution by UK Open University's OER Research Hub towards Indian OER.

35. For instance, the Bangalore-based NGO 'IT for Change' established how online mailing groups accompanied by state-level workshops can provide a supportive environment for teachers and teacher educators (Iyengar et al., 2014).

36. Their own words.

37. Protection of Children from Sexual Offences (POCSO) Act, 2012.

38. DoE, Delhi government http://www.edudel.nic.in/ssa/2ngo_dt_07062012.htm accessed 18 March 2022.

39. Special Training Centres http://edudel.nic.in/ssa/7.pdf accessed 18 March 2022.

40. List of STCs: http://www.edudel.nic.in/mis/ssa/ssa_28072014/nonresistcrunbyngo201415.htm accessed 18 March 2022.

4

Teachers and the Delhi classroom: what has changed?

I am the primary in-charge for the past two years, and I have the entire freedom, and other teachers, too, have the freedom. We have K-YAN in our school, and we connect it with YouTube to show to students, for curriculum and storytelling. We use projectors and Tabs [tablets], whatever we want to do … like … We don't have to take them for the picnic. In our school, we have a garden, and there is a farm near our school, so we take them there, and our principal never stops [us] doing anything (FT3 Primary SV8).

Introduction

The previous chapter presented how the AAP government has altered the structure of in-service teacher training and institutionalised the structure of on-site support. Mentor teachers provide on-site learning support and organise workshops to strengthen the academic and pedagogic capacities of their fellow teachers. Teachers' work in Delhi classrooms has been undergoing change because of the shifting landscape of school education, with a magnified focus on teachers' roles and calls for accountability in policies and public debates as school quality becomes redefined in terms of efficiency and measurable outcomes. To understand the impact of school reforms, it is vital to know what teachers do. This chapter presents teachers' narratives in the context of pedagogic reform in government schools in Delhi. As theoretical lenses with practical implications, the concepts of agency and autonomy have been valuable in attempting to understand the ways teachers think, act and learn, and how they accommodate or resist change in their classrooms and schools

(Sherman and Teemant, 2021). This chapter starts by defining teacher agency – a concept that has emerged in recent literature as an alternative means of understanding how teachers might enact practice and engage with policy (Priestley and Biesta, 2013; Priestley et al., 2015). Teacher agency is interpreted as the willingness to engage in iterational, practical-evaluative, projective and transformative action, despite the existence of practical, personal and institutional constraints. It then outlines how the quality of dyadic relationships between headteachers and teachers influences teacher agency, which has helped to build creative, curious and participative learning environments. The autonomy and discretion of teachers to use innovative techniques are negotiated in the classrooms to facilitate a conducive environment of learning for students. Such agency, therefore, aids in the improvement of the teachers themselves as well as impacting students. Finally, this chapter reviews how the HC and the EMC – both additions by the AAP government[1] and taught from kindergarten to class VIII – support the teachers' approach in constructing personal connections to deliver experiential teaching as well as building co-scholastic skills of mindfulness, instilling moral values and offering opportunities to motivate students towards vocational education.

The status of teacher agency and professional autonomy in India

The concept of teacher agency has emerged in recent literature as an alternative means of understanding how teachers might enact practice and engage with policy in classrooms (Lasky, 2005; Leander and Osborne, 2008; Ketelaar et al., 2012; Priestley and Biesta, 2013; Priestley et al. 2015). Agency is an inadequately conceptualised construct, and it is frequently unclear whether the term refers to the individual capacity of teachers to act 'agentically' or to an emergent 'ecological' phenomenon dependent upon the quality of individuals' engagement with their environments (Biesta and Tedder, 2007). In the context of professional learning, teacher agency is defined as 'the capacity of teachers to act purposefully and constructively to direct their professional growth and contribute to the growth of their colleagues, (Soundararaj, 2019, 29). It is imperative for the process of implementing educational reforms (Hamid and Nguyen, 2016). To successfully implement reforms, teacher professional agency is required: to shape a creative, curious and participative learning environment that aids design and practice of innovative teaching methods; and to put theoretical knowledge into practice through classroom teaching, school enhancement and self-development (Lipponen and Kumpulainen, 2011). In addition, autonomy and agency are positively related to teacher motivation and engagement in teaching (Lennert da Silva and Mølstad, 2020). Teacher autonomy is a key aspect of the teaching profession (Wermke and Höstfält, 2014) that is positively related to perceived self-efficacy, job satisfaction and a positive work climate (Cribb and Gewirtz, 2007; Wermke et al., 2019). These factors are crucial to teachers' motivation and commitment to providing effective learning opportunities for students (Cribb and Gewirtz, 2007).

In India, Poonam Batra has written extensively about teacher agency and professional autonomy (2005; 2006; 2009; 2011; 2014; 2017), which she acknowledges as the most unaddressed issues in Indian education reform. While Batra does not offer a single definition of what teacher agency entails, she highlights issues such as the system's view of teachers as passive recipients expected to mindlessly implement predefined content designed elsewhere, and its failure to engage with teachers' sociopolitical context or imbibed sociocultural beliefs (Brinkmann, 2016). Scholars (O'Sullivan, 2006; Schweisfurth, 2015; Tabulawa, 1998) have pointed out that often pedagogical models are developed by a central team with no attention to the actual process of change, the complexities of ground realities and what teachers themselves know and think about their classroom practice, yet the team expects the model to be rigidly implemented by the teachers. Often reformers tend to be unrealistic in what they expect teachers to do, and how quickly they expect change to happen.

Ramachandran et al. (2008, 6) maintain that the crux of the problem in Indian pedagogical reform lies in how the education system views teachers as 'lowly recipients and implementers of instructions and content designed elsewhere', who are expected to comply with predefined tasks rather than to analyse their own teaching practices in view of student learning. Batra (2005) argues that this top-down discourse moves into the National Curriculum Framework 2005, which, despite its commendable vision, views teachers more as 'passive agents of the state who are expected to be persuaded and trained to magically translate the vision of the NCF 2005 in schools' (43–9). By failing to articulate the processes and programmatic interventions needed to operationalise its ambitious vision, the NCF 2005 (like many policy reforms in India) unfortunately undermines its own fulfilment. Teachers who themselves have never been enabled to exercise autonomy or critical thinking can hardly be expected to develop these skills in children (Batra, 2006; Kumar, 2005). Teachers' lack of autonomy creates a culture in which they feel compelled to strictly follow a prescribed curriculum and textbooks, restricting their ability to adapt teaching content and methods to local needs, as expected by child-centred pedagogies. Batra views focusing on teacher agency and empowering teachers as public transformative intellectuals as 'the most important component of reform of Indian public education without which very little can be achieved' (Batra, 2006, 9).

A number of factors have contributed to shaping and reinforcing teachers' low degree of professional agency in India. Kumar (2005) traces its roots to the bureaucratic colonial system, which enforced centralisation in both employment-related matters and academic matters such as the design of the curriculum, textbooks and examinations. Another oft-cited factor has been the policy decision by several states to introduce a system of professionally unqualified and underpaid, locally recruited para-teachers (Ramachandran et al., 2008). Teachers' professional status and motivation are further undermined by the low status of teaching as a profession, increasingly chosen as a last resort by unemployed youth or women seeking a part-time, socially acceptable occupation. Often, honest and motivated teachers are the ones saddled with non-teaching assignments or transferred to difficult areas (Ramachandran et al., 2008). The various complexities of teachers' working realities are rarely confronted in public documents, yet, as Ramachandran points out, 'a demoralised, unmotivated and burdened teacher cannot turn the system around' (2005, 2144). Batra's main recommendation for uplifting teacher agency is to restructure teacher education and training to make it an interdisciplinary programme with a longer duration, grounded in broader critical academic discourses (Brinkmann, 2016).

The status of teacher agency and professional autonomy in Delhi after the reforms

In 2015 the Delhi government reduced the administrative bureaucracies for routine matters in its schools and offered more autonomy to headteachers for removing bottlenecks so that basic facilities could be provided to the students (Kaur, 2019). The AAP government recognised the state of teacher agency and lack of empowerment and with this the need to unburden teachers of non-educational duties, facilitating vibrant professional communities and giving them more autonomy in the classroom. As mentioned in the previous chapter on teacher training, the proposed transformation started with in-service teacher training and capacity development. To make the approach to teaching and learning more interactive, teacher-training programmes were evaluated and classrooms and other school facilities were equipped with contemporary teaching aids and classroom equipment (Kaur, 2019). Besides that, the HC and the EMC were introduced to develop the areas of transformative learning. The Delhi education reforms journey was guided by specific principles, as reviewed by Bhat (2020). First, decentralising control and building agency, which includes investments in long-pending initiatives around school-leadership development, teacher professional development and giving agency back to school leaders, teachers, parents and students – ideas that have modelled their success. Second, upskilling teachers and mentor teachers, clearing pathways for school leaders to perform their primary function and giving them supporting funds, resources and people, has led to far-reaching shifts in mindset around their role. Third, creating a collaborative culture by removing age-old 'silos' between the different government departments delivering educational services and enabling a clear shift in the realisation of educational outcomes. Lastly, recognising that reforms have only been possible because of the government's deep sense of engagement and involvement with all the stakeholders involved (Bhat, 2020). A recent report published by the Boston Consulting Group (BCG)[2] (2020, 96–8) found that 95 per cent of surveyed teachers reported an improvement in the quality of education, along with 91 per cent of them feeling more motivated about teaching. The introduction of a new holistic curriculum was notably the most impactful academic change for teachers. The report states that headteachers have become more encouraging, promoting collective ownership and visiting classrooms more often – which was cited as among the most impactful of the academic changes. Teachers' voices on these factors will be discussed in the following paragraphs.

Teachers' 'professional' agency and the work environment

Within the discourse of agency, teacher agency is considered a specific form of professional agency – teachers' active contribution to shaping their work and its conditions is assumed to be an indispensable element of good and meaningful education (Biesta et al., 2015). The sociocultural perspective on agency (Giddens, 1984) gives ample opportunity to understand the role of teacher agency in professional development and school reform: from this perspective, interdependence between the individual and the social context is central (Imants and Van der Wal, 2020).

Teacher agency is realised within sociocultural constraints – for example, national and school curricula, professional and power relationships with colleagues and management, and the dominant culture in the school. When asked whether they received freedom from the headteachers to try new things in the classroom, a teacher shared, 'I teach science to 8th, 9th and 10th, [and] we have to use models to explain various phenomena or other activities in science; for instance, to teach the theory of relativity, we used a model. Though I paid from my pocket, there was no restriction to use different methods by the principal' (MT1 Science SV7). A teacher shared her experience to explain what made her school different from others, saying: 'I have worked only for 2–3 months in other DG [Delhi government] schools, so they may differ. We get teaching aids here … we have got a tablet, for online teaching, or digitalisation; technically, we get lots of help here from the headteacher and colleagues' (FT5 Mathematics RPVV1). Another teacher echoed: 'I was posted in some another school where I didn't like the work environment. I wanted to change that school … Now I got an opportunity to work with [principal's name redacted] … generally he is …, actually, a good leader, a very good principal' (FT6 Primary RPVV1). When probed on what motivated her to teach at this school, she shared that 'like goal achievers … they give us new strategies, and techniques. They share with us, those techniques and strategies, so that we can work on them and kindly get the results that we are … looking for' (FT6 Primary RPVV1). An experienced teacher expressed that 'it was not like that, in the past 10 years, the freedom for teachers has increased. A system is established where teachers are heard, they are connected, dialogues are heard, whatever policies are made; as a teacher I feel the work that is being done in the education sector … is based on the will of the teacher. So, I have freedom as a teacher to say what I want to say. The higher authorities are also working teachers well this is what I feel' (MT6 Mathematics SV11). From the interviews, it emerged that teachers' professional agency is nurtured by their relationship with headteachers, which helps them to build creative, curious and participative learning environments. This was possible because the Delhi government built on insights about what held headteachers back from having a vision for their schools – the lack of an enabling environment. Headteachers were sent on leadership development programmes and exposed to the best teaching-learning institutions nationally and globally to inspire them and show them what might be possible (Talreja and Bhat, 2020). Headteachers articulated an increased sense of empowerment and ownership over their schools due to the devolved financial and administrative powers and the development training. They had the freedom to allocate budgets to improve both schools and learning outcomes. Headteachers felt they were trusted to make decisions in the best interest of their schools, and encouraged to have a five- to 10-year vision for their school and students

(Talreja and Bhat, 2020). They also reflected on their growth as school leaders and expressed a strong conviction that self-improvement was leading to tangible improvements in school governance and learning outcomes (BCG, 2021).

At the same time, teacher agency is restricted by the availability of resources like classroom equipment, instructional methods and ICT devices. However, these constraints are not completely out of the control of teachers. Depending on a teacher's interpretation of these contextual constraints and boundaries, and depending on their agency, teachers can enact the curriculum as per the environments within their school and outside the school (Imants and Van der Wal, 2020). Teachers commented that the administration and headteacher are supportive in terms of arranging teaching aids. A science teacher shared: 'to explain a concept, for example to teach students about [the] digestive system, I draw it on the [black] board, however, students will understand it better if I show them a video and explain through that. So, if I ask headteacher sir to provide me with a projector or [if] I need the computer lab he readily supports me. He is very supportive' (FT7 Science SV3). Another teacher explained how the headteacher supports her self-efficacy and motivation; she said: 'He [the headteacher] has asked us not to worry about completing the syllabus. If a task is needed to be done, which we consider will improve the quality of the school, we have full support from HoS to implement it without hesitation. Whatever we need, equipment or anything, we ask our HoS to provide, and he ensures that we get it. Our HoS is from a science background, so he is always ready to take classes. He has asked us to inform him if he needs to take any classes, he has no issue … He always told us that if he visits our classroom, that does not mean he is there to find shortcomings in our teaching. Instead, he is there to support us. He says that a teacher knows how to teach – he is there only to support us, and we can ask him to help us whenever we need. A better environment is essential to teach, which we get here' (FT11 Social Science RPVV3). Furthermore, recognising the critical role that teachers play in shaping the values, beliefs and world views of learners, the Delhi government created spaces for teachers to be heard by strengthening their relationship with headteachers.

In addition to the social, emotional and interpersonal relationship between teachers and students, a teacher requires substantial freedom and autonomy from headteachers to be able to try out new things in the classrooms (Lennert da Silva and Mølstad, 2020). Teacher autonomy concerns the relations between teachers' scope of action and the state's role in providing resources and regulations that extend or constrain this scope of action (Lennert da Silva and Mølstad, 2020).

Looking at Delhi government school practices, one teacher feels that 'a system is established where teachers are heard, they are connected, dialogues are heard, whatever policies are made … I feel it is based on the will of the teacher. So, I have freedom as a teacher to say what I want to say' (MT6 Mathematics SV11). The autonomy and discretion of teachers to use innovative techniques are negotiated in the classrooms to facilitate a conducive environment of learning for students. For instance, a teacher negotiated their teaching 'space', stating that 'during biology class, the headteacher felt uncomfortable in showing the garden as some chaos would prevail, but I thought that it is essential because one cannot learn everything from theory; practical knowledge is also necessary … then she gave us a full hand to implement that in the classroom or school level. So, this is the way she gives us full freedom' (MT9 Science SV1). Teachers made references to resources that can be viewed as material factors in the practical-evaluative dimension of professional agency and can also include the physical environment and other resources (Priestley et al., 2015). These voices imply that agency can be 'partly shaped by the availability of physical resources and the nature of physical constraints' (Priestley et al., 2015, 25).

Overall, data demonstrates that the quality of dyadic relationships between headteachers and teachers influences teacher agency and is key to teachers feeling supported in their work. Analysis of teachers' voices in this section revealed how positive engagement with headteachers and colleagues can impact teachers' professional agency. Their voices suggest that professional agency can be enabled through the collective actions of teachers in strong and collegial relationships (Ramberg, 2014; Robinson, 2012). In addition, this reduces teacher isolation and helps teachers design and practise innovative teaching methods, transforming theoretical knowledge into classroom practices, school enhancement and self-development. The autonomy and discretion of teachers to use innovative techniques are also negotiated in the classroom to facilitate a conducive environment of learning for students. Such agency, therefore, aids in the self-improvement of teachers as well as impacting the children, as shall be explored below.

Teacher's self-efficacy and agency in classrooms

The supportive teacher–headteacher relationship, as highlighted in the previous section, directly influences individual teachers' efficacy over either the school- or classroom-level curriculum. Existing studies confirmed that support from the principal, colleagues and students is essential for individual teachers to implement and sustain changes brought about by the reform policy (Brezicha et al., 2015; Min, 2019). In addition, the teachers' self-efficacy directly influence their agency towards implementing education reform. Self-efficacy refers to the perception of one's ability to perform certain actions at a desired level (Ross et al., 2016). The teacher level of self-efficacy regarding student engagement and child-centred approaches was associated with their willingness to enact reforms in their classrooms.

Before the AAP reforms, to complete a lengthy syllabus, teachers focused more on teaching than on learning (BCG, 2021). In this design, 'completing a chapter' became more important than ensuring that students learnt something as a result of the chapter. To change this mindset, AAP made a conscious effort to shift the vocabulary of education towards developing teachers' efficacy and competencies. This was achieved by, first, ensuring that the new material was offered in simple and easy-to-understand language (for example, through Pragati books) and by, second, reducing the curricular burden on teachers. As early as 2015 the Delhi government reduced the curriculum for students in classes I to VIII by 25 per cent. Students in some learning groups were also allowed to focus on just 20 to 60 per cent of the syllabus (BCG, 2021).

The department also conducted an at-scale teacher consultation process (by inviting inputs through online channels) to determine how to reduce the syllabus. On teachers' recommendations, the Delhi government opted to reduce the syllabus by 25 per cent (BCG, 2021). This increased teachers' ability to teach by different methods such as 'recapitulation', 'testing previous knowledge' and mind mapping. When asked to provide examples from their classroom before the pandemic, a teacher shared: 'I gave [the students] the word flower, now, [asking] what they think about it. Many students whose parents are working mandi (market) said, *hum in foolon ki mala banate hai or phir bechte hain* (we prepare garlands to sell)' (FT8 Primary SV12). Mathematics and science teachers use K-Yan games as well as the activity-based method which they have learnt during in-service teacher training (see Chapter 2). This shows teachers' self-efficacy and motivation to do their best for their students, as these are important in shaping the form aspirations will take (Priestley et al., 2015).

A supportive headteacher–teacher relationship, as highlighted in the previous section, increased teachers' self-efficacy to teach in classrooms. A teacher shared that 'our principal has told us that the lessons can be delivered in any way which we like, but students should be able to understand. The principal has told has that we have to interact with the students, and ... because of the principal's support, I could perform in the classroom and our school has an all-India 5th ranking' (FT4 Primary RPVV2). When asked how teachers use child-centred teaching methods[3] in order to develop critical thinking, a teacher gave this example: 'taking children for outdoor activities such as research or for showing pollination, which I cannot make them understand only by drawing diagrams on the board or by showing colourful pictures in the book. Children enjoy watching things if there is scope to watch – like, during flowering days, I like to take them to the garden to have a look at flowers such as rose or hibiscus' (FT3 Science SV12). This shows teacher empowerment, which means teachers have the right to exercise efficacy and professional judgement about what and how to teach (Bolin, 1989).

A science teacher expressed enthusiasm for using software applications to teach scientific concepts: 'I can try different methods now such as the Visible Body is an app [software application] for doctors, but I have it. I do screen sharing and show ... a dissection that when we remove the upper layer, the lower layer is like that. Students are not interested in that [in this method]. I enjoy practising my methods' (FT4 Science SV3). Language teachers expressed self-efficacy in using bilingual teaching methods to make their subjects understandable. They expressed that it has increased their students' comprehension skills.

This may be explained by suggesting that headteachers and teachers are supportive of improvements in students' learning and their own professional development through embracing reform. The teacher narratives in this section show how teacher self-efficacy was celebrated and never constrained by a lack of support from headteachers for innovative teaching methods. The voices here show that the teachers could practise their self-efficacy by repositioning themselves as implementers of child-centred teaching activities. Teacher narratives reflect that their efficacy in creating a friendly learning environment was further strengthened through the HC and EMC, which will be discussed below.

Teachers' professional agency via the Happiness Curriculum and the Entrepreneurship Mindset Curriculum

HC and EMC have received significant appreciation from all stakeholders, especially teachers, who shared that they have contributed to their agency. Teachers commented that both the HC and the EMC help them connect with students and achieve their teaching goals. The HC and EMC were introduced by AAP to increase student retention and teacher–student engagement, in particular to improve the well-being of children in domains of learning and mainstream subjects (Kondalamahanty, 2019). The main objective is to develop self-awareness among students, and this is done in a fun and engaging manner to enable students to understand themselves and each other. Every week, on one day, students take a break from teacher-facilitated activities and practise building communication skills through debates and 'just-a-minute' talks. This shifts student attitudes towards risk-taking, collective problem-solving and self-belief (Kondalamahanty, 2019).

HC adds the goal of creating a stimulating environment for learners, with a child-centred pedagogy that focuses on children's experiences and active participation. The premise of this curriculum is that helping students develop essential skills associated with happiness improves students' learning and life outcomes (SCERT Delhi, 2018). In the classroom teachers get a lot of opportunities to exercise their efficacy by connecting knowledge to life outside of school, encouraging students to apply skills in their lives and using a variety of engaging teaching strategies to elicit active participation. They expressed that the curriculum brought joy and happiness to students' lives and provided enabling conditions for them to practise creativity, which motivated them in other subjects. Teachers observed that HC changed student behaviour, such as student willingness to share perspectives in other classes. HC has also changed teachers' teaching orientation; they see the flexibility of curriculum as a positive development. In the absence of required standardisation in content, timeline and assessment, teachers have the freedom to design classes according to student needs and interests. The social-emotional learning assessment is feedback-based. While this eases the burden on students, it has increased the considerable curricular burden upon teaching staff.

Along with the happiness classes, Delhi schools now also provide an opportunity for students to gain real life-based experience through the EMC. This focuses on enhancing the entrepreneurial mindset of the students to enable them to 'apply, challenge and innovate' (PTI, April 2021). EMC was started in 2019 as a pilot aimed at instilling an innovation mindset among class XIII students, enabling them to take their ideas to the next stage, creating future 'job-providers' in the country. Under EMC, each day, students from classes IX to XII in 1,024 schools spend 40 minutes picking up soft skills such as speaking with confidence, problem-solving and understanding how businesses work

(Kondalamahanty, 2019). While EMC is compulsory, it is a non-graded subject, so students don't face the same performance pressure as in subjects with examinations. Students are each given INR 1,000 as 'seed money' with which to develop their ideas, and they get to keep it if their ideas grow into a money-making business (Kondalamahanty, 2019). Manish Sisodia, whose brainchild this project is, said: 'This will open up multiple new possibilities for students in Delhi government schools, as they explore various options and choose their profession.' Sisodia has said that EMC will help in dealing with joblessness, economic slow-down and unemployment. EMC was created by educator, serial entre-preneur and software analyst Tarak Goradia and Bengaluru-based entrepreneur and member of AAP, Prithvi Reddy (Kondalamahanty, 2019). The Delhi government states that it aims to equip young people with knowledge and skills for employment through school. The devel-opment community sees entrepreneurship education as one practical solution to the double-edged problem of inadequate education and few jobs. Entrepreneurship education is aligned with a governing ration-ality of neoliberalism that requires individuals to create their own livelihoods with government social supports (DeJaeghere, 2017). EMC thus strengthens the concept of entrepreneurial citizens – those who utilise their innovative skills and behaviours to claim the economic and social rights they had been excluded from previously. EMC sessions provide spaces for the teachers to provide experiential teaching and give them opportunities to motivate students towards vocational edu-cation. In terms of practical activities, through EMC teachers' efficacy has also been nurtured. They 'interact with entrepreneurs who studied at government schools such as Arjun Thakral, Rajiv Thakra, and other famous personalities' (FT8 Science SV2). It helps teachers to 'think cre-atively, out-of-box and make them [students] imaginative' (FT5 Social Science SV5).

Even in the online mode of learning during the Covid-19 pan-demic,[4] teachers used creative approaches such as social media and online interventions to implement these additions to the curriculum. For the students without internet access, teachers designed the interactive worksheets on the HC and EMC (Srinivasan, 2021). In April 2021 in a keynote address, Manish Sisodia commented that a number of students attending the Delhi government schools helped to grow their family businesses in the pandemic based on their learning from EMC (PTI, 2021). He recounted a story from his visit to a government school before the pandemic, when a female student shared that after attending entre-preneurship classes, she was able to help her father by drafting an online marketing system for a mobile repair business. According to Sisodia, EMC inspires the youth and changes mindsets via teachers (PTI, 2021).

The idea of an entrepreneurial citizen is also evoked in Prime Minister Narendra Modi's speeches on making 'job creators' through innovation (2018) and giving youth the capabilities to make it an 'Indian century' (2016) (cited in Maithreyi, 2021, 20). In 2018, speaking at the 'valedictory' function of the 125th anniversary of Swami Vivekananda's Chicago speech at Coimbatore, organised by the Shri Ramakrishna Math,[5] Modi emphatically articulated the importance of developing 'skills, confidence, and entrepreneurialism' in India's youth. The speech reflects the 'global culture within which skills and individual personalities have come to be seen as the appropriate developmental solutions' (Maithreyi, 2021, 20).

Alongside this, significantly, the 'hyper-masculine religious nationalism' (Pathak, 2019, 10) that has come to dominate the state's policies and practices also deeply embeds a neoliberal ethic of 'responsibilisation' and entrepreneurialism in strangely novel ways. The ideology of entrepreneurialism is more clearly seen in the calls for skills development to harness India's youth demographic, in order to make them 'employable' (MoSDE, 2015 cited in Maithreyi, 2021). With entrepreneurialism tightly wedded to nationalism, as seen through the prime minister's 'clarion' calls on 'Atmanirbhar Bharat', 'Make in India' and 'Skill India', the ideal young person is called upon to engage themselves unquestioningly and productively through education and employment, and demonstrate resilience by pulling themselves up by the 'bootstrings', even under worsening structural conditions of unemployment (Mitra and Singh, 2019).

This section shows how skilling has become the new 'training gospel' (Swift, 1995 cited in Maithreyi, 2021, 30). EMC targets the development of technical or vocational knowledge, while HC focuses on the cultivation of new personalities, attitudes and mannerisms. Tracing these changes to the neoliberalisation of education and training shows how a range of skills development programmes such as HC and EMC, from social and personality development skills to employability and vocational skills, seek to cultivate ethics of self-responsibility through up skilling, to overcome structural disadvantage among marginalised youth (Sandhu, 2021).

The neoliberal logic not only governs the state, the economy and civil society, but also behaviour and the subjective identity of the self. The curriculum reforms by the AAP government cannot be seen in a vacuum, as they have the potential to promote new values, leading to the construction of new identities, which draw their genesis from particular economic rationales (Sandhu, 2021 Lall and Anand, forthcoming 2022).

Teacher autonomy and teacher agency in relation to state control and regulations

Teacher autonomy is also dependent on the regulations and resources provided by the state, which can empower (Cribb and Gewirtz, 2007) or deprofessionalise teachers (Ball, 2003; 2010). Cribb and Gewirtz (2007) showed that experienced teachers know that official rules, guidance and norms are important resources in framing and supporting decisions; it does, however, depend on the kinds of rules and regulations. Wermke and Forsberg (2017) added that teachers may see state frameworks as forms of complexity reduction that define particular standards guiding teachers' work but that do not necessarily define the teaching profession itself. In consonance with this argument, teachers in Delhi face barriers that limit their ability to practise autonomy and agency in the classroom, which will be discussed below.

Participating teachers generally experienced the frameworks provided by the state as unhelpful. They explained that it limits their autonomy to teach and devise their teaching strategies. Teachers in Delhi shared that they are forced to enact activities as dictated by the governments. A teacher shared, 'there were lots and lots of problems. We needed a Fit India certificate, [and] had to fill out the ten different forms for physical education teachers [as they] do not understand those forms' (FT2 English RPVV2). The teacher emphasised that the central and state governments planned activities differently: 'the state came up with one circular [and] the centre came up with [another] circular for three months' (FT2 English RPVV2). This creates confusion and low efficacy among teachers and students. In terms of implementing activities, teachers mentioned nonacademic duties and how this affected their work: 'I was out of my school for 80 days, I could not go to my school' (FT5 English SV12). These non-teaching activities require time and teachers feel overburdened, their autonomy constrained.

The constraints in practising autonomy led to a culture of performativity, where tensions between professional commitments and beliefs and the imperative to meet performative requirements affect teachers' subjectivities, causing a lack of creativity, diminished professional integrity and less fun in teaching and learning. Such changes occur in very different national contexts, as noted by Ball (2003; 2010) in England, and Dias (2018) in Brazil. In Delhi teachers stated that there was a policy under which they have to teach every student, check their books, conduct the weekly test, record their attendance and find out the reasons for their absenteeism. There is evidence to suggest that many teachers in Delhi schools have reacted to bureaucratic pressures by increasing performativity in schools, which compromises teachers' professional autonomy. Sachs (2016) asserts that the current focus on regulation is fixated on compliance, and accountability has the negative effect of restricting the enacted curriculum, as teachers increasingly use time to prepare students for examinations. Similarly, in Delhi, a teacher reported that by 'hook or crook, we have to get the best results and high performance of our students. The main focus is only on that. We have to show that we are one of the best government schools' (FT7 Science SV3). Another teacher articulated, 'As teachers, we have to do a lot of hard work for motivating children and getting a good result' (FT5 Social Science SV5). A teacher expressed that 'we are only centred on the marks and whatever' (FT1 English RPVV3). Teachers' voices show that they are teaching to get results for their schools. Ball (2003) points out that the performativity measures claim to increase the freedom for managers and organisations by removing unnecessary constraints; this is, however, a new form of control that encourages teachers to add value to themselves solely by improving their productivity and thereby negating the worth of commitment and service. In terms of internal control, Delhi schools have cameras in the classrooms or hallways, now a common surveillance practice. The teachers explained that the headteachers justified the use of cameras by saying it was a protective measure to avoid violence by students against teachers and peers, and for parents, but some teachers experienced the use of cameras in classrooms as a form of internal control. School leadership will inspect teaching when parents complain about certain teachers. Therefore, teachers feel that even if they have pedagogical freedom, they struggle over teaching practices because of the use of cameras in the classrooms. This reflects Ball's (2003) 'fabrications', which suggests that teachers' responses to accountability and surveillance is performativity to meet the requirements.

Notwithstanding the Delhi government's innovations in education, which enhanced teacher agency, the following paradox still arises: why is the universal provision of autonomy and agency for teachers still a fundamental challenge? Aiyar et al. (2015; 2021) advocate a move in conceptual understandings of why policies or reforms fail, by utilising a political economy framework[6] to uncover why education policy implementation tends to distort. This is illustrated in Delhi. Through the political economy lens, state actors in Delhi are driven by self-interest, with an aspiration to maximise their own power at any given opportunity. Similarly, Riddell (1999) and Grindle (2004) assess policy implementation as a procedure of agenda setting that explores connections and negotiations which 'shape or alter' the political agenda for education and the comparative powers of alternative interest groups (Kukreja, 2019). This might explain why teacher autonomy is still limited, even under the AAP education reform agenda, due to CCTV surveillance, non-administrative duties and state regulations.

Conclusion

The implementation of the AAP initiatives on teacher training and teaching strategies saw some noteworthy results. The improved learning outcomes suggested a steady increase in CBSE board results (reaching 98 per cent pass rate of class XII students) in 2020.[7] It also saw a growth in fundamental literacy and numeracy among students in classes VI to VIII (BCG, 2021, 17). HC and EMC have been received positively by both students and teachers. The student attendance has improved and students attested to increased teacher attendance, efficacy and creativity. Teachers' voices revealed that their experiences of professional agency were dependent on the times and contexts in which they worked. Their experiences uncovered enablers (such as the relationship with headteachers) and constraints (such as state control and regulations) as having a significant impact on professional agency and autonomy. The teachers complained about having a lack of time and energy for work, due to the documentation tasks assigned to them for accountability and performativity purposes. This happens because performativity can change the teacher's identity, as their focus narrows down to performance goals, inhibiting more natural, fluid, rich and flexible thought (Ball, 2003; Liu and Meng, 2009). Teachers' absence for in-service training workshops (as mentioned in Chapter 2 and this chapter) also means that they have less time to teach. This affects their relationships with students (students' agency) and their parents. Manish Sisodia said that in the post-Covid scenario, when schools reopen, the SMCs would play a major role. AAP is focusing on strengthening the role of SMCs in the post-Covid era and bridging the gap between parents and teachers (ANI, Jan 2021). Sisodia said that 'the real success will be when every child leaves the school with a passion to do something for their country and commit to driving a change'.

Notes

1. In 2021, AAP also instituted a Deshbhakti Curriculum; however, this has not been examined in this volume, as it has not yet taken root in classrooms. See Epilogue for more details.
2. Delhi Commission for Protection of Child Rights through BCG was evaluating the impact of educational reforms implemented by the Government of Delhi between 2015 and 2020. https://www.bcg.com/en-in/school-education-reforms-in-delhi-2015-2020 accessed 18 March 2022.
3. Teachers didn't define the methods as child-centric. Some critiques (Lall, 2011; Smail, 2014; Tarmo, 2018) ask challenging questions about whether it is suitable for all cultural or resource contexts. Lall (2011, 219) said that 'CCA is a better approach to teaching and learning, the principal issue identified by teachers, head monks and parents is the fact that this western approach undermines traditional hierarchical structures of respect for teachers and elders, leading to a culture clash at home and in the classroom.'
4. More on the effects of Covid-19 in the last chapter of this volume.
5. https://www.youtube.com/watch?v=QCtvJY5cA50 accessed 18 March 2022.
6. By exploring the cognitive elements integral in the day-to-day decisions of political actors at various reform levels, such research can shed light on the roles that rationality and conflicting interests play in determining the scope of policy.
7. This is not without controversy, as the improvements in results are partly due to a setting strategy that is discussed in the next chapter.

5
Teachers and inclusion: success for all?

'I think inclusion is [when] all kinds of students are getting an opportunity to study together, whether they are slow learners, god-gifted children or children with special needs' (MT3 Social Science SV9).

Introduction

This chapter engages with teachers and inclusion. Given Delhi's diverse background and deep inequalities, inclusion in and through education is of paramount importance. The interviews revealed that teachers have a limited understanding of inclusion as a policy term that was mostly focused on disability, which in turn they felt was the responsibility of special educators. They do, however, work to support children from disadvantaged backgrounds, developing particular strategies for support. Once the label of 'inclusive education' was dropped, teachers explained how they engaged with hard-to-reach children, especially those involved in child labour or from migrant families.

The AAP education policies, including the summer camps of Mission Buniyaad, have helped some of the most marginalised children catch up, provided they can attend the sessions. Teachers were generally supportive of the summer programme, but much more critical of the procedures of setting that have taken hold due to the pressures of achievement: entire class sections have been relegated to the lowest 'Neo-Nishtha' category, where only part of the syllabus is completed, and teachers do not expect students to be able to read or write. This chapter engages critically with this phenomenon, outlining how the setting procedures are divisive and counter to the 'education for all' ethos that permeates AAP education policy.

The long discussions with the respondent teachers allowed a deeper exploration of the issues of inclusion, including the challenges they face. In her work on inclusive education, Singal points out that teachers' voices on this subject are rarely heard or heeded:

> Glaringly absent in debates on inclusive education, particularly in India, is a respect for teachers' concerns, and an acknowledgement of their real struggles … teachers in many mainstream schools' work in classrooms with limited teaching and learning resources, high pressures of non-teaching duties, and low levels of support. Teachers are 'knowers' of their classroom. There needs to be a deeper acknowledgement of the sometimes very limited real choices that they are working with, while also understanding the situated values and priorities that determine their actions … There is a need to create a space for dialogue with teachers, where they are viewed as partners in the inclusive education agenda, rather than as a problem (Singal, 2019, 837).

This chapter aims to bring some of these voices to the fore, the interviews creating that much-needed space for the dialogue which, as Singal explains, is missing.

Inclusion, hard-to-reach children and education – India's policy context

Inclusive education was prominently mentioned in India's District Primary Education Programme (DPEP) in the 1990s. The DPEP report states: 'Inclusion is a philosophy … bringing children with special needs well within the purview of mainstream education … recognizes the diverse needs of the students and ensures quality education to all through appropriate curricula, teaching strategies, support services and partnerships with the community' (DPEP, 2000, 5, cited in Singal, 2006, 365). At this time India emphasised the development of separate, special schools for children with disabilities as well as non-formal education centres. Sen and Dreze (1995) criticised the low quality of these alternative systems. In her decades-long work on the education of children with disabilities, Singal (2006) emphasised the perpetuation of social inequalities as well as the issue of effective use of resources that such a parallel system underpins. 'Taking a purely economic standpoint it can be argued that the development of alternative school systems takes away precious resources that could be channelled into bringing about new developments in the general education system' (365).

After the 1994 Salamanca Statement (UNESCO, 1994), India reformulated its policies to support the inclusion of students with disabilities and other special needs in mainstream schools. The advent of SSA in 2001 shifted the responsibility for children with special needs to the schools. Emulating the US, SSA established a zero-rejection policy. SSA's focus of inclusion was specifically on children with disabilities, who had been at the margins of education for so long (MHRD, 2003). This policy change resulted in a significant increase of children with disabilities being accepted in mainstream schools (Singal, 2006).[1] The new approach was subsequently supported by the Right to Education Act of 2009 (Ministry of Law and Justice, 2006 cited in Singal, 2006) that guarantees education as a fundamental right to all children until the age of 14. The Rights of Persons with Disabilities Act 2016 (Ministry of Law and Justice, 2016) commits India to 'inclusive education', wherein 'students with and without disability learn together and the system of teaching and learning is suitably adapted to meet the learning needs of different types of students with disabilities' (Section 18 of 23).

While the law guarantees the right of disabled children to free education in a neighbourhood school or a special school of their choice, the implementation of inclusion of disabled children in Indian schools has been uneven, or even poor (Tiwari et al., 2015; Armstrong and Sahoo, 2020). SSA supported the new model as it increased access; however, it also promoted a combination of home-based education and alternative educational settings to address the educational needs of children with severe intellectual/physical disabilities (SSA, 2007, cited in Singal, 2019, 829).

Inclusion's change of focus

Over the last few years, the focus of inclusion at a global level has shifted beyond children with disabilities to include all marginalised children. Sustainable Development Goal 4 (SDG4) ensures 'inclusive and equitable quality education' and promotes 'lifelong learning for all' and is part of the pledge of the United Nations 2030 Agenda for Sustainable Development to leave no one behind. The agenda promises a 'just, equitable, tolerant, open and socially inclusive world in which the needs of the most vulnerable are met' (United Nations, 2015). This global process has shifted the debate from the right to inclusive education, in Article 24 of the 2006 UN Convention on the Rights of Persons with Disabilities (UN, 2006), to the inclusion of people who are marginalised on account of gender, age, poverty, ethnicity, language, religion, migration or displacement status. Antoninis et al. (2020) argue that inclusive education is both a process and a result – whereby 'actions that embrace diversity and build a sense of belonging, rooted in the belief that every person has value and potential and should be respected, regardless of their background, ability, or identity' (104) lead to a result – of inclusive education. Inclusive education has become part and parcel of the wider international discourse of education. The Global Education Monitoring (GEM) report dedicated its 2020 edition to the theme of inclusion (Antoninis et al., 2020, 104). The report makes 10 recommendations for achieving inclusion targets by the 2030 deadline. The first underscores the widening of the agenda beyond disability and the eight recommendations for the role of teachers in the process.[2] Teachers are therefore key in making the policy shift a success.

In India, the National Education Framework 2005 – already discussed above in Chapters 1 and 2 – followed the global trend, emphasising the implementation of the 'policy of inclusion' in all schools and the education system. The policy ensures that 'all children, especially the differently-abled children from marginalised sections, and children in difficult circumstances, get the maximum benefit of this critical area of education' (NCERT, 2006, 85). The policy aims to engage all students in the process of learning. Consequently, the Delhi government developed and rolled out particular programmes to engage different sections of hard-to-reach children. Teachers are the crucial 'cog in the wheel', as they are the ones who have to make sure there is education for all in their classrooms, no matter what the circumstances. Given the barriers of high PTRs and limited parental involvement, this is often quite difficult; however, as shall be seen below, the extra resourcing and programmes in Delhi have made a difference.

Delhi teachers' understanding of inclusion – the issue of disability

As has been seen, inclusive education is not a new concept in India. The Kothari Commission (1964) mentioned in Chapter 1 aimed to develop an education system that would serve all, 'irrespective of the caste, creed, background, or ability equally in one environment and one classroom' (cited in Thamarasseri, 2008). The responding teachers clearly believed

we have 35 students. We can recognize those children comfortably. When I join the teaching at that time, there used to be vast classes of 100–125 students. In that class, it was a little challenging to identify such children' (FT13 Sanskrit RPVV3). Teachers also explained that this was the role of special educators who had the required training and knowledge. 'There are so many physically challenged students in our class. And as I told you that we keep a special teacher there. And in infrastructure also so many things are kept in mind while designing the building for them like we have ramps, special toilets for them, and we try that their classrooms are on the ground floor only (FT5 English SV12).

As long as school infrastructure was adequate and there were specialists to help 'special' children, teachers felt that the school was doing its bit to meet the legal and governmental requirements. However, in many Indian schools, the infrastructure is inadequate. Kundu and Rice point to the teachers they engaged with in West Bengal, who generally perceived that the physical infrastructure and instructional resources were inadequate for supporting students with special needs and that school management was not adequate to ensure inclusive education (Kundu and Rice, 2019).

Offering inclusive education also depended on the type of school. One teacher remembered:

> in this school it is there, but in MCD schools … We had only one special teacher for five to six schools. Moreover, he used to come one day a week. For that one day, he will take care of the students who are not in a position to go to the toilet for themselves. But at this school, we have a special teacher for students with special needs. Mainstreaming of these students is there. And they learn things with other students. These students take time to learn, but if you teach them with extracurricular activities … These children have more creativity in them. There was a girl in the 5th standard. She was even having problems with her speech. There was a dance competition, and she was not able to dance, and she was standing with a flag in her hand. She was made to sing Vande Mataram [National Song]
> (FT2 Social Science SV10).

In the case of schools that had no such facilities, teachers felt it was left to them to manage, an extra burden for them as well as the other students in their class. Although none of the participating teachers specifically advocated separate schooling, they did feel that special educators were required and other studies point to teachers citing special schooling as more appropriate, especially with regard to the curriculum and the required individual attention (Elton-Chalcraft et al., 2016). Singal reminds us that without special educators or adequate specialist support, young disabled people who had attended mainstream school felt isolated and neglected (Singal et al., 2018). Before the pandemic, in 2019, the child rights body of the Delhi government had issued 'show-cause' notices to 151 government schools which did not have special educators. In this notice, the Delhi Commission for Protection of Child Rights warned these schools of strict action if they failed to recruit a special educator within six weeks of the notice (Press Trust of India, 2019).

The role of special educators

In schools where there was extra support for children with special needs, teachers pointed to the special educators or children with special needs teachers: 'Some students are blind. We have special educators' (MT3 Social Science SV9). In these cases, the problem was 'solved' and they did not feel that it was their responsibility. 'I had a student in 6th standard, that student is coming with normal students, classes are going on, but they require a special teacher. That student is learning something, but those students require proper counselling and separate teachers; it is difficult to teach them basic things' (FT7 English SV4).

A few teachers pointed to the fact that children with and without disabilities needed to learn to engage with each other. 'These students stay in the school just like the normal students. That way the students come to know how to deal with them, and they also develop an acceptance for them, and they are their buddies and help them too' (FT12 Science SV11). Teachers also thought that SEN students benefitted from certain aspects of mainstream education. 'It is a good as well as bad concept. Good in the sense that the children do not feel alienated. They feel that they are also part of the same milieu. And the bad part is they do not get to learn the things which they would have received in special schools' (FT14 Hindi SV11).

In 2017, in its mission to achieve inclusive and quality education for all (SDG 4.7), the Government of Delhi in association with the UNESCO Mahatma Gandhi Institute of Education for Peace (MGIEP) organised a capacity-building workshop for special educators in 'screening different learners'. The main objective of the workshop was to enhance the skills of special educators in identifying and addressing students who learn differently (UNESCO MGIEP, n.d.). Even then, those teachers trained as special educators had problems in that they might not have had the right training for the disabilities they were facing. Colleagues pointed out that those supporting blind and deaf students might not know how to help dyslexia dyslexic students or anyone termed as 'slow' by the teachers, and that different disabilities needed more support: 'In our school, there are thirteen children with special needs. They all have different needs and requirements. They all learn through different techniques and methods. They all are on different levels and of different ages. So, we need more special educators to fulfil the need of all such children' (FT14 Hindi SV11).

The examples abound, but some teachers were less familiar with inclusive education: 'Inclusion? Sorry, I am not getting this term … (pause) What you mean to say, do you want to know about special children or the poor? There are children from a poor family' (FT2 Primary SV4).

This allowed the discussion to widen to include the education not only of those children with a disability but also of those whom one can loosely term as 'hard to reach' or those from families generally discriminated against in Indian society, based on caste or creed. One teacher put it succinctly: 'There are three types of students in inclusive education: first, students with special needs, secondly students who have difficulty in studying, for example, students with dyslexia – that is, students who are physically OK but have challenges in their mental health where [and] take time to understand or have difficulty to understand things. And lastly, students who come from different castes or race sections of the society. Inclusive education means including all these three categories of students in the class along with other children and giving them equal opportunity to study' (MT10 Social Science SV10).

The next section will explore teachers' views on hard-to-reach children, including the poor, working and migrant children.

Teachers' views on hard-to-reach children

Inclusion in India has to mean more than education for disabled children. In the context of a country and particularly a city with such stark levels of wealth inequality, reinforced by migrant labour moving from rural areas to city slums, traditions of caste discrimination, and child labour, Delhi government schools have for decades struggled to keep children from dropping out. Yet, Delhi teachers did not see the 'inclusion' of poor(er) hard-to-reach children as 'inclusion'. They just saw it as part of the context they lived and operated in. Despite the lack of an 'inclusion label', teachers had developed specific strategies to help such children, which they shared; these are discussed further below. Discussing 'hard-to-reach' children, teachers spoke of the poor, the migrant families from other states and children who had to work to support their families.

A few participating teachers did not think that poverty made much of a difference. 'In class, one cannot recognise who is poor and who is not, just who is active and who is not' (FT4 Science SV9). This was possibly the case because government schools no longer serve the middle classes. India has termed poor families as EWS – Economically Weaker Sections of society. With the rise of private schools across the country, many families in the middle classes and aspiring middle class send their children to private, often low-cost schools. The middle classes have largely abandoned the public education system (Lall, 2013). This means that government provision is generally only for the most disadvantaged and marginalised in society – the EWS. One teacher explained that 'we don't have that category; that is meant for the private school only, I think. There is no EWS category in government school. … mostly the students are from that space' (FT3 Mathematics RPVV1). Other teachers agreed that there could not be any special arrangements for EWS students, as 'they mostly come from poor families' (FT7 Science SV3). 'In our government schools, I would say that most of them, students, and you can say 98 per cent are from EWS. … They only need the motivation, that is for the whole class because 98 per cent of them are poor' (FT2 English RPVV3).

However, a clear aim of AAP policy has been to bring the quality of government schools to the level of private provision, so that lower and aspiring middle-class families do not have to spend money on fees and face hard choices sometimes. There has been some evidence (Dhawan, 2019) that lower-middle-class families in some areas of Delhi are now leaving the low-fee private alternatives and returning to government provision. One teacher explained that things had changed drastically at her school since she had herself been a student there:

> … nowadays, children from private schools are coming here to get admission because the school has changed drastically. Now the government schools are no more the same government school which they used to be. An image of a government school has been built that it is not good, but many good children are coming to our school who have not dreamt of joining government school. This is the reality. I am not lying; I am sitting in the school, many facilities

Hard-to-reach children were seen to do less well than their peers because of their circumstances. Teachers distinguished between them and low-achieving students, who were unable to follow the pace of the class. Sometimes these categories overlapped, but in general, these issues were treated separately and teachers developed specific strategies to support different types of students.

Caste and gender

Education has also acted to mediate and reproduce class, caste and gender inequalities. The unequal allocation of resources and opportunities in a socially stratified society sharpens the 'tenuous' links between education and gender equality (Manjrekar, 2021). Gender segregation was ubiquitous in all organisational arrangements in schools in Delhi. Manjrekar describes a typical school day, starting with the morning assembly held in the playground. 'Girls and boys of each class stood in separate rows facing the portico on which six or seven "older" girls sang patriotic songs. ... In the classroom, girls and boys sat separately, an aisle acting as both a physical and symbolic divide between them – a "gender boundary" as it is' (Manjrekar, 2021, 24). The 'motif of gendered spaces within the classroom and playground pervaded in the observations. Whether teacher-directed or not, the cues of the differentiated system are effectively internalised by the children' (Manjrekar, 2021, 24).

Issues of inclusion and equity concerning gender and caste persist as major concerns in classrooms in India (Tiwary et al., 2017) and were reflected in the Delhi-based interviews as well. A teacher described the role of pedagogy as the socialiser in shaping gender equity in the classroom:

> ... inclusive education should also focus on boys' and girls' education, because these genders need a different kind of approach, and we should handle them with gentle care. First of all, because if you are studying in a class where there are many boys, you will have a different kind of temperament altogether. And if you are teaching in a class where there is equal strength, then you must have a different kind of temperament ... The girls are not being taught that they should have confidence in themselves; for their own struggles, it is required. If you have a particular gender, then it is fine, then it will be very simple, but your basic struggle comes when there are two genders in your class, and you have to regulate your own behaviour first, and then you have to monitor the behaviour and those study

patterns in that particular class. So according to me, inclusive education should also go beyond the weaker sections … You can say it should also enter the zone where girl and boy education should also be monitored, because in recent times, we have a different kind of pattern in our schools (FT1 English RPVV3).

Some teachers explained the gender differences in dropout and academic achievement. A teacher mentioned:

There is a dropout from some classes. We try to contact the parents, you can understand. If the girl is deviating from the studies, then parents make them sit at home; if the student is in 9th and 10th, then they feel that they will make her do household work and marry her off in two years. Then we talk to parents, and it depends on their parents; sometimes they understand too. But they say, we will continue the study but will not send her to the school. There are around one or two cases when they take their ward out from the school (FT3 English SV10).

There also exists some evidence of gender differences in academic performance. A teacher voiced: 'Around 75 per cent of girls in my school are who help their mothers in the household work in the morning or in the evening. Their performance is lesser than the other students as they are not able to pay attention to their studies in comparison to other students.' When asked about teaching strategy, the teacher elaborated: 'I explain to parents that make [their children] take out some time for studies too. Household work should not stop them from doing their schoolwork' (FT2 Primary SV2). Poverty is directly related to girls' burden of labour within the home, sharing responsibilities for cooking, cleaning and minding younger children and caring for the aged and sick (Khan and Lall, 2020).

Young school-age girls from poor communities (disproportionately represented by non-Savarna,[5] Adivasi[6] and Muslim communities) contribute to household survival and sustenance by labouring in waged as well as unpaid work. The opportunity costs of educating girls are therefore high. Since gender relations are primarily socioculturally sanctioned, a cultural 'relativist' position runs the risk of extending processes of primary socialisation to schools, legitimising and consolidating the learning of existing gender roles and divisions in wider society (Khullar, 1991). A teacher explained:

through. A teacher noted that for the whole year she tries to explain, but when they near the exam, she asks them to use rote learning – '*beta ye important questions hai raat dalo* (these are the important questions, memorise it)' (FT8 English SV5).

The No Detention Policy, challenges to basic literacy and numeracy and ability setting

One of the biggest complaints by Sarvodaya school teachers was regarding the NDP.[8] This means that students move up every year to the next class even if they have not reached the required level – sometimes including basic writing and counting. The first time students are faced with exams that can hold them back is in class IX, by which time it is often too late to catch up. Across India, dropout rates after class VIII are very high. Teachers reported that due to the NDP some students take their studies for granted, leading to low engagement in class. A teacher stated that, due to the NDP, 'sometimes their mindsets become that they will pass' (FT6 Social Science SV8). This was confirmed by another teacher: 'When they come to class IX, they cannot suddenly become serious' (FT9 Social Science SV2).

Because of the automatic progression, teachers find that suddenly in class XIII they have to teach children basic literacy and numeracy, creating a massive challenge. 'They have not learnt reading or writing correctly' (FT9 Social Science SV2). One teacher reported age-appropriate admission as part of the problem: 'for example, an eleven-year-old who never went to school gets admission to the Vth standard. The child lacks the basic literacy to read or write.' The teacher shared her frustration over whether to teach the child '1, 2, 3, 4 or A, B, C, D or the syllabus of the Vth'. Both teachers and students face difficulties. 'But without base, how will the child learn the things?' (FT2 Social Science SV10). One teacher flagged that in her class, students who 'had cleared VI, VII, and VIII because of the no-detention policy, and out of 110 students, 75 students had failed [in class IX]' (FT2 English RPVV2).

Teachers generally have a negative view of the NDP due to the lack of accountability it creates. Children as old as 14 do not know how to read or write, as there is no checking at the primary level, leading to low student engagement and dropouts later. 'The no-detention policy has ruined our system of education. Why was there no accountability at a level for a class V?' (FT2 English RPVV2). This in turn means that teachers have to devote extra hours to teaching the basics to students who have passed one class after another due to the NDP.

In order to deal with the wide variety of achievement levels within the classroom, from those fluent in English to those who cannot read or write, Delhi schools have resorted to a settings policy. The schools divide students into two or three groups, depending on their level. As this teacher explains, much of this is directly linked to the NDP:

> Nishtha is where students … came from primary education, who did not know how to read or write or do basic maths and due to the No Detention Policy they got promoted to class IX. Now in this class, the teachers did not want to spoil their records, they passed them to 10th. In tenth also the teachers promoted them due to CCE. Now they have come to 11th, we got to know that they can't even read Hindi. This was the case that the student has [been] promoted to the next class from primary and has come to class 11 but does not know how to read or write (MT1 Science SV7).

The negative labelling of erroneous actions or practices generalises to the negative labelling of the learner and their abilities. Actions and practices can be problematised and modified, but labelling the person and not the behaviours can have long-term negative consequences and in educational contexts can certainly result in negative self-perceptions, inevitably leading to learner disengagement. This setting methodology has its proponents and its critics, as discussed below.

Ability setting

Setting students according to ability has been a part of education reforms globally. This kind of 'triage' system is linked to overall school achievement, with more resources such as teacher attention being put towards students in the middle group, who are likely to perform better and lift the grade average of the school. Gillborn and Youdell (1999) examined the effects of this on students in the UK and found that those in the lowest group of achievement were largely from ethnic minority groups and hard-to-reach families. The setting culture might have improved school achievement on the surface but led to the creation of a permanent underclass of undereducated children, classified as 'losers', who had no chance of catching up and getting into higher education. In India the setting practice has become part of the support system for teachers. It was developed and provided by one of India's most prominent NGOs, of students, they can learn from each other. If we segregate, they will not learn. If we have a mixture, we can apply peer learning and they will learn from each other. Mission Buniyaad is amazing

(FT8 Science SV2).

Teachers pointed out that Mission Buniyaad, discussed in the next section, is a better model to support children. Although meant as a programme for catching up, Mission Buniyaad does not segregate based on ability and works particularly well.

So, I said the students should not be segregated based on Nishtha or Pratibha. Like in Mission Buniyaad, all different kinds of students with different abilities for learning can sit and study in the same class. Because I feel there is a loss for Neo-Nishtha students, as they don't get their education altogether. Also, for example, in class IX, if I have to bring Neo-Nishtha students to the level of Prathiba students, I will take some extra time to complete the syllabus, and that is also an issue. So I feel that Neo-Nishtha, Pratibha should be eliminated and Mission Buniyaad should be kept

(FT7 Social Science SV10).

In 2019 a plea filed by the Parents' Forum for Meaningful Education alleged the children were facing discrimination due to their segregation. The AAP government informed the Delhi High Court that students have been segregated under the Chunauti scheme merely to enable teachers to address the learning needs of different groups of children systematically and effectively. In an affidavit filed before Delhi Court, the government commented that the students are allocated to groups based on their foundational learning ability within their class so that teachers can strengthen their basic reading, writing and numeric abilities. The students also benefit because teachers are able to focus more on those students whose learning levels need to be upgraded most, thus reducing the accumulated learning deficit (Banka, 2019).

Mission Buniyaad

The programme of Mission Buniyaad[13] is generally organised during the summer vacations, when teachers offer extra classes for the 'weaker' students. The focus is on the basics. 'In April, they get admitted. In May–June, we run Mission Buniyaad classes. Our focus is to clear their basic till June. We can see the result in the VIIIth standard. In fact, from July onwards, we can see the difference. … Slowly, slowly we move from easy to advanced level' (FT8 English SV9). Mission Buniyaad seems to help both teachers and students, especially with improving writing skills as well as mathematics. '[In] the time this [Mission Buniyaad] was not there, we used to filter students and give them extra work. But from the past two–three years, the Mission Buniyaad project is going, and we have to see their progress in mathematic sums, reading and writing' (FT3 Primary SV8).

As seen above, many teachers praised the scheme and preferred it to the setting policy. But the mission is not without its critics, who point out that the summer is hot, and teachers end up without a summer break. Students from migrant families also leave Delhi to return home, and because of the reverse migration, the programme loses much of its targeted population.

> Mission Buniyaad did not help those who needed it the most. Because those students are from other states, and they visit their villages when this Mission Buniyaad project is running during summer vacations. Most of the time, they go for one or two months, and in Mission Buniyaad, you have only two or three students in the class who are regular. I don't think it will work if they do it in summer vacation. It should be done in the classes with regular school
>
> (FT4 Primary SV1).

Conclusion – is AAP really offering 'Education for All'?

The teacher voices in this chapter show how the inclusion of children in any classroom is ultimately up to the teachers themselves and their ability, as well as the environment they are in. The task of teaching children with special needs is often just delegated to special educators – if they are available. Where they are not, teachers find themselves unprepared and lacking the support and infrastructure for inclusive education, thus finding it difficult to respond to the diversity of learners' needs (Goyal, 2020). This further marginalises children from the teaching-learning process. Studies (Bhatnagar and Das, 2013; Shah and Veetil, 2006), using both attitude surveys and qualitative interviews, capture a positive shift in teacher attitudes towards children with special needs. However, as reflected in the voices above, there is growing dissatisfaction with poor infrastructure, large class sizes and lack of paraprofessional staff. Reflecting on the issues faced by Delhi teachers, teachers in government schools in rural Haryana emphasised the need for better training (Singal et al., 2018). This is ultimately a policy problem. Inclusive education for children in Delhi has been hampered by policy inconsistencies as well as the scarcity of assessment of achievements and quality, resulting in serious gaps in implementation and untargeted interventions. While the right to inclusive education has been recognised by the Right of Children to Free and Compulsory Education Act 2009, SSA, the Rights of Persons with Disabilities Act 2016 and the New Education Policy 2020, there is no uniform framework for inclusive education in the country.

Reflecting on what the teachers expressed, it is possible that teacher attitudes towards inclusive education could be related to preservice and in-service training, which lack a structuralist perspective (see Chapter 2). As discussed, the practical experience in schools is largely absent in pre-service teacher training, and it is unclear how much theory on inclusion is imparted, making it harder to overcome the theory–practice divide (Resch and Schrittesser, 2021).

The findings can also be explained by Thomas Skrtic's theory of bureaucracies within the school organisation which compares and analyses different forms of interprofessional cooperation and schools' organisations of special educational work. Education policy is therefore emphasised as important for understanding the conditions under which school staff are responsible for inclusion (Resch and Schrittesser, 2021). Education policy is a constraining factor for the cooperating actors in their efforts to achieve inclusive classrooms. Flexible cooperation was hindered by curricular constraints and standardised testing. Teachers and special educators in this chapter felt pressure to cover a large amount of curricular content and prepare their students for standardised tests, which hindered their flexibility and their opportunities to adapt instruction and use alternative child-centred teaching methods.

The pressure experienced by teachers and special educators in different national contexts, highlighted in this chapter, can be understood in relation to the global spread of audit cultures and educational standardisation, along with the growing significance of the Programme for International Student Assessment (PISA) and other international standardised tests (Sellar and Lingard, 2013). Conflicting policy demands, for inclusion on the one hand and competition and performativity on the other, often emphasise the dominance of the latter (Barton and Slee, 1999). Magnússon (2019) points out that even the Salamanca Statement allows for several different interpretations of the meaning of inclusion, which range from narrow definitions focused on the placement of pupils to wider ideals of creating communities. A highly standardised and competitive education system encourages an interpretation of inclusion focused on individuals' access to the general curriculum and classrooms rather than on community, adaptations and meaningful participation.

By once again returning to Skrtic (1991), the constraints on interprofessional cooperation inflicted by education policy would be a sign of a strong machine bureaucracy that shapes the work of professionals in schools (Bishop and Kalogeropoulos, 2015). Based on the analysis, the authors argue that 'adhocracy' (also suggested in the research by Bishop and Kalogeropoulos, 2015) is a possible way forward to achieve inclusive classrooms, but that professional and, above all, machine bureaucratic structures hinder professionals' opportunities for flexible cooperation. In the light of the discussion, the question of how much responsibility for inclusion can be placed on teachers, special educators and principals is a legitimate one.

As shall be seen in the Epilogue, the NEP 2020 acknowledges the crucial role played by teachers in the identification of certain disabilities. However, it only includes specific learning disabilities and completely neglects other developmental and intellectual problems, or any other issues children might face based on caste, class, language or parental background. The policy discourse on inclusive education in India has confused integration and inclusion, focusing on solutions that allow children to integrate into the system rather than questioning and evaluating existing practices, based on the recognition of disability as a result of structural and attitudinal limitations (Goyal, 2020). Consequently, the approach towards inclusive education in Delhi government schools has placed a disproportionate amount of attention on issues of access and enrolment, concomitantly disregarding the quality of education imparted and the learning outcomes for children with special needs as well as hard-to-reach children.

The wider question on inclusion remains: to what extend are the AAP reforms really offering education for all?[14] Could a focus on inclusive approaches to the pedagogy change the engagement situation positively? The Pratham-supported ability-setting policy is contested by the teachers themselves, as they understand the long-term consequences of creating an underclass of students who remain in the lowest ability group. However, teachers are caught in the structure imposed upon them from above, through their schools. Given the lack of teachers' voices and feedback, the policy is likely to continue uncontested, despite the damage it could incur.

Notes

1. SSA data from 2003 to 2008, showing the number of children with MHRD in 2012, stated that 3.26 million children with disabilities had been identified, of which 87.38 per cent were enrolled in school. In total, 95.33 per cent of children with disabilities have been covered through various strategies, such as the School Readiness Programme. These figures need to be seen in contrast to those available prior to 2003. For example, Mukhopadhyay and Mani (2002) noted that: 'the picture (of school enrolment for children with disabilities) is dismal since less than one per cent of children with disabilities attend school' (101). However, high enrolment figures mask a range of important challenges. Based on an analysis of data from the U-DISE, Singal et al. (2017) noted significant disparities in enrolment according to the type of disability, as children with autism and cerebral palsy were least likely to be enrolled in school. Additionally, transition rates for all children with disabilities remain very low, even to upper-primary levels, let alone secondary education and beyond. A deeper analysis highlights a range of concerns in relation to the implementation of inclusive education in India. We critically examine these issues using Fraser's notion of justice, given that inclusive education is about building a socially just educational and social system (UNESCO, 1994).
2. Widen the understanding of inclusive education: it should include all learners, regardless of identity, background or ability; and prepare, empower and motivate the education workforce: all teachers should be prepared to teach all students (UNESCO, 2020).
3. According to Das et al. (2013), the results showed that nearly 70 per cent of the regular schoolteachers in Delhi had neither received any training in special education nor had experience teaching students with disabilities. It was even more troubling to see that nearly 87 per cent of the teachers did not have access to support services in their classrooms. It is therefore not surprising to see teachers rating themselves as not competent in each of the 10 competency categories. Research indicates that negative attitudes of teachers and their lack of skills impede the successful implementation of inclusive education programmes.
4. More on this in the section on settings in this chapter.
5. Non-Brahmins.
6. Scheduled Tribes.
7. It is, of course, possible that such students are dyslexic or have dyspraxia; however, there is no mechanism to diagnose such disabilities in most government schools.
8. As discussed in Chapter 1, the Sarvodaya schools select their students through a lottery, while the RPVVs hold admission tests. Hence, RPVV schools already get high-performing students. So, only the teachers from Sarvodaya schools reported that due to the NDP, students in class IX did not know how to write their names in English.
9. This was part of the Nobel Prize-winning work of Banerjee and Duflo (2011). Also see Banerjee et al., 'Remedying Education' (2007). For more information on Pratham's setting methodology, see https://www.pratham.org/about/teaching-at-the-right-level/
10. It is interesting to note that the BCG report does not include the voices and views of teachers, but rather focuses on a parental survey and the views of headteachers and politicians.
11. According to the Delhi government (2016), there is an enormous failure rate; this means almost 50 per cent of students were failing, which was attributed to four main reasons. Firstly, the NDP; secondly, 'years of accumulated learning deficit'; thirdly, 'pressure on the teachers to complete the syllabi leading to inability to bring weaker children to the desired level and lastly, 'huge variances in basic skills like reading/writing within a single classroom' (Delhi Government, 2020). Regrouping students of classes VI, VII and VIII according to the levels of basic learning was facilitated by the teachers with an understanding that the teachers will 'not have to tackle huge variances in learning levels of students in the same class' (Delhi Government, 2020).
12. Students who have failed class IX twice and have had to leave school.
13. To conduct the Mission Buniyaad classes, the DoE provides manuals to HoS and teachers. It also provides copies of students' learning material, which are shared with teachers during the training for Mission Buniyaad classes. The learning material includes 'Classes III to V: (a) Kahaniyan hi Kahaniyan and (b) Number Cards for all students studying in classes III to V. And for classes VI to VIII, (a) Kahaniyon ka Khazana (b) Hamara Ganit-For students of classes VI to VIII who are below Advance reading in Hindi/Urdu and/or below division level in maths' (DoE, n.d.).

14. What is not engaged with here is the question posed by Geetha Nambissan (2021) of how children who live in unrecognised or illegal settlements access education. The fact that Delhi has a large number of these settlements and that their residents do not have access to basic services such as water or electricity (and therefore only reduced and difficult access to government schools, often relying on low-cost private alternatives) should be part of a wider inclusion debate when discussing the Delhi education reforms. This volume, however, focuses on what teachers have to say, and this was not mentioned by them.

6
Teachers and Covid-19: challenges of a pandemic

In India, the quality of education worsens as you go down the economic spectrum, but during Covid-19, the gap deepened even more. What we have had in the last year was that a very large segment of children could not access formal education. I think this gap that has been created is a very serious one. Education in elite private schools has been virtually uninterrupted, but in government schools, there has been a lack of laptops, mobile phones, or Wi-Fi at home. Children have missed an entire year. We will be able to open schools in July–August 2021, but our biggest challenge then will be how to deal with the learning loss

(Atishi Marlena,[1] IANS, Feb 2021).

In March 2021, exactly one year after the Covid-19 pandemic hit Delhi, Manish Sisodia took part in the State Teachers Award ceremony. He publicly declared that teachers impact thousands of lives and are the biggest contributors towards nation-building: 'teachers ensured that learning never stops by reaching to out their students through innovative means. Teachers who did not know how to use a smartphone equipped themselves with the knowledge of how to use it. Their efforts are really praiseworthy' (Daily Pioneer, March 2021). The Delhi government honoured 98 teachers and headteachers for their invaluable contribution to school education during the pandemic. Teachers and headteachers were congratulated by Deputy Commissioner Udit Prakash, who echoed this sentiment in saying 'our education system was badly hit by the pandemic, as school closures left everyone clueless about the teaching-learning during the Covid times. But our teachers and school principals really stepped up to the occasion and showed unparalleled grit and determination in responding to this situation' (Daily Pioneer, 2021). For the future, Sisodia also urged teachers to reconsider assessment and learning strategies, saying: 'We need to build correct approaches and develop 360-degree assessments for our students. The premise of rote learning evaluated through an end-of-year three-hour exam is an injustice to our students and teachers. The challenge is to eliminate rote-learning practices, and this is why we are at the juncture of establishing the Delhi Board of Education' (Digital Learning Network, 2021). He added that the Delhi Board of Education will develop continuous and comprehensive assessments, augmenting a holistic learner profile of students and enabling teachers to refine their teaching practice. He announced that the Delhi Virtual School would be developed with the support of teachers in order to strengthen access to education across India (Digital Learning Network, 2021).

Teachers' voices and experiences are important to develop a framework for virtual schools. This is because, during a crisis like the Covid-19 pandemic, teachers play an important role in establishing educational partnerships with parents and communities to ensure an inclusive and effective approach to mending the learning loss and socioemotional damage to child development. UNESCO's GEM report (2020) presents a rich picture of how the pandemic has been very disruptive to disadvantaged students across all levels of education, a fact that may have long-lasting implications for intergenerational mobility, income inequality and health disparities. Throughout the pandemic, children from poorer communities as well as girls, the disabled, immigrants and ethnic minorities in many countries have been impacted more severely than others for a multitude of reasons, including poor connectivity and a lack of parental support. Teachers are projected as having the technical proficiency to cope with the challenges of school closures in crisis situations. Such professionalism requires collective agency: the ability of individual teachers to act collectively and draw on systems of mutual support. It also requires personal agency: the mindset and dispositions to respond to changing conditions in order to serve the learning and well-being needs of students appropriately (Ehren et al., 2021).

India's experience of the Covid-19 pandemic started with a national lockdown in April 2020. The chapter looks at the significant variation in the ways that young people could access, navigate and use the internet and other new technologies, including an important minority who were excluded entirely (Williamson, 2020). As schools closed due to the Covid-19 outbreak, many teachers turned to digital means to connect with their students but found that teaching and learning slowed significantly. The chapter looks at how teacher engagement with online teaching affected their digital agency, and the digital pedagogies used across Delhi government schools. Engaging with the more recent publications on education in a pandemic and the wider literature on education in emergencies, the chapter looks at how technological solutions are no panacea, as not all young people have internet access and digital know-how. Overall, the teachers' voices revealed the loopholes (such as lack of sustained internet availability/connectivity or digital training for teachers) in the online education system as well as some positive aspects of offline or classroom teaching. This last chapter of the volume, though focused on the effects of the pandemic, allows for a review of the AAP education policies at a time when the system was under significant stress.

Background

Covid-19 severely disrupted the Delhi education system. The closure of schools, universities and other educational institutions affected 990 million (UNESCO, 2020, 1) students worldwide and over 320 million in India – estimated 16 lakhs of whom were in Delhi (Iftikhar, Feb 2021). Covid-19 significantly affected the lives of children from marginalised and vulnerable backgrounds, especially children with special needs and from low-income families, as the lockdown deprived these children of physical learning opportunities and the social and emotional support available at school (Bonal and González, 2020). The pandemic and government response to it also revealed many underlying vulnerabilities and inequalities in the education system. Online education strategies were found to have five key themes: the development of online learning platforms, ensuring a good internet connection, increasing access to internet-capable devices, teacher training and solving non-infrastructural impediments to learning.

India's large population made dealing with Covid-19 particularly challenging. During the countrywide lockdown, the Indian government had to resort to online classes for education. Teachers in India have been using the 'chalk and talk' method for a long time, but the lockdown compelled them to shift education online (Lederman, 2020). Online teaching became 'victor ludorum' amid the chaos; no longer an option but a necessity (Dhawan, 2020, 7). As a result, there has been a boom in the e-learning sector. Software applications like Zoom, WebEx, Google Meet and WhatsApp have become the norm for students, teachers and parents. With that came the need for ownership of a smart device and a reliable internet connection, which is not always guaranteed in India (Khanna and Kareem, 2021).

Many of the teachers had not been trained in teaching online (Jain et al., 2021). Teachers lacked technical support in using ICT for teaching; in turn, some felt a sense of anxiety about using ICT to stimulate the classroom experience (Khanna and Kareem, 2021). Furthermore, as far as younger children are concerned, Mahoney (2020) asserts that teaching primary-class students online involves significant challenges, as it generally requires hours of screen time, which hampers child development and does not allow for hands-on learning. Moreover, the children's low attention span compounded the problems. The lack of human touch, the absence of opportunities for collaborative learning and most importantly the lack of hands-on learning for complex subjects like mathematics and science were big concerns for achieving 'quality' education (Chari, 2020). Teaching from home created challenges for teachers as well. For example, teachers with children found it challenging to have a work-life balance and to teach their classes while supporting their own children.

Looking at the challenge of schools being closed, the government of India as well as different state governments and private players methodically published information on initiatives undertaken by ministries such as the MHRD (now renamed Ministry of Education), Department of Technical Education, the NCERT and others to support both teachers and students. MHRD was at the forefront of provisioning technology-enabled learning through audio-video mode or e-books and journals. It promoted a number of ICT initiatives such as the National Repository of Open Educational Resources (NROER),[2] ePathshala[3] for school textbooks and resources, and DIKSHA[4] for higher education, which provides access to e-content for 80 undergraduate courses. The pre-existing multilingual DIKSHA platform (National Digital Infrastructure for Teachers) was expanded and now contains e-learning content for students, teachers and parents aligned to the curriculum, including video lessons, worksheets, textbooks and assessments. The software application has more than 80,000 e-books for children of classes I to XII and is available to use offline. In addition, the pre-existing SWAYAM platform for free massive open online courses was expanded with new material covering a variety of topics. SWAYAM covers material from class IX upwards. The 'PM e-VIDYA' platform has 12 new direct-to-home (DTH) channels and offers one for each class, to reach out to all strata of society. The 'Bharat Padhe Online' campaign crowdsourced designs for improving the online education ecosystem of India, Young India Combating Covid with Knowledge, Technology and Innovation (YUKTI)[5] and YUKTI 2.0[6] emerged to help keep the teaching-learning process going (Jain et al., 2021). In order to increase accessibility, Swayam Prabha, a national television service, broadcast programmes aimed at children who were not connected to the internet and had limited access to radio and television (Wood et al., 2021). This is encouraging. But the moment online education moves from being an option to becoming the mainstream mode of learning, a disturbing side becomes evident, which will be discussed in the following section.

'Pathology' of remote learning in a hierarchical society: 'pandemic-induced' changes

Remote learning involves either live synchronous online classes for students or digital content which can be accessed at any time – offline or online. Many South Asian countries (such as India, Pakistan and Bangladesh) lack a reliable internet infrastructure and the cost of online access can be prohibitive for poorer communities (Menon, 2020). The UN says that at least 147 million children are unable to access online or remote learning in South Asia. In India only 24 per cent of households have access to the internet, according to a 2019 government survey (Menon, 2020). In rural parts of India the numbers are far lower, with only 4 per cent of households having access to the internet. The whole of India enjoys geographic and cultural diversity, but it also suffers from a massive socio-economic divide. As education went online, a new hierarchy of students and teachers would emerge based on what technological facility they could muster. This was not only an issue of differentiating between urban and rural communities – even in India's capital, digital access varies tremendously. In a teacher survey conducted in Delhi in 2020 it was found that only about 17 per cent of government schools had digital facilities, and many had not been fully equipped digitally – and this in the nation's capital (Jain et al., 2021, 65). This reflects that only a small majority of the Delhi population has access to online education – interrupted power supply, weak or non-existent internet connectivity and inability to afford the necessary devices are among the major factors.

Accessing education in Delhi during the pandemic

Without access to mobile phones, the internet and laptop or desktop computers, approximately 1,600,000 (16 lakh) children from poor families, studying in government (including municipal) schools in Delhi, experienced disruptions to their studies (Bedi, 2020b). Students from

EWS were the ones most affected by the lockdown. In November 2020 a survey[7] was conducted by Delhi-based NGO ChildFund India[8] among 1,725 children, 1,605 parents and 127 teachers in those states that had witnessed the heaviest inflow of migrant labourers and their children returning home from urban areas, where their work had been stopped by the lockdown. These children faced immense challenges in re-enrolling in schools due to a lack of documents (India Education Diary, 2021). More than 50 per cent of parents witnessed increased negative behaviour in their children, and more than 60 per cent of children themselves also expressed experiencing changes in their own behaviour. These included an increase in anger and irritability, and lack of concentration, the survey stated. The prolonged closure of schools further exacerbated their situation, as it resulted in a decline in nutrition levels among the children, who otherwise would have had midday meals; online learning came with severe challenges and the psychological well-being of the children was badly affected (India Education Diary, 2021).

According to the data collected by the education department of Delhi, large numbers of children have fallen off the map – the schools cannot trace them. Over 166,000 students in Delhi's government and municipal schools are missing (Iftikhar, 2021). According to the government officials and school authorities, the migration of thousands of families to their home states during and after the lockdown and the sudden shift to online education are the main reasons for this (Iftikhar, 2021). From October to December 2020, the government and municipal schools attempted door-to-door visits, sending letters and assignments to addresses on their records and forming peer groups to locate missing students (Iftikhar, 2021). A headteacher shared that 'at least 40 students are completely unreachable at our school. Of them, 25 are in class VI. We have taken all possible steps, but these children were not found at the addresses mentioned in our records. We got to know from the neighbourhood that these families returned to their villages after the lockdown and have not returned yet'. The director of NGO CHETNA said: 'Extensive steps need to be taken to trace students who have been pushed into child labour due to financial difficulties wrought by the pandemic. The priorities of parents have also changed amid the financial crises. The switch to online education is also responsible for the situation. There is a possibility of more drop-outs if this situation continues' (Iftikhar, 2021).

For those not able to access the virtual classrooms through phones and laptops, Finance Minister Nirmala Sitharaman had announced a line of new initiatives including 12 new television channels (one for each class, from kindergarten to XIII) – 'a step towards increasing the reach of educational content for Indian households, especially the ones which lack access of high-speed internet connection for unhindered consumption of learning content' (Pandey, 2020). Delhi government school teachers were also encouraging simple activities that are easier for parents to monitor. A senior official of the Delhi education department said: 'We are trying to overcome challenges and hence started an SMS system to assign work, as even if families don't have internet, nearly every household has a phone' (Bedi, 2020a). However, the official said there were constraints, such as households with three students having just one phone (Bedi, 2020a). A son of a domestic worker in South Delhi could no longer use his father's secondhand phone, as it had broken. When the father's employer offered to buy him a smartphone, he realised delivery of 'non-essentials' was not doable amid the lockdown. The employer said: 'I felt very bad, so I give my phone every morning when my domestic worker's son has his classes. The teacher now has my number' (Bedi, 2020a). While the Delhi government has distributed tablets to 17,000 students of RPVVs and Schools of Excellence, others don't have the devices required for online classes. A class XII student at a government school in South Delhi, the son of a newspaper vendor, was worried because the household doesn't have a computer or a smartphone. 'I have to write the boards next year, but I don't know how I'll be able to complete the syllabus. We don't even have books, else I would've tried to study by myself' (Bedi, 2020a). The difficulties of limited resources and poor connectivity are worse still for students with disabilities. A visually impaired student at a Delhi government school said: 'Assignments on WhatsApp were not possible for me. I don't have parents and my grandparents are too old to use WhatsApp' (Bedi, 2020).

Teachers' views on student access to digital infrastructure and engagement

When asked about students, teachers pointed out that many students did not have a proper device and a stable internet connection. Parents were required to buy a high-speed internet connection in order for their children to be able to access classes smoothly; however, most of the students came from low-income families that had difficulty paying for any extras. A teacher shared: 'very low class … those who do not have clothes to wear and books to read. They are in a pretty bad state, even for online classes, they do not have a phone at their homes. They are putting an effort to buy a phone,' (FT13 Social Science SV3). Another teacher said, 'if we ask students to explore something, then they do not have internet. Or some students are not very fast … or internet is not very fast' (FT1 Science RPVV1). In terms of children of migrant parents, a teacher said:

> … in lockdown, students have gone to village if parents don't have employment. They are not in contact for so long, we are not going to cut their names. We are waiting for them, and we will continue. For them, there is nothing special. If we feel their performance is getting low, then we give them worksheets and handwritten notes that you read them, if you are not able to understand the chapter, then read this (FT3 Social Science SV5).

In terms of parental support and engagement, a teacher stated that 'parents can't help with their homework or lessons as they are illiterate, this student is praying to come back to the school' (FT2 Hindi RPVV1). Another teacher related a story of a child of migrant parents who had no provision for online classes. She said, 'her family is very poor, which does not allow this girl to access the privilege of online classes' (FT5 Social Science SV5). Shockingly, teachers also shared that the management teams of certain schools has asked teachers to block such students from the classes.

In terms of student agency, a teacher said that 'in online classes, I am also aware of the reasons why they are not completing the worksheets sent by the DoE; there is a girl who is not doing her work. We have to do a lot of hard work for motivating children and getting good results' (FT5 Social Science SV5). Another teacher commented, 'students have to work in the lockdown. They can't participate' (FT2 Hindi RPVV1). Most of the teachers pointed out that primary-class students from EWS have a low attention span (Mahoney, 2020).[9] In order to mitigate this, teachers said that the government has given a worksheet and they follow the teaching pattern listed in that. A teacher explained: 'I give homework to students for a week which is supposed to be finished on a day-to-day basis' (FT7 Social Science RPVV2). Students who have smartphones, teachers shared, are sent the worksheets on WhatsApp. 'I need to call up students on their parents' phones who do not have smartphones and tell them their homework' (FT5 Social Science SV5). When probed, a teacher imparted that 'teaching online is okay but follow-up via phone is challenging, especially with students from lower-income groups' (FT1

Science RPVV1). Another teacher commented: 'I spend a lot of time making calls to these students every morning; some parents have given me wrong numbers' (FT3 Social Science SV5). To ease the gap, teachers explained that the management fixed one day a week where students could come to the school, ask questions and get their worksheets from teachers. Moreover, classes such as physical education, arts and crafts were not a part of the timetable anymore. They added that primary-class students used to have an active learning session in the school, but now teachers had to change their methodology, as they were mostly sitting in front of the screen. Online learning has made the students less active, and teachers felt that an online classroom hampered the child's physical development and socialisation.

For poor families, who may have lost their source of income because of the lockdown and have little in the way of savings, there will be additional costs of regular online classes, such as the internet and higher electricity bills. For some, these costs may be unaffordable and education will seem to be less of a priority as the struggle to put food on the table begins. Such circumstances will not only affect their children's grades but will also have a detrimental impact on their confidence and self-esteem. Being cut off from their teachers and peers means that their mental health will suffer too, and this will have a negative impact on their motivation to study. The key feature of distance education is that it requires discipline and dedication from the student. However, it also demands a conducive environment for study, and this is a luxury for many.

Teachers' narratives imply that the support and motivation that students from the EWS require are completely absent from online teaching. The young children from lower classes with differential experience of lockdown and education raise pertinent questions regarding the valorisation of technology as a medium of social transformation. These narratives also question the logic of education which negatively affects the sociocultural context. Technology seems to contain in it the possibility of overcoming social, economic, political and geographical barriers and radically transforming the forms of human engagement. However, the ability to access technology and the conditions for its smooth operation are unequally distributed among members of society. The societal inequalities in terms of class, caste, gender and race do impinge on the ownership and control of technology. There is a sense of in-built inequality in terms of access to, and control of, technology. Rather than being a medium of social transformation, technology can often perpetuate existing inequalities. The middle-class obsession with online education is short-sighted, as it doesn't acknowledge the basic fact that large sections of the population are unable to access such education. The ability to access online education is a privilege in a hierarchical society like India (Shahdeo, 2020), a testimony to the socioeconomic perpetuation of inequality through the means of technology.

While the inequalities created by the pandemic shine through, it was also interesting to see how teachers developed locally adapted solutions to continue to deliver education to their students regardless of their socioeconomic background. The section below reviews how Delhi teachers experienced the pandemic, how it affected their teaching and their lives.

Access, skills and usage gaps – realities for teachers during Covid-19

In the first weeks of the pandemic and at the start of the lockdown teachers were asked to move their teaching online. In order to deliver online classes, teachers needed to invest money to access the necessary technology – suitable devices, adequate internet connectivity and a reliable power source. Research involving the collection of data from teachers based in Delhi and the National Capital Region via an online survey demonstrated a shortfall in access; teachers were facing internet and network issues while responding to the administered questionnaire, and teachers without a smartphone or laptop would have been excluded (Jain et al., 2021). The survey conducted by Jain et al. revealed that while teachers reported that their schools had the supporting infrastructure for online work, it turned out that this was mainly the case for the private school teachers and only 17 per cent of the representative government schools had such facilities, indicating that government school teachers had not been digitally equipped. This had a number of implications for teachers and their students from different socioeconomic backgrounds. In the same research, when teachers were asked how well they were equipped for their online classes, including details on the kind of device used, if they had a high-speed internet connection at home, if they faced any issues with the devices or internet connection and what they would do if faced with any such difficulty – all the responding teachers said that they were not fully equipped or prepared with regard to the resources required for online sessions. It also took them a while to get used to the system. A teacher commented, 'I use my phone to take classes, but I do not have high-speed data, and this affects my teaching' (FT1 Science RPVV1). Another teacher echoed a similar concern: 'I use my laptop for teaching and use my mobile data, but my students are sometimes unable to join, and I don't have enough resources' (FT7 Social Science RPVV2).

Teachers had to switch between prepared videos and PowerPoint lessons and hosting live teaching via Google Classroom, Zoom, Microsoft Teams and other platforms. They needed to adapt their lesson plans, worksheets, assessment sheets and other materials (The Hindu, 2020; Kundu, 2020). A large majority (75 per cent) of teachers surveyed by Jain et al (2021) found that teachers interacted with their students regularly. Most from private schools did so on all working days; only 25 per cent of those teachers engaging with students on all working days came from government schools. This again reflects socioeconomic and digital access differences across society.

Part of the problem was that teachers were not trained and had difficulties in quickly becoming proficient at using technology. In that same survey, 15–25 per cent of government school teachers not only reported a lack of preparedness for conducting online classes but also raised concerns about engaging with a disadvantaged group of students, some of whom had returned to home villages (Jain et al., 2021). Though most teachers and students are digitally literate, full-time online education is still a new experience for them (The Hindu, 2020). Teachers recognised that online teaching required a specialised form of pedagogy with which they were not familiar. Online classes proved more problematic for middle-aged teachers who were finding it challenging to maintain discipline in the digital class and were subject to online bullying and harassment from students (Sharma, 2020). When they voiced concerns, teachers were accused of being unwilling to adapt to online teaching (Mudi, 2020). Some teachers resorted to sending assignments to students and, subsequently, being available to address their questions, rather than conducting classes online (Jain et al., 2021). In other cases, teachers just transferred classroom materials onto slide presentations or gave lectures through the online platform of their choice. Rather than being learner-centric, most Covid-19 education has been a series of one-way teacher-centric provisions.

Teacher digital agency, accountability, efficacy and confidence

In the same way that teachers require agency for the physical classroom, in the virtual classroom, for teachers to be effective, they need 'digital agency'. Digital agency provides an outline for guaranteeing that teachers can employ technology in a 'meaningful and capital enhancing way', instead of only 'functioning with technology' (Pearce and Rice, 2017, 2). It is the teacher's capacity to regulate and alter a digital world. Digital agency advances awareness and interplay between educators and digital technologies. This section deals with three aspects of digital agency, digital competence, digital confidence and digital account-ability (Passey et al., 2018), to highlight the pedagogical issues faced by teachers and students and how teachers' engagement in online teaching has affected their digital agency (Anand and Lall, 2021).

Teacher and student spatial limitations

Spatial limitations in teachers' home environments affect their digital accountability in online teaching. In Delhi, teachers felt they had a low level of accountability[10] due to less familiarity with the digital world and its ethical issues (such as guaranteeing security and privacy for students) and the impact of their digital actions. From March 2020 onwards, spatial interactions between teachers and students and their families were totally transformed. Across India and other parts of the world, online classes on platforms such as Zoom or Microsoft Teams provided opportunities for parents as well as headteachers to observe teachers' pedagogical practices. Some teachers stated that it was difficult to teach with disruptions both in their own homes and in the homes of their students. Many teachers described the overall teaching experience as 'awkward' (Anand and Lall, 2021, 65). A few teachers voiced that their family members occasionally observed them teach, or access students' records, which raises additional accountability issues. Female teachers in particular faced low efficacy due to spatial constraints. A teacher stated that her online classroom is in the 'pooja [prayer] room with all textbooks and notebooks [taken out] only after my mother-in-law finishes her prayer' (FT7 Social Science RPVV2, cited in Anand and Lall, 2021, 65). When asked to elaborate, she voiced that it is problematic for a daughter-in-law to negotiate space to teach (Anand and Lall, 2021, 65). Teachers explained that families did not recognise the importance of online teaching. Confidentiality and propriety-related concerns established key issues – teachers commented on how family members of students logged into the online classroom to confirm the identity of teachers (Sharma, A.K. 2020; Jain et al., 2021). In addition, during online classes, most teachers stated that students' parents 'peep in', 'record the lectures' or 'take pictures' which affected their engagement with students. Besides infrastructural concerns, language, mathematics and science teachers explicitly shared the inability to teach concepts (without markers or teaching aids) and to express themselves in the same way as in the physical classroom. Though there were digital resources or tools offered by the government, these were not sufficient, as explained below.

Teachers' adaptations of digital resources or tools

As mentioned above, teachers were provided with a number of digital resources by the NCERT and CBSE.[11] In addition to these resources, the content of government material encompassed the NCERT-issued Alternative Academic Calendar,[12] videos of teaching and digital editions of textbooks. In online teaching, teachers can choose the digital tool to teach and select the digital resources to complement learning that they feel will work for them and their students. Digital resources incorporate hardware, software and infrastructure. Resources do not simply function based on their programmed intention but can operate as gatekeepers to social practices or societies or cultures (Passey et al., 2018). When asked, teachers stated that they were teaching online without training and consequently faced difficulties in using digital tools (such as Google Meet or Zoom) in their pedagogical practices. When they were asked what digital tools they employed, a majority of teachers explained they used tools such as WhatsApp or text messages. A teacher used WhatsApp to segregate students into two groups – the ones owning smartphones and those with cell phones – in order to reach out to both groups individually. She also said, 'I can now use WhatsApp, share files, making group video calls or a broadcast group' (FT3 Social Science SV5 cited in Anand and Lall, 2021, 65). Another teacher echoed a similar experience: 'the WhatsApp features are difficult, and it took time to learn video calls but now I use it to send worksheets and mark the students' (FT3 English SV10 cited in Anand and Lall, 2021, 65). For students who did not have access to WhatsApp or phones, teachers asked their parents to visit the school and gave out worksheets and homework for a week. Overall, teachers articulated that online teaching had been reduced to 'one-way delivery', with 'little or no personal contact', no method of 'checking who's getting it and who's not' and 'no engagement' (cited in Anand and Lall, 2021, 65). In addition, teachers started sharing videos over WhatsApp or YouTube so that students could watch them at their convenience. Nevertheless, this engendered problems for students to understand the concepts of lessons and thus promoted rote learning. Prerecorded sessions aired on the television (such as Swayam Prabha DTH channels) and radio (such as audio lessons, All India Radio) catered to a wider student population that could not access live online classes (Anand and Lall, 2021), these again serving the one-way delivery culture.

As far as the teacher-training initiatives on navigating or handling digital tools or resources are concerned, a teacher said, 'These online trainings just focus on the role of parents and content and learning outcomes and ask us to use the e-pathshala and DIKSHA, but we don't know how to teach' (FT5 Social Science SV5 cited in Anand and Lall, 2021, 65). In the absence of classroom teaching, most students were left waiting for tuition classes or schools to reopen in order to study appropriately and clear their doubts. A class VIII student said: 'I am waiting for my tuition classes to restart so that I can clear my doubts. Taking lessons through WhatsApp is not very helpful. There are many things that I do not understand, especially in Maths' (Sharma, 2020, 8). This section underlines how teacher competency played a significant role not just in handling the digital resources or tools, but in using them confidently in the enactment of the curriculum to meet the diverse needs of students.

Teacher digital self-efficacy and confidence

Digital confidence is the foundation of digital autonomy and exercising control over social changes arising from the use of digital tools (Passey et al., 2018). It is about having the efficacy and confidence to skilfully navigate digital realms in a 'transferable' manner (Passey et al., 2018). As mentioned above, teachers reported teaching using digital resources or tools as 'ineffective', 'exhausting' and a 'demotivating' experience. Some teachers stated that online teaching needed autonomy and skills but that the 'hardship' was not acknowledged by headteachers (Anand and Lall, 2021, 66). Some schools commenced teaching class XII students over Zoom; nevertheless, most of the students in primary schools were struggling, as they either had no access to assignments or found it virtually impossible to study mathematics and other subjects via WhatsApp or similar platforms. Language teachers elucidated that during in-person teaching they employ bilingual communication to resolve students' queries. This is because the physical involvement of sight and sound becomes an effective medium for a language teacher to teach confidently. The online medium lacks the pedagogical contact that enables the teacher to evaluate the level of students' understanding (Anand and Lall, 2021). Likewise, mathematics and science teachers voiced a low level of efficacy and self-confidence in clarifying concepts without chalk or experiments in the laboratory. Teachers said that evaluating students' understanding became challenging in online teaching. Due to low confidence, teachers shifted their focus from child-centred methods to rote-memorising methods, 'tricks' or 'important questions' to remember to attain good marks in an examination (Anand and Lall, 2021, 66).

Beyond teaching responsibilities, teachers were also expected to complete other duties imposed by the AAP government. During the first lockdown, a few teachers explained that they were unable to teach due to nonacademic duties which included distributing rations, surveying settlements and occasionally working in containment zones or quarantine centres located in government schools – all of which took huge amounts of time and affected their capacity to support students (Anand and Lall, 2021).

Pedagogical solutions for online teaching

As discussed above, many teachers shared that they could not replicate their offline teaching practices in the new online setup. Instead of delivering notes and introducing students to something new, teachers had to sometimes create their multimedia content and share it with students beforehand.

Teachers also shared a number of innovative practices and pedagogies to teach students online in order to convert students from passive receptors to active learners. Teachers adjusted and devised new teaching strategies during the lockdown (Anand and Lall, 2021). Among the most common changes adopted by teachers were the use of multimedia content, reduction of pen-and-paper work during classes and changes in homework and how it was assigned. A majority of the respondents believed the pandemic redefined the role of the teacher in Delhi, from disseminating knowledge to mentoring. When asked about pedagogical innovations and decisions, a teacher said: 'I use YouTube videos, storytelling and experiments. Currently we are learning about diet and nutrition; I bring food packets and also ask them to bring it. This way they [students] learn visually' (FT1 Science RPVV1). Another teacher explained using puppetry and storytelling to teach English lessons. 'I introduced skills – conversational, voice manipulation, how to write a script and narrate a story. Then I give them [students] a chance to present their stories. Narrating their stories builds their confidence and improves creativity' (FT7 Social Science RPVV2). When probed on the impact of these techniques on students, a teacher shared that 'such activities improve the imagination skills of the students and storytelling only helps to make classes exciting and fun but also improves the imagination of young students' (FT4 Science SV3). In addition, one of the teachers used different activities in the class for different kinds of learners. For instance, 'a game pink toe for kinaesthetic learners, a rapid math problem for logical learners, memory games and tongue twisters for verbal learners' (FT5 Social Science SV5). The teacher added that, under lockdown, she would have a quick dance session to lift the students' mood.

Certain teachers were making use of the autonomy they had been given and the truncated contact hours to guide students in their learning process through activity-based learning, rather than trying to replicate the face-to-face teaching model. This flipping of responsibility, putting students in charge of their learning, albeit with different degrees of guidance from teachers and support from parents, did help to develop student agency (Wadia, 2020). A few teachers also related that activity-based online learning and digital homework were common teaching strategies used during the pandemic. A science teacher shared that teaching new scientific concepts without a laboratory was a hard task until she started finding alternative modes of explaining the same concepts through things that are easily available at home: 'physical and mechanical changes through boiling milk and put lemon into it and defined indicators by putting red cabbage in boiling water' (FT5 Social Science SV5). A language teacher claimed that to explain things better to students online, teachers needed to speak in their language. 'When I started talking in Hindi, I found that students feel connected. We need to give Hindi an upper hand, even as we move back to physical classes. This way students feel instantly connected. They have shown more interest in solving online assignments than doing the same in pen and paper way' (FT3 English SV10). Even though the lockdown cost a lot emotionally and physically, these teachers did their best to keep students' spirits up by using innovative, interactive and inclusive teaching practices.

In the semi-structured interviews, a few teachers also revealed that a blended learning environment increased students' engagement in an elementary classroom when teachers were supported with necessary digital proficiencies. In blended learning classrooms, children access the digital curriculum and receive traditional instruction in a physical setting; hence, implementing intricately blended learning requires working closely with teachers to help them determine rhythms and patterns for their classrooms (Kundu et al., 2021). Blended learning – the integration of student-directed online learning with a teacher-led offline component – leverages digital technologies to provide children with more control over the time, place, path and pace of their learning (Staker and Horn, 2012). Overall, teachers commented that the time spent in a blended learning environment had a positive effect on children's classroom engagement irrespective of gender, and these effects emerged for only a few weeks. The implication is that blended learning is potent in bringing positive changes in students' classroom learning engagement provided teachers are getting the necessary encouragement, even in schools with low-standard technological infrastructure and underprepared but willing teachers (Kundu et al., 2021). When asked to describe their blended classrooms, teachers explained that children access the digital curriculum and also receive traditional instruction in a physical setting, thereby receiving the benefits of both mediums (Rao, 2019). Their pedagogical goal for blended learning is to combine the social opportunities of a physical classroom with personalised, technologically enhanced active learning in an online environment (Powell et al., 2015). This was also viewed as an opportunity to redesign how courses are developed, scheduled and delivered, through a combination of physical and virtual instruction: 'bricks and clicks' (Vaughan, 2014, 247). Norberg et al. (2011) found joining the best features of in-class teaching with the best features of online learning promotes active, self-directed learning opportunities with the added flexibility that should be the goal of this redesigned approach. Garrison and Vaughan (2008) echo this sentiment when they say that 'blended learning is the organic integration of thoughtfully selected and complementary face-to-face and online approaches and technologies' (148). In order to make online education effective, accessible and safer, besides the training programmes and schemes, the teaching community also started the Discussion Forum of Online Teaching[13] to initiate discussion on different aspects of online teaching and create repositories of useful resources.

Edtech and inequalities

Edtech companies in India saw the pandemic as a big market opportunity (Ghosh, 2020).[14] Online, virtual, e-learning education in India has been a booming industry and with the pandemic has witnessed rapid growth (Ghosh, 2020). Well-established companies such as Vedantu, Toppr, BYJU'S and Simplilearn as well as start-ups like Eupheus Learning were suddenly in demand from schools as well as students and their families (Verma, 2020). According to media reports, edtech start-up BYJU'S witnessed 7.5 million new users on its platform, and in April 2021 the firm grossed Rs.350 crore (Medhi, 2020a) or c.GB£35 million. Toppr and Vedantu also witnessed a surge in enrolment for their live classes during the lockdown (The News Minute, 2020). By leveraging the limitations emerging out of the pandemic, these start-ups have managed to raise funds. For example, Bengaluru-based online edtech start-up Vedantu raised US $12.56 million from Chinese venture firm Legend Capital in April. In the same month, it raised US $6.8 million of funding from the South Korea-based KB Global Platform Fund (Medhi, 2020b).

But it was not only families; there was also a sudden rise in schools approaching business-to-consumer companies to develop digital interventions and curriculum-driven solutions like online reference books and learning tools. Some of the edtech companies like Vedantu were providing free access to their learning platform for students and parents, as well as teachers, in New Delhi, Bengaluru, Kerala and Hyderabad (Mishra, 2020). Big companies such as Apple, Google and Microsoft were offering services like iCloud, Google Classrooms and Microsoft Teams for free to schools (Chakravarty, 2020). Because of the increasing demand and Asia's growing youth population, the industry is expected to triple in value from just over $100 billion in 2015 to $350 billion by 2025 (Gilchrist, 2020). Edtech companies have thus come in at three levels: getting parents to subscribe directly, getting schools to subscribe and use their services, and in some cases offering training to teachers to improve their capabilities in the virtual classroom. During the pandemic, edtech firms saw a massive expansion of online learning engagement on their platforms. According to a report by the Broadcast Audience Research Council, there has been a 30 per cent increase in the time spent on education software applications since the lockdown commenced (Biswas, 2020).

This could have important implications for the future, as discussed by Ben Williamson (2020) in his article on how big technology companies are creating new power networks, which are emerging as active part-ners in the pedagogic process. In the long run, these companies could affect classroom teaching practices in a very profound way. According to Williamson, datafication and analytics are going to replace the decision-making power of teachers in terms of the needs of students and, con-sequently, devising learning models for students. This would in effect disempower teachers.

In fact, edtech solutions are unlikely to work across the whole of India. Newspaper articles praised the edtech companies, discussing the 'new normal' and how students might not need to return to their classrooms, but this is problematic, not least for poorer students who do not have access to technology. As seen above, not everyone has stable electricity, an internet connection or a separate room for study, creating inequalities in access to education and the ability to remain engaged with the syllabus. According to a study conducted by edtech platform Buddy4Study, of the 250 million (25 crore) students affected by the lockdown, 80 per cent fall into the EWS category (Mahesh, 2020). Other data, cited from Statista 2018, shows that only 27 per cent of the Indian population have smartphones. The same article cites data from the National Sample Survey Office's 75th round of key household indicators of 2018 indicating that only 23.8 per cent of households have internet facilities (Rajeshwari, 2020).

Despite the issues discussed above, the Delhi government is planning to launch its virtual school to provide education and personalised remote learning to students through cutting-edge technology. A year into Covid-19, AAP proposed in its 2021–2 budget to establish virtual schools, as the pandemic increased the need for remote learning amid uncertainty over the duration of the lockdown. A six-member committee of schoolteachers, headteachers and government IT officials was formed in April 2021 to study global best practice for remote schooling and is expected to submit a blueprint for virtual schools to the government (Hindustan Times, 2021). The first meeting of the committee was headed by Education Minister Manish Sisodia, who outlined the scope of the Delhi model of virtual schools in overhauling the remote-learning experience for students. The virtual schools would employ education technology, personalised teaching-learning methodologies and modern assessment. These Delhi Model Virtual Schools would be just like any other school, with ID cards, dedicated staff and assessments. The schools are expected to operate with the principle of 'anywhere living, anytime learning, anytime testing' (Hindustan Times, 2021). Sisodia further added that Indian teachers have effectively learnt how to use technology during the pandemic and that this has set fertile ground to establish India's first virtual school in Delhi (Hindustan Times, 2021). Given the second wave of the pandemic described below, such virtual schools might indeed be required. However, the Delhi government does not seem to have taken on board the issues that arose during the first wave, and lessons on the lack of access to technology and the lack of digital pedagogy are yet to be learnt.

The second Covid-19 wave in Delhi

With Covid-19 cases spiking once again in Delhi at the beginning of 2021, teachers of government and municipal schools went back on pandemic-related duties, causing several schools to raise concerns over the deployment of teachers for non-teaching work at a time when practical exams of board classes had begun and the evaluation process of the other classes was underway. However, in January 2021 Manish Sisodia directed Chief Secretary Vijay Dev to issue an order reducing the number of government school teachers deployed on Covid-19 duty, to ensure that teachers re-engaged in academic work, following which a large number of teachers were released from pandemic-related work. With cases increasing again, teachers, as well as other government employees, had been asked to undertake a door-to-door mobilisation for the ongoing Covid-19 vaccination drive. For instance, in the Shahdara district in Delhi, around 124 teachers were asked to join the survey work on vaccination (Hindustan Times, 2021).

The deployment did not go down well with schools. A headteacher of a government school in Old Delhi said their only physical education teacher was called back on Covid-19 work on a Tuesday:

> We have our class XII physical education practical exam on Friday. How will we do that without our internal examiner? Besides, at least seven teachers who were busy uploading internal marks of students on to the Directorate of Education (DoE)'s portal have been assigned survey work and duty at the airport (Hindustan Times, 2021).

The general secretary of the government school teachers' association said, 'the government should not allow the district administrations to deploy teachers on Covid-19 duty at such a crucial time – the academic session is ending, and students need teachers the most right now' (Hindustan Times, 2021).

The headteacher of another government school said their only IT professional had been deployed at Delhi airport to screen passengers: 'Our staff are completely dependent on the IT person for uploading student marks and preparing results. The government has already asked schools to declare results up to class VIII by March 31. How will we finish the work in such a situation?' Similar concerns were raised by headteachers of municipal schools. A headteacher of the East Delhi municipal body in

Gandhi Nagar said, 'The result of the classes where teachers are on duty is not prepared yet. Another teacher will have to finish the work of his/her class first and then complete the work of others. So, half the students will be getting their results soon while the other half will have to wait a while' (Hindustan Times, 2021).

Teachers were involved with Covid-related activities for months, increasingly going beyond their role as educators. At the beginning of May 2021, a teacher was posted as a nodal officer at an oxygen refilling centre in Dwarka (Baruah, 2021). Some teachers were allotted duty for the 'monitoring of dead bodies' at hospital mortuaries. However, after an outcry from teachers' unions, the order was withdrawn. One of the teachers who had been allotted this duty was then posted to a dispensary, doing contact tracing. Schools were actually supposed to be at work preparing the marks of class X students in the absence of board exams, an almost impossible task. A headteacher shared:

> my school is currently a vaccination centre and 15 of my teachers are involved in that. There is one doctor supervising the five rooms in which vaccinations are happening, and one nurse administering the vaccines in each room. All data entry work is being done by teachers. Five teachers at my school are on vaccine duty in hospitals … There are 19 centres in my district which are once again functioning as hunger relief centres (Baruah, 2021).

The escalation of the Covid crisis, the imposition of lockdown and the halting of teaching-learning all went hand-in-hand in Delhi and led to schools and teachers completely losing touch with students. With the entire education department diverted elsewhere, education officials said they could not focus on keeping track of students – including whether or not their families may have left the city (Baruah, 2021). Teachers were just expected to juggle their Covid-19 duties with their teaching responsibilities. Teachers who did not report for their Covid-19 duties were threatened with action under the Delhi Disaster Management Act.[15] Sant Ram, an elected member of the Government School Teachers' Association said, 'If teachers are going on Covid-19 duties, who is teaching?' (Sarfaraz, 2021). It seems that the Delhi government deprioritised education during the second Covid wave. This chapter's depiction of the realities on the ground calls for the Delhi education reforms to be reimagined and reconfigured around the survival of the teaching and learning process, even in healthcare crises.

Conclusion and parting thoughts

Online education opens up a lot of possibilities for students and teachers alike. Yet it may also widen the inequalities in the socioeconomic fabric of India. The pandemic and the ensuing lockdown disrupted the lives of many, and the effects on young people have been massive. The pandemic exposed the large fault lines that exist in the digital infrastructure of India. The transition to online classes was not smooth, as there is massive inequality in access to electricity, the internet and laptops and mobiles, between rural and urban India and between rich and poor families, even in the national capital. This period will leave its mark on the academic progress of many students.

The AAP government's policies and interventions regarding online education are striving to be inclusive. But its determination has been shaken by the pandemic lockdowns, which closed many schools and reduced incomes. Even though government schools are free, many families facing poverty had no resources for switching to remote learning. The experience of the pandemic has shone an unambiguous spotlight on educational disparity – while most well-resourced private schools have been able to cope with Covid-19, most government and low-resource schools have struggled, even those supported by the AAP reforms. The pandemic also forced many children out of school and caused many to relocate to farms and factories to work, thereby worsening the child labour problem and increasing gender disparities (Khan and Lall, 2020); these changes are unlikely to be reversed soon, even under the stewardship of a reform-minded government.

The school closures also created a rapid shift to alternative modes of educational delivery (online learning and teacher-supported home-schooling) which revealed deep inequities in education systems worldwide, as many children lost access to teachers and schooling. Finding an effective response to these changes has tested teachers' capacities and individual and collective agency intensely (Hindustan Times, 2021). The state governments adopted online solutions in the early stages of the pandemic. Since then, many of these initiatives have been rolled back and state education departments have begun to endorse more context-based, direct teaching-learning solutions (Bedi, 2020a; 2020b). The other issue is that teachers (in rural India and government schools) are unequipped to teach through a digital platform, as they lack the requisite pedagogical skills and sometimes don't even have access to a stable internet connection. Hence, education in certain areas will not be available and students will be cut off completely. In such a scenario their learning will be stalled for a long period and they might be forced into child labour or marriage. For primary school children and parents, another problem surfaced: the lack of physical schooling will deprive them of the midday meal they would otherwise receive. This will impact their nutritional intake (Bedi, 2020a; Hindustan Times, 2021).

This chapter also showed how the digital infrastructure (and associated factors such as external distraction or family interruption) in Delhi is in contention with the accountability and efficacy of teachers, as well as the overall purpose of education. It is evident that digital agency is reliant on teachers' digital competencies and confidence; however, online teaching in India restricts the prospects for teachers to get the right balance between the needs of students and teachers and the opportunities provided by the digital technologies.

Lastly, education is not simply about completing the syllabus, taking classes and meeting deadlines, but is as much to do with engaging, social exchange, being involved in classroom discussions and physical activity. It is crucial to understand that though the pandemic has limited teacher capacity in many ways, teachers were doing their best to make virtual classes inclusive and successful. The pandemic has exposed gaps in the Delhi 'education revolution', which must be addressed to deal with such unprecedented situations in the future – such as future waves of the pandemic – without compromising quality and access to education for all. In doing so, education systems must support the enhancement of teachers' personal and collective agency in the face of continued disruption to schooling and ongoing challenges to educational equity.

Notes

1. MLA for AAP.
2. NROER is a digital initiative launched by the Ministry of Education which offers students access to e-books, e-libraries and e-resources.
3. Through this portal, students from classes I to XII can access the audio and video material and e-books of different subjects. This digital initiative is a venture of the NCERT.
4. The Ministry of Education has launched the National Digital Infrastructure for Teachers (DIKSHA) portal to equip teachers from class I to class XII for the world of e-learning. The platform is available for both teachers and students requiring learning material.
5. YUKTI was launched to identify ideas relevant to the Covid-19 pandemic.
6. YUKTI 2.0 is an extension of YUKTI to create a database of technologies and innovation in edtech.
7. Across 20 backward districts in 10 states – Bihar, Chhattisgarh, Delhi, Jharkhand, Madhya Pradesh, Maharashtra, Odisha, Rajasthan, Uttar Pradesh and West Bengal.
8. https://childfundindia.org accessed 18 March 2022.

9. This could be linked to nutrition issues. The midday meal scheme in India exists for this very reason – poor families do not have enough resources to adequately feed their children, who come to school hungry. When schools are closed, there is no midday meal for these children.
10. Digital accountability includes responsibility for oneself and others regarding one's digital actions, knowledge of the digital world and its ethical issues, understanding concerns and ensuring security and privacy (Passey et al., 2018 cited in Anand and Lall, 2021).
11. Teachers shared that the DoE of the Government of Delhi has also launched a blog targeting primary teachers and students across the 449 Sarvodaya Vidyalayas. The blog uploads weekly worksheets in various subjects and there are separate blogs for teachers of English and maths. It is being used additionally to promote online teaching; however, they found it hard to enact online.
12. https://bit.ly/3kE5nCN accessed 18 March 2022.
13. https://sites.google.com/view/dfot2020/home accessed 18 March 2022.
14. A key aspect of coping with Covid-19 is ensuring that the learning remains a continuous process. "Connecting students and teachers through digital platforms and necessary software through the use of laptops or phones is the latest transition in education, trying to eradicate the need for physical classrooms and in-person teachers. This is an ideal time to accept technology and its latest offerings to make education delivery to students more efficient and more productive through online learning and assessments ... Technology is turning education from teacher-centric education to both teacher and student-centric education. Virtual classrooms and various online tools today allow us to make the engagement between the teacher and students as close to a real, in-classroom like experience, as possible (Kiran Dham, CEO of Globus Infocom Ltd)" (Dhawan, 2020).
15. https://dmnewdelhi.delhi.gov.in/ddma/ accessed 18 March 2022.

Epilogue: was it a revolution?

Education and 'soft Hindutva' as a basis for AAP's election campaigns beyond Delhi

Since the research for this book concluded, AAP has continued and expanded its education reforms in Delhi schools. In January 2021, the Delhi government announced the restructuring of the SCERT and DIET in order to further improve the facilities for teacher training in the national capital. The government is planning to set up a cadre of teachers who are specialists in collaborative professional development and shared lesson planning, and will provide teachers with agency and autonomy in order to improve teacher training, along with increased interaction with parents, to reduce student dropout rate (Hindustan Times, 2021). One newly introduced programme is Business Blasters, a practical component of the EMC for classes XI and XII, to give students the experience of working in teams, brainstorming and identifying social challenges or business opportunities (Bhalerao, 2021). Business Blasters is a television show that will give these students an opportunity to present their start-up ideas to investors and obtain investment capital to take them to the next level. The show recently featured the finalist business ideas of 51,000 submissions from 300,000 students (Bhalerao, 2021). The programme seems to be a key part of the education revolution that AAP wants to launch in Delhi and eventually across India. After the first episode, Sisodia's feedback was positive: 'It was encouraging to see children pitch some creative ideas, which when scaled have the potential of bringing about tremendous social impact. This programme for students of classes XI–XII is going to form the basis of the country's progress. Through this, children will not run after jobs, but jobs will come to these children' (cited in Bhalerao, 2021).

AAP is currently preparing to introduce the International Baccalaureate (IB) curriculum in Schools of Specialised Excellence at junior levels in East Delhi (NDTV Education, 2021). Sisodia tweeted: 'IB

Board shall be the knowledge partner of DBSE [Delhi Board of School Education] to provide support in curriculum, assessment and teachers training. This is a big step to ensure a world-class education for every child including the kids coming from the poorest families [sic]' (NDTV Education, 2021). Sisodia added that the DBSE will discourage rote learning, as it is a 'partner of learning and not an authority of testing' (cited in Bhalerao, 2021). The aim of this programme is additionally to advance 'future pathways' among students and increase their access to higher education via the newly established Delhi Skill and Entrepreneurship University (Bhalerao, 2021). Teacher feedback on this was rather negative. At the point when teachers found out that they would need to teach IB from nursery to Class VIII, a teacher reacted: 'They [the department] should have oriented us from the start because I can't fully understand what's happening.' Among the teachers of the less privileged schools, a teacher shared: 'We have close to 70 students per section and when all children come to school, they'll be knocking into each other for lack of space' (cited in Bhalerao, 2021). Teachers found the circulars, memorandums and meetings confusing, as they are still reeling from the effects of the pandemic. As one teacher said: 'Forty out of 60 teachers will be engaged in administrative or data work daily. In the midst of all this, they are bringing IB. If it fails, it will be the teachers' fault' (cited in Bhalerao, 2021). As discussed in this volume, adding the IB will require practical measures, for instance developing teacher training that encompasses leadership opportunities, to engage and understand the new curriculum agenda. These are at an early stage in Delhi and, according to the teachers' feedback, the implementation plan requires significant amendments.

It is clear that the AAP education reforms have made an impression at the centre. Some of the AAP initiatives have inspired the NEP 2020, such as the more robust teacher-training programme, teacher mentoring and school governance and infrastructure. The education reforms are also slowly being taken up by other states – for example, the Happiness Curriculum (HC) has been implemented in Kerala, with the purpose of easing students into the post-pandemic learning environment. Teachers have been given online training by the Kerala SCERT on how to go about implementing the HC (The Hindu, 2021b). As Chief Minister Yogi Adityanath in Uttar Pradesh announced plans to launch the HC in primary schools as a pilot venture to make the students more sensitive towards nature, society and the nation, Kejriwal accused Yogi of 'copying' AAP's HC project, ahead of the Assembly elections (Prabhu, 2021).

This debate has now spread into the state election campaigns across India. Although AAP's power base is in Delhi, its political aims have always been India-wide.

Having won the Delhi State Assembly elections in February 2020, AAP started to campaign in the states of Goa, Uttar Pradesh, Uttarakhand and Punjab, which held State Assembly elections in early 2022 (Aswani, 2021). In order to lure voters, education was used for comparative purposes. In December 2021, AAP challenged BJP voters to compare education in BJP-administered municipal corporation schools in Delhi with the work done by AAP in the Delhi government-run schools. In a press conference, Sisodia said: 'If you like their [BJP's] model of education, then vote for them ... AAP's education model built schools and increased enrolment, but BJP's education model shut down schools and lost students' (The Hindu, 2021a). In the BJP-ruled states such as Haryana and Uttar Pradesh, there has been a decline in the number of government schools. Even in the Congress-ruled states such as Punjab, there has also been a decline in the number of government schools.

Kejriwal is trying to win in other states such as Punjab and Goa by pitching his election campaign on similar themes, including education. In Punjab, where AAP won power, Kejriwal promised free electricity and free health treatment and medicines at government hospitals (The Siasat Daily, 2021). In November 2021, he promised cash transfers to the account of every adult woman in Punjab. He urged women to give him and his party a chance to rule Punjab. Kejriwal also announced that AAP would provide high-quality free education in government schools if his party formed the government (The Siasat Daily, 2021). In response, Pargat Singh, the Punjab Education Minister commented that:

> he [Kejriwal] is trying to mislead people on the same land where Vedas and Upanishads were written long before people knew how to read and write. What revolution can he bring in Punjab where the bani of great Gurus are imbibed in Sri Guru Granth Sahib ji ... Punjab has one of the most transparent transfer policies in India which is completely online ... From teacher transfer policy to school data, everything can now be done with the click of a mouse, which even the Kejriwal government couldn't do in the past ten years in Delhi
>
> (Express News Service [Indian Express], 2021).

In Goa, Kejriwal promised cash transfers and described it as the 'world's biggest women empowerment programme' (Aswani, 2021). He also made a promise to increase access to education for children of Dalit background.

However, more recently, AAP's commitments to education have seemed secondary to their bid to engage Hindu voters, with the party indulging in explicit Hindu rhetoric and promising free pilgrimages to Hindu temples, even as its leaders are visiting temples. The religious rhetoric had been employed in the run-up to the Delhi State Assembly election, as Chief Minister Kejriwal told a television news channel that he is a 'kattar Hanuman bhakt',[1] following which he recited the 'Hanuman Chalisa'.[2] Kejriwal's articulation of Hindu rhetoric and his 'Jai Hanumam' (victory to Hanuman) slogans are aimed not only at matching the BJP's long-standing 'Jai Shri Ram' but also at making Kejriwal and AAP more attractive to Hindu voters (Aswani, 2021). While trying to take the political fight to the BJP, AAP even organised a Tiranga Yatra[3] in Ayodhya in September 2021, with stopovers at the Ram temple and Hanuman Garhi temple (the temple of Lord Hanuman in Uttar Pradesh). AAP is endeavouring to draw on BJP ideas and ideologies of Hindu supremacy and patriotism via education to expand its mandate beyond Delhi (Aswani, 2021; Sarkar, 2021). Sarkar (2021) remarked that AAP seems to lack ideological clarity and political diplomacy – its experiment risks yielding to the failures of 'soft Hindutva' strategies that have been tried by non-BJP parties in the past.

Regardless of its core anticorruption platform, AAP is now also drawing on patriotism, already successfully used by the BJP (Aswani, 2021; Sarkar, 2021). In Uttarakhand, AAP has named Ajay Kothiyal, a retired colonel of the Indian Army, as its chief minister candidate because 'Kothiyal has been a true warrior who served the nation fighting Pakistan in Kargil war, and terrorists in Jammu and Kashmir without caring for his own life' (Kejriwal cited in Aswani, 2021). Simultaneously, AAP is publicising Kothiyal's work in rebuilding the Kedarnath Temple in Uttarakhand. On similar lines, the AAP government also introduced a Desh Bhakti curriculum in Delhi to deliver a daily dose of patriotic sentiments (Sarkar, 2021). Kejriwal commented that 'We need to develop an environment wherein all of us and our children constantly feel patriotic' (Sarkar, 2021). The curriculum is meant to motivate the younger generation to take pride and realise their duty towards shaping the future of India. Pathak (2020) argues that the patriotism curriculum will sharpen the students' sociohistorical imagination, to know and understand the mission for *swaraj* (self-governance). However, a major concern is the lack of training among teachers to transform history or civic lessons into a fascinating experience using creative, sensitive and dialogic pedagogical styles (Pathak, 2020; Anand, 2019).

The AAP government has tried to transform education by harnessing the capacities of teachers but failed to address teachers' evolving needs. Consequently, teachers are struggling to make sense of education reforms and meet the demands of the state. The pandemic has also limited teacher capacity and uncovered gaps in Delhi's education revolution. It is how AAP addresses teacher needs in the future that will determine the success of their education revolution, even as this model is scaled up across other states. It remains to be seen whether the policies proposed in Delhi and elsewhere will meet the needs of teachers as they have been presented in this book.

Notes

1. Hard-core devotee of the Hindu deity, Hanuman.
2. A Hindu prayer to Hanuman.
3. Rally round the national flag.

References

Aggarwal, A. 2019. 'J&K not the first, Delhi too, was stripped of statehood once.' India Today. https://www.indiatoday.in/india/story/article-370-statehood-delhi-jammu-and-kashmir-1577629-2019-08-06 Accessed 15 March 2022.

Ahmad, S. 2019. 'AAP Govt Fixed A Broken State Schooling System, But Glitches Remain.' Outlook India. https://www.outlookindia.com/magazine/story/india-news-a-for-aaplause-b-for-boos/301297 Accessed 15 March 2022.

Aiyar, Y. 2020. 'NEP and the classroom consensus.' *Hindustan Times*. https://www.hindustantimes.com/columns/nep-and-the-classroom-consensus/story-T6Nz5sqVLKooBylFZsOFBJ.html Accessed 15 March 2022

Aiyar, Y. and Bhattacharya, S. 2015. The post office paradox: A case study of the block level education bureaucracy. Delhi: Accountability Initiative, Centre for Policy Research.

Aiyar, Y., Davis, V., Govindan, G. and Kapoor, T. 2021. Rewriting the Grammar of the Education System: Delhi's Education Reform (A Tale of Creative Resistance and Creative Disruption). *Research on Improving Systems of Education (RISE)*. https://doi.org/10.35489/BSG-RISE-Misc_2021/01 Accessed 15 March 2022.

Aiyar, Y., Dongre, A.A. and Davis, V. 2015. 'Education reforms, bureaucracy and the puzzles of implementation: A case study from Bihar.' *Bureaucracy and the Puzzles of Implementation: A Case Study from Bihar (September 1, 2015)*.

Alexiadou, N. and Essex, J. 2016. Teacher education for inclusive practice – responding to policy. *European Journal of Teacher Education*, 39 (1), 5–19.

Altinok, N. and Kingdon, G.G. 2012. 'New evidence on class size effects: A pupil fixed effects approach.' *Oxford Bulletin of Economics and Statistics*, 74 (2), 203–234.

Alderman, H., Orazem, P.F. and Paterno, E.M. 2001. 'School quality, school cost, and the public/private school choices of low-income households in Pakistan.' *The Journal of Human Resources*, 36 (2), 304–326.

Anand, K. 2019. *Teaching India and Pakistan relations: Teachers' pedagogical responses and strategies* (PhD diss., UCL (University College London)).

Anand, K. and Lall, M. 2021. 'Teachers' Digital Agency and Pedagogy during the Covid-19 Crisis in Delhi.' In *States of Emergency: Education in the Time of Covid-19,* NORRAG Special Issue 6.https://resources.norrag.org/resource/659/states-of-emergency-education-in-the-time-of-covid-19 Accessed 15 March 2022.

Anand, K. and Lall, M. (Forthcoming) 2022. The debate between secularism and Hindu nationalism: How India's textbooks have become the government's medium for political communication.

ANI. Jan 2021. 'Need to develop strong mindset among children to have confident, conscientious citizens.' Sisodia. *Sify*. https://www.sify.com/news/need-to-develop-strong-mindset-among-children-to-have-confident-conscientious--citizens-sisodia-news-national-vbluahciifbfc.html Accessed 15 March 2022.

Antoninis, M., April, D., Barakat, B., Bella, N., D'Addio, A.C., Eck, M. and Zekrya, L. 2020. 'All means all: An introduction to the 2020 Global Education Monitoring Report on inclusion.' *Prospects*, 49 (3), 103–109.

Anwer, N. 2019. 'Teachers and Parents on the Delhi Govt's Big Bang Education Reforms.' *The Citizen*. https://www.thecitizen.in/index.php/en/NewsDetail/index/9/17067/Teachers-and-Parents-on-the-Delhi-Govts-Big-Bang-Education-Reforms Accessed 20 March 2022.

Armstrong, F. and Sahoo, P. 2020. 'Disability, policy and education: Contrasting perspectives from India and England.' In *Education and Social Justice in the Era of Globalisation* (102–127). Routledge India.

Arya, A. 2018. '11 NGOs You Can Get In Touch With To Ensure Every Child In India Has A Chance At A Better Future.' *Scoopwhoop*. https://www.scoopwhoop.com/children-ngos-india-volunteer-donate/ Accessed 15 March 2022.

ASER. 2015. Annual Status of Education Report (Rural) 2014. *ASER Centre*. New Delhi.

ASER. 2016. Annual Status of Education Report (Rural) 2015. *ASER Centre* New Delhi. http://img.asercentre.org/docs/Publications/ASER%20Reports/ASER%202016/ase_2016.pdf [Page not found]

ASER. 2018. Annual Status of Education Report (Rural) 2017. http://img.asercentre.org/docs/Publications/ASER%20Reports/ASER%202017/aser_2017.pdf [Page not found]

Aswani, T. 2021. 'Aam Aadmi Party's Right-Turn.' *The Diplomat*. https://thediplomat.com/2021/12/aam-aadmi-partys-right-turn/ Accessed 15 March 2022.

Azim Premji Foundation. 2017. Teacher Absenteeism Study. Research Group. https://azimpremjiuniversity.edu.in/SitePages/pdf/Field-Studies-in-Education-Teacher-Absenteeism-Study.pdf [requires login]

Babu, N.M. 2020. 'AAP sets sights on other States.' *The Hindu*. https://www.thehindu.com/news/cities/Delhi/aap-sets-sights-on-other-states/article32650632.ece Accessed 15 March 2022.

Ball, J. 2010. Educational equity for children from diverse language backgrounds: Mother tongue-based bilingual or multilingual education in the early years. Summary. http://dspace.library.uvic.ca/handle/1828/2457 Accessed 15 March 2022.

Ball, S.J. 2003. 'The teacher's soul and the terrors of performativity.' *Journal of Education Policy*, 18 (2), 215–228.

Banerjee, A.V. and Duflo, E. 2011. 'Why aren't children learning.' *Development Outreach*, 13 (1), 36–44.

Banerjee, A.V., Cole, S., Duflo, E. and Linden, L. 2007. 'Remedying Education: Evidence from two randomized experiments in India.' *The Quarterly Journal of Economics*, 122 (3), August, 1235–1264. https://doi.org/10.1162/qjec.122.3.1235 Accessed 15 March 2022.

Banka, R. 2019. 'Government defends segregation of students in Chunauti format.' *Hindustan Times*. https://www.hindustantimes.com/cities/govt-defends-segregation-of-students-in-chunauti-format/story-YPBLtBh5gMbQFS3DptqY6O.html Accessed 15 March 2022.

Banks, F. and Dheram, P. 2012. 'India: Committing to change.' In *Teacher Education and the Challenge of Development* (92–106). Routledge.

Barton, L. and Slee, R. 1999. 'Competition, selection and inclusive education: some observations.' *International Journal of Inclusive Education*, 3 (1), 3–12.

Baruah, S. May 2021. 'Delhi: With teachers on Covid duty and no online classes, schools lose touch with students.' *The Indian Express*. https://indianexpress.com/article/cities/delhi/delhi-with-teachers-on-covid-duty-and-no-online-classes-schools-lose-touch-with-students-7308419/ Accessed 15 March 2022.

Batra, P. 2005. 'Voice and agency of teachers: Missing link in national curriculum framework 2005.' *Economic and Political Weekly*, 4347–4356.

Batra, P. 2006. 'Building on the National Curriculum Framework to enable the agency of teachers.' *Contemporary Education Dialogue*, 4 (1), 88–118.

Batra, P. 2009. 'Teacher Empowerment: The education entitlement–social transformation traverse.' *Contemporary Education Dialogue*, 6 (2), 121–156.

Batra, P. 2011. 'Teacher education and classroom practice in India: A critique and propositions.' In *epiSTEME-4* conference.

Batra, P. 2014. 'Problematising teacher education practice in India: Developing a research agenda.' *Education as Change*, 18 (sup1), S5–S18.

Batra, P. 2017. 'Inertia in teacher education and the need for judicial intervention.' *Learning Curve*, (26), 25–28.

Batra, P. 2020. 'NEP 2020: Undermining the Constitutional Education Agenda?' *Social Change*, 50 (4), 594–598.

Bawane, J. 2019. 'Paradoxes in teacher education: Voices from the Indian context.' In *Teaching and Teacher Education* (49–70). Switzerland: Palgrave Macmillan, Cham.

Bazeley, P. 2007. *Qualitative data analysis with NVivo*. London: SAGE Publications.

Bedi, A. 2019. 'Kejriwal's report card – how Delhi's AAP govt fared on its 70 manifesto promises from 2015.' *The Print*. https://theprint.in/politics/kejriwalsreport-card-how-delhis-aap-govt-fared-on-its-70-manifesto-promises-from-2015/288453/ Accessed 15 March 2022.

Bedi, A. 2020a. 'No gadgets, no studies: What online classes mean for 16 lakh poor students in Delhi schools.' *The Print*. https://theprint.in/india/education/no-gadgets-no-studies-what-online-classes-mean-for-16-lakh-poor-students-in-delhi-schools/406837/ Accessed 15 March 2022.

Bedi, A. 2020b. 'Delhi govt starts online lessons for Class 12 but only a handful of students are logging in.' *The Print.* https://theprint.in/india/education/delhi-govt-starts-online-lessons-for-class-12-but-only-a-handful-of-students-are-logging-in/397880/ Accessed 15 March 2022.

Beteille, A. 2001. 'The Indian Middle Class.' *The Hindu.* http://www.hinduonnet.com/2001/02/05/stories/05052523.htm [Page not found]

Béteille, T. 2009. 'Absenteeism, Transfers and Patronage: The Political Economy of Teacher Labor Markets in India', unpublished PhD diss., Stanford University.

Bhalerao, S. 2021. 'This State Govt Launches TV Show For Helping Class 11, 12 Students Pitch Startup Ideas; Rs 60 Crore Up For Grabs!' *Track in.* https://trak.in/tags/business/2021/11/30/this-state-launches-tv-show-for-helping-class-11-12-students-pitch-startup-ideas-rs-60-crore-up-for-grabs/amp/ Accessed 15 March 2022.

Bhanj, J.D. 2018. 'Mission Buniyaad' launched. *The Hindu.* https://www.thehindu.com/news/cities/Delhi/mission-buniyaadlaunched/article23506965.ece Accessed 15 March 2022.

Bhat, D. 2017. '"Harbinger of a New Era"? Evaluating the effect of India's Right to Education Act on learning outcomes.' *M-RCBH Associate Working Paper*, 76.

Bhat, S. 2020. 'Lessons From The Delhi Education Reform Journey.' *Dream a Dream.* https://dreamadream.org/lessons-from-the-delhi-education-reform-journey/ Accessed 15 March 2022.

Bhattacharjee, S. 2019. 'Ten Years of RTE Act: Revisiting Achievements and Examining Gaps.' *ORF Issue Brief.* https://www.orfonline.org/research/ten-years-of-rte-act-revisiting-achievements-and-examining-gaps-54066/ Accessed 15 March 2022.

Bhattacharya, D. 2001. 'Civic Community and Its Margins: School teachers in rural west Bengal.' *Economic and Political Weekly*, 36 (8): 673–683.

Bhatnagar, N. and Das, A. 2013. 'Nearly two decades after the Implementation of Persons with Disabilities Act: Concerns of Indian teachers to implement inclusive education.' *International Journal of Special Education*, 28 (2), 104–113.

Biesta, G.J.J. and Tedder, M. 2007. 'Agency and learning in the lifecourse: Towards an ecological perspective.' *Studies in the Education of Adults*, 39, 132–149.

Biesta, G., Priestley, M. and Robinson, S. 2015. 'The role of beliefs in teacher agency.' *Teachers and Teaching*, 21 (6), 624–640.

Bishop, A.J. and Kalogeropoulos, P. 2015. '(Dis) engagement and Exclusion in Mathematics Classrooms – Values, Labelling and Stereotyping.' In *Diversity in Mathematics Education* (193–217). Springer, Cham.

Bissoyi, S.K. 2018. 'The perils of inequality – the ugly face of Delhi.' *Dialy O.* https://www.dailyo.in/politics/delhi-poverty-aam-aadmi-party-education-rteanganwadi-bjp-odf-water-swachh-bharat/story/1/27180.html Accessed 15 March 2022.

Biswas, V.S. 2020. 'Ed-tech platforms cash in on pandemic; posts surge in users and time spent.' *Financial Express.* https://www.financialexpress.com/brandwagon/ed-tech-platforms-cash-in-on-pandemic-posts-surge-in-users-and-time-spent/1947135/ Accessed 15 March 2022.

Bolin, F. 1989. 'Empowering leadership.' *Teachers College Record*, 91 (1), 81–96.

Bonal, X. and González, S. 2020. 'The impact of lockdown on the learning gap: Family and school divisions in times of crisis.' *International Review of Education*, 66 (5), 635–655.

Boston Consulting Group. 2020. School Education Reforms in Delhi 2015–2020, an independent report. BCG. https://www.bcg.com/en-in/school-education-reforms-in-delhi-2015-2020 Accessed 15 March 2022.

Brezicha, K., Bergmark, U. and Mitra, D.L. 2015. 'One size does not fit all: Differentiating leadership to support teachers in school reform.' *Educational Administration Quarterly*, 51 (1), 96–132.

Brinkmann, S. 2015. 'Learner-centred education reforms in India: The missing piece of teachers' beliefs.' *Policy Futures in Education*, 13 (3), 342–359.

Brinkmann, S. 2016. The role of teachers' beliefs in the implementation of learner-centred education in India. (PhD diss.) University College London.

Brinkmann, S. 2019. 'Teachers' beliefs and educational reform in India: From "learner-centred" to "learning-centred" education.' *Comparative Education*, 55 (1), 9–29.

Britannica. n.d. Anna Hazare. https://www.britannica.com/biography/Anna-Hazare Accessed 15 March 2022.

British Council. 2019. The School Education System in India – An overview. *British Council.* https://www.britishcouncil.in/sites/default/files/school_education_system_in_india_report_2019_final_web.pdf Accessed 15 March 2022.

Britzman, D.P. 2012. *Practice makes practice: A critical study of learning to teach.* New York: Suny Press.

Bruns, B., Filmer, D. and Patrinos, H.A. 2011. *Making Schools Work: New evidence on accountability reforms. Human Development Perspectives*, World Bank, Washington D.C.

Burakowski, A. and Krzysztof, I. 2017. India's Aam Aadmi (Common Man's) Party: Are the Newcomers Rocking National Politics? *Asian Survey,* 57 (3), 528–547.

Bushe, G.R. 2010. 'Commentary on "appreciative inquiry as a shadow process"'. *Journal of Management Inquiry*, 19 (3), 234–237.

Byker, E. 2014. 'ICT oriented toward nyaya: Community computing in India's slums.' *International Journal of Education and Development Using ICT*, 10 (2), 19–28.

Byker, E.J. and Banerjee, A. 2016. 'Evidence for Action: Translating field Research into a large scale assessment.' *Current Issues in Comparative Education*, 18 (1), 42–53.

Calvert, L. 2016. 'The power of teacher agency.' *The Learning Professional*, 37 (2), 51.

Cater, J.K. 2011. 'Skype: A cost-effective method for qualitative research.' *Rehabilitation Counselors and Educators Journal*, 4 (2), 1017–1019.

Central Square Foundation. (2020). 'Private Schools in India.' https://www.centralsquarefoundation.org/state-of-the-sector-report-on-private-schools-in-india/ Accessed 15 March 2022.

Census 2011. NCT of Delhi – Administrative Divisions 2011. *Census India*. https://censusindia.gov.in/2011census/maps/administrative_maps/DELHI1.pdf Accessed 15 March 2022.

Centre for Policy Research. 2015. Categorisation of settlement in Delhi. Cities of Delhi – Policy Brief. https://cprindia.org/briefsreports/categorisation-of-settlement-in-delhi/ Accessed 15 March 2022.

Chakravarty, A. 2020. 'Indian school heads discuss switching to virtual learning during corona panic.' *Scoonews*. https://www.scoonews.com/news/indian-school-heads-discuss-switching-to-virtual-learning-during-corona-panic-8859 Accessed 15 March 2022.

Chandran, M. 2021. 'Teacher accountability and education restructuring: An exploration of teachers' work identities in an urban school for poor in India.' *International Studies in Sociology of Education*, 1–20.

Chari, R. 2020. 'Challenges of quality in online learning.' *The Times of India.* https://timesofindia.indiatimes.com/blogs/edutrends-india/challenges-of-quality-in-online-learning/ Accessed 15 March 2022

Chennat, S. 2014. 'Internship in preservice teacher education programme: A global perspective.' *Australian Journal of Teacher Education*, 15 (1).

Clarke, J., Gewirtz, S. and McLaughlin, E. (eds). 2000. *New managerialism, new welfare?.* London: SAGE Publications Ltd.

Clarke, P. 2003. 'Culture and classroom reform: The case of the district primary education project, India.' *Comparative Education*, 39 (1), 27–44.

Corbridge, S., Williams, G., Srivastava, M. and Véron, R. 2005. *Seeing the state: Governance and governmentality in India* (Vol. 10). Cambridge University Press.

Cribb, A. and Gewirtz, S. 2007. 'Unpacking autonomy and control in education: Some conceptual and normative groundwork for a comparative analysis.' *European Educational Research Journal*, 6 (3), 203–213.

Daily Pioneer. Mar, 2021. 'Teachers honoured for imparting edu during pandemic lockdown.' *Daily Pioneer.* https://www.dailypioneer.com/2021/state-editions/teachers-honoured-for-imparting-edu-during-pandemic-lockdown.html Accessed 15 March 2022.

Dakin, J., Tiffin, B. and Widdowson, H.G. 1968. *Language in Education: The problem in commonwealth Africa and the Indo-Pakistan sub-continent.* Oxford: Oxford University Press.

Darling-Hammond, L. 2006. 'Constructing 21st-century teacher education.' *Journal of Teacher Education*, 57 (3), 300–314.

Darling-Hammond, L. 2014. 'One piece of the whole: Teacher evaluation as part of a comprehensive system for teaching and learning.' *American Educator*, 38 (1), 4.

Das, A.K., Kuyini, A.B. and Desai, I.P. 2013. 'Inclusive Education in India: Are the teachers prepared?' *International Journal of Special Education*, 28 (1), 27–36.

Datnow, A. 2000. 'Power and politics in the adoption of school reform models.' *Educational Evaluation and Policy Analysis*, 22 (4), 357–374.

Davies, P. 2000. 'The relevance of systematic reviews to educational policy and practice.' *Oxford Review of Education*, 26 (3–4), 365–378.

Dayal, S.R. 2018. 'Emerging Concerns in Preservice Teacher Education.' *Educational Quest: An International Journal of Education and Applied Social Sciences*, 9 (2), 181–186.

De, A., Noronha, C. and Samson, M. 2005. 'The New Private Schools.' In Banerji R. and Surianarian, S. 2005 *City Children, City Schools: Challenges of Universalising Elementary Education in Urban India*. 95–113, Pratham Resource Centre Working Paper (in collaboration with UNESCO).

Deakin, H. and Wakefield, K. 2013. 'Skype interviewing: Reflections of two PhD researchers.' *Qualitative Research,* 14 (5), 603–616.

DeJaeghere, J.G. 2017. *Educating entrepreneurial citizens: Neoliberalism and youth livelihoods in Tanzania*. London: Routledge.

The Delhi Government. 2020. Special Training for Out of school children – PAB (2015–16). http://edudel.nic.in/ssa/7.pdf Accessed 17 March 2022.

Deloitte. 2013. A report: Urgent needs of NGOs in the education sector. Deloitte, GiveIndia, *CII*. https://www2.deloitte.com/content/dam/Deloitte/in/Documents/IMO/in-imongo's-in-the-education-sector-noexp.pdf [Page not found]

Dhawan, P.D. 2019. 'By reforming its public education system, Delhi govt is setting an example of good governance.' *The Logical Indian*. https://thelogicalindian.com/story-feed/awareness/good-governance/?infinitescroll=1 Accessed 15 March 2022.

Dhawan, S. 2020. 'Online learning: A panacea in the time of Covid-19 crisis.' *Journal of Educational Technology Systems*, 49 (1), 5–22.

Dias, V.C. 2018. 'Integral education program of São Paulo: Problematizations about the teaching work.' *Educação e Pesquisa*, 44.

Digital Learning Network. March 2021. '98 teachers, principals of Delhi govt, private schools honored for contribution.' *Digital Learning*. https://digitallearning.eletsonline.com/2021/03/98-teachers-principals-of-delhi-govt-private-schools-honored-for-contribution/ Accessed 15 March 2022.

Directorate of Education, Government of NCT of Delhi. (n.d.). '2015 And Beyond. Delhi Education Revolution.' *Edudel*. http://www.edudel.nic.in/welcome_folder/delhi_education_revolution.pdf Accessed 15 March 2022.

Department of School Education and Literacy, MHRD. 2012. *Vision of teacher education in India: Quality and regulatory perspective, report of the high-powered commission on teacher education constituted by the Hon'ble Supreme Court of India*. New Delhi: Government of India MHRD.

District Primary Education Programme. 2000. *Empowerment through education: Identification and enrolment of children with special needs in DPEP*. Noida: Education Consultant of India Limited.

Diwakar, R. 2016. 'Local contest, national impact: Understanding the success of India's Aam Aadmi Party in 2015 Delhi assembly election.' *Representation*, 52 (1), 71–80.

Duflo, E., Rema, H. and Stephen, R. 2012. 'Incentives Work: Getting teachers to come to school.' *American Economic Review*, 102 (4), 1241–78.

Dwivedi, S. 2018. 'Support Grows for Atishi Marlena, Fired by Centre as Delhi Advisor.' *NDTV*. https://www.ndtv.com/india-news/support-grows-for-atishi-marlena-fired-by-centre-as-delhi-adviser-1840652 Accessed 15 March 2022.

Dyer, C., Choksi, A., Awasty, V., Iyer, U., Moyade, R., Nigam, N. and Sheth, S. 2004. 'Knowledge for teacher development in India: The importance of "local knowledge" for in-service education.' *International Journal of Educational Development*, 24 (1), 39–52.

Economic Survey of Delhi. 2018–19. Planning Department Government of NCT of Delhi. http://delhiplanning.nic.in/sites/default/files/Final%20Economy%20survey%20English.pdf Accessed 15 March 2022.

EduDel. 2020. Education Department, Government of NCT Delhi. http://www.edudel.nic.in/samagrashiksha/content/2schmanagementwise.pdf Accessed 15 March 2022.

Education World. 2016. 26 NGOs Enabling Indian Education. https://www.educationworld.in/26-ngos-enabling-indian-education/ Accessed 15 March 2022.

Education Booklet. 2018. Quality Education for All: Initiatives and innovations –transforming Delhi education. https://aamaadmiparty.org/wp-content/uploads/2018/01/Education-Booklet-2018.pdf Accessed 15 March 2022.

Egan, T.M. and Lancaster, C.M. 2005. 'Comparing appreciative inquiry to action research.' *Organization Development Journal*, 23 (2), 29–49.

Ehren, M., Madrid, R., Romiti, S., Armstrong, P.W., Fisher, P. and McWhorter, D.L. 2021. 'Teaching in the Covid-19 era: Understanding the opportunities and barriers for teacher agency.' *Perspectives in Education*, 39 (1), 61–76.

Elton-Chalcraft, S., Cammack, P. and Harrison, L. 2016. 'Segregation, integration, inclusion and effective provision: a case study of perspectives from special educational needs children, parents and teachers in Bangalore, India.' *International Journal of Special Education*, 31 (1), 2–9.

Enright, E., Hill, J., Sandford, R. and Gard, M. 2014. 'Looking beyond what's broken: Towards an appreciative research agenda for physical education and sport pedagogy.' *Sport, Education and Society*, 19 (7), 912–926.

Estimates of State Domestic Product of Delhi. 2018–19. Directorate of Economics & Statistics, Government of NCT of Delhi. http://des.delhigovt.nic.in/wps/wcm/connect/c16676004 96211a6a319bb26edbf4824/Estimates+of+State+Domestic+Product+of+Delhi-201 819+%28Base+Year+201112%29.pdf?MOD=AJPERES&lmod=587268366&CACHEID= c1667600496211a6a319bb26edbf4824 Accessed 15 March 2022.

Flåten, L.T. 2017. 'Spreading Hindutva through education: Still a priority for the BJP?' *India Review*, 16 (4), 377–400.

Flores, A.M. and Fernandes, P.S.S. 2014. 'Preservice Teachers Views of Their Training: Key issues to sustain quality teacher education.' *Journal of Teacher Education for Sustainability*, 16 (2), 39–53.

Forbes India. 2020. 'The rise, fall and rise of AAP: A timeline.' *Forbes India.* https://www.forb esindia.com/article/special/the-rise-fall-and-rise-of-aap-atimeline/57681/1 Accessed 15 March 2022.

Freire, P. 1970. 'Cultural action and conscientization.' *Harvard Educational Review*, 40 (3), 452–477.

Garrison, D.R., and Vaughan, N.D. 2008. *Blended learning in higher education: Framework, principles, and guidelines.* San Francisco, CA: John Wiley & Sons.

Gewirtz, S. 2002. *The Managerial School.* London: Routledge.

Gewirtz, S. and Ball, S. 2000. 'From "Welfarism" to "New Managerialism": Shifting discourses of school headship in the education marketplace.' *Discourse: Studies in the cultural politics of education*, 21 (3), 253–268.

Ghosh, D. 2020. 'For Ed-tech start-ups, it's raining money.' *Fortune India.* https://www.fortu neindia.com/bengaluru-buzz/for-edtech-startups-its-raining-money/104233 Accessed 15 March 2022.

Giddens, A. 1984. *The Constitution of Society: Outline of the theory of structuration.* University of California Press.

Giddens, A. and Dallmayr, F.R. 1982. *Profiles and Critiques in Social Theory.* Los Angeles: University of California Press.

Gilchrist, K. 2020. 'These millennials are reinventing the multibillion-dollar education industry during coronavirus.' *CNBC.* https://www.cnbc.com/2020/06/08/edtech-how-schools-educat ion-industry-is-changing-under-coronavirus.html Accessed 15 March 2022.

Gillborn, D. and Youdell, D. 1999. *Rationing Education: Policy, practice, reform, and equity.* McGraw-Hill Education (UK).

Glewwe, P. 2002. 'Schools and skills in developing countries: Education policies and socioeconomic outcomes.' *Journal of Economic Literature*, 40 (2), 436–482.

Goddard, C. and Evans, D. 2018. 'Primary preservice teachers' attitudes towards inclusion across the training years.' *Australian Journal of Teacher Education*, 43 (6), 122–142.

Government of India. 2012. Restructuring and Reorganisation of the Centrally Sponsored Scheme on Teacher Education: Guidelines for Implementation. New Delhi: The Government of India.

Goel, C. 2019. 'Improving professional practices of in-service teachers in Delhi.' *International Online Journal of Education and Teaching*, 6 (3), 432–441.

Government of India. 2013. Twelfth Five Year Plan (2012–2017) Social Sectors Volume III. New Delhi. Planning Commission, Government of India.

Government of India. 2014. Indian Standard Classification of Education. https://www.education. gov.in/sites/upload_files/mhrd/files/statistics/InSCED2014_1.pdf Accessed 21 April 2022

Government of India. 2019. Draft of National Policy of Education 2019, Ministry of Human Resource Development, New Delhi.

Government of India. 2020. National Education Policy 2020. Retrieved from Ministry of Human Resources Development. https://www.mhrd.gov.in/sites/upload_files/mhrd/files/NEP_Fina l_English_0.pdf Accessed 15 March 2022.

Gorur, R. and Dey, J. 2021. 'Making the user friendly: The ontological politics of digital data platforms.' *Critical Studies in Education*, 62 (1), 67–81.

Govinda, R. and Josephine, Y. 2004. *Contract teachers in India: A review.* Paris: IIEP UNESCO.

Goyal, D. 2020. 'Assessing the level of inclusive education at the school level in India.' *ORF.* https:// www.orfonline.org/expert-speak/assessing-the-level-of-inclusive-education-at-the-school- level-in-india/ Accessed 15 March 2022.

Goyal, S. 2009. 'Inside the house of learning: The relative performance of public and private schools in Orissa.' *Education Economics*, 17 (3), 315–327.

Goyal, S. and Pandey, P. 2009. *How do government and private schools differ? Findings from two large Indian states.* World Bank.

Gratch, A. 2000. 'Teacher voice, teacher education, teaching professionals.' *The High School Journal*, 83 (3), 43–54.

Gray, L.M., Wong-Wylie, G., Rempel, G.R. and Cook, K. 2020. 'Expanding qualitative research interviewing strategies: Zoom video communications.' *The Qualitative Report*, 25 (5), 1292–1301.

Grewal, K. 2020. 'What the Delhi school education model is and why Maharashtra is looking to emulate it.' *The Print.* https://theprint.in/india/education/what-the-delhi-school-education-model-is-andwhy-maharashtra-is-looking-to-emulate-it/350356/ Accessed 15 March 2022.

Grindle, M.S. 2004. 'Good enough governance: Poverty reduction and reform in developing countries.' *Governance*, 17 (4), 525–548.

Guichard, S. 2010. *The construction of history and nationalism in India: Textbooks, controversies and politics.* (Vol. 17). London: Routledge.

Guichard, S. 2013. 'The Indian nation and selective amnesia: Representing conflicts and violence in Indian history textbooks.' *Nations and Nationalism*, 19 (1), 68–86.

Gupta, L. 2018. 'Discourse of teacher education in India.' In *Routledge Handbook of Education in India: Debates, Practices, and Policies,* edited by Kumar, 248–269. Taylor and Francis.

Gupta, S. and Ahmad, F. 2016. 'Teaching and the transformative promise of public education: What went wrong? Have we lost our way? A perspective from two government school teachers.' *Contemporary Education Dialogue*, 13 (2), 266–272.

Hamid, M.O. and Nguyen, H.T.M. 2016. 'Globalization, English language policy, and teacher agency: Focus on Asia.' *International Education Journal: Comparative Perspectives*, 15 (1), 26–43.

Hanushek, E.A. and Woessmann, L. 2011. 'Overview of the symposium on performance pay for teachers.' *Economics of Education Review*, 30 (3), 391.

Härmä, J. 2009. 'Can Choice Promote Education for All? Evidence from Growth in Private Primary Schooling in India.' *Compare: A Journal of Comparative and International Education*, 39 (2), 151–165.

Harrison, L.M. and Hasan, S. 2013. 'Appreciative inquiry in teaching and learning.' *New Directions for Student Services 2013,* (143), 65–75.

Heller, P., Mukhopadhyay, P., Banda, S. and Sheikh, S. 2015. 'Exclusion, Informality, and Predation in the Cities of Delhi – An Overview of the Cities of Delhi Project.' https://cprindia.org/workin gpapers/exclusion-informality-and-predation-in-the-cities-of-delhi/ Accessed 15 March 2022.

Heyneman, S.P. and Stern, J. M. 2014. 'Low cost private schools for the poor: What public policy is appropriate?' *International Journal of Educational Development*, 35 (1), 3–15.

Hill, J., Sandford, R. and Enright, E. 2016. '"It has really amazed me what my body can now do": Boundary work and the construction of a body-positive dance community.' *Sport in Society*, 19 (5), 667–679.

The Hindu. 2020. 'Corona Virus: In the time of pandemic classes go online and on air.' *The Hindu.* https://www.thehindu.com/news/national/in-the-time-of-the-pandemic-classes-go-online-and-on-air/article31264767.ece Accessed 17 March 2022.

The Hindu. 2021. 'AAP to fight elections in six States: says Delhi CM Kejriwal.' *The Hindu.* https://www.thehindu.com/news/cities/Delhi/aap-to-fight-elections-in-six-states-says-delhi-cm-kejriwal/article33683078.ece Accessed 17 March 2022.

Hindustan Times. 2017. 'Delhi govt to start five English-medium "schools of excellence" next year.' *Hindustan Times – Delhi News.* https://www.hindustantimes.com/delhi-news/delhi-govt-to-start-five-englishmedium-schools-of-excellence-next-year/story-p8zAUAydjZS2RKcY3v4MgP.html Accessed 15 March 2022.

Hindustan Times. 2018. 'Student-classroom and pupil-teacher ratios of govt schools have improved, shows Economic Survey.' *Hindustan Times.* https://www.hindustantimes.com/education/economic-survey-says-student-classroom-and-pupil-teacher-ratios-of-govt-schools-have-improved/story-mND5dp9DKcBkyIsKeoX3JM.html Accessed 15 March 2022.

Hindustan Times. 2020. '61% prefer sending kids to Delhi government school, says survey.' *Hindustan Times.* https://www.hindustantimes.com/education/61-prefer-sending-kids-to-delhigovernm ent-school-says-survey/story-2baF9nJo0uxunPLGfrK4yL.html Accessed 15 March 2022.

Hindustan Times. March, 2021. 'Govt to work on enhance teacher training and cutting dropout rates: Manish Sisodia.' https://www.hindustantimes.com/cities/delhi-news/govt-to-work-on-enhance-teacher-training-and-cutting-dropout-rates-manish-sisodia-101610918101525.html Accessed 15 March 2022.

Hoy, W.K. and Woolfolk, A.E. 1993. 'Teachers' sense of efficacy and the organizational health of schools.' *The Elementary School Journal*, 93 (4), 355–372.

IANS. Feb 2021. 'Unequal access to education worsened during Covid-19: Atishi.' *Daijiworld*. https://daijiworld.com/news/newsDisplay?newsID=804204 Accessed 15 March 2022.

Iftikhar, F. Feb 2021. '166k students in Delhi fell off grid as schools moved online.' *Hindustan Times*. https://www.hindustantimes.com/cities/delhi-news/166k-students-in-delhi-fell-off-grid-as-schools-moved-online-101612385072733.html Accessed 15 March 2022.

Imants, J. and Van der Wal, M.M. 2020. 'A model of teacher agency in professional development and school reform.' *Journal of Curriculum Studies*, 52 (1), 1–14.

India Education Diary. Mar 2021. '64% Children worry that without additional educational support they will not be able to cope up with curriculum and may drop out.' ChildFund Assessment Report. *India Education Diary*. https://indiaeducationdiary.in/64-children-worry-that-with out-additional-educational-support-they-will-not-be-able-to-cope-up-with-curriculum-and-may-drop-out-childfund-assessment-report/ Accessed 15 March 2022.

The Indian Express. 2021. 'Tiranga yatra is an attempt to take the fight to BJP. But AAP will have to navigate strategy's pitfalls.' *Indian Express*. https://indianexpress.com/article/opinion/edi torials/aap-tiranga-yatra-hindutva-politics-7479092/lite/ Accessed 17 March 2022.

INEE. 2012. 'Preservice and in-service teacher training.' *INEE*. https://inee.org/resources/pre-and-service-teacher-training-strategy-document Accessed 15 March 2022.

Indian Express. 2020. 'Over 12,000 rooms in Delhi schools will be ready by April: Manish Sisodia.' *Indian Express*. https://www.edexlive.com/news/2020/feb/18/over-12000-rooms-in-delhi-schoolswill-be-ready-by-april-manish-sisodia-10280.html Accessed 15 March 2022.

India Today. 2019. What is the difference between a state and a union territory? https://www.ind iatoday.in/education-today/gk-current-affairs/story/what-is-the-difference-between-a-state-and-an-union-territory-1577445-2019-08-05 Accessed 21 April 2022

India TV News Desk. 2020. 'AAP sweeps Delhi in another landslide win – 10 reasons that contributed to Kejriwal's victory.' *India TV*. https://www.indiatvnews.com/elections/news-arvind-kejri wal-aap-aam-aadmi-party-victory-reasons-delhi-election-result-2020-588069 Accessed 15 March 2022.

Ishak, N. and Bakar, A. 2012. 'Qualitative data management and analysis using NVivo: An approach used to examine leadership qualities among student leaders.' *Education Research Journal,* 2 (3), 94–103.

Iyengar, R., Witenstein, M.A. and Byker, E. 2014. 'Comparative Perspectives on Teacher Education in South Asia.' *Annual Review of Comparative and International Education 2014,* 99–106. Emerald Group Publishing Limited, Bingley. https://doi.org/10.1108/S1479-36792014000 0025010 Accessed 15 March 2022.

Iyer, G. 2019. 'The effectiveness of the Right to Education (RTE) Act in unrecognised schools of Delhi, India.' A thesis submitted in candidature for PhD. Newcastle University. https://the ses.ncl.ac.uk/jspui/bitstream/10443/4627/1/Iyer%20G%202019.pdf Accessed 15 March 2022.

Jaffrelot, C. and Jairam, P. 2019. 'BJP has been effective in transmitting its version of Indian history to next generation of learners.' *Carnegie Endowment*. https://carnegieendowment.org/2019/ 11/16/bjp-has-been-effective-in-transmitting-its-version-of-indian-history-to-next-generat ion-of-learners-pub-80373 Accessed 15 March 2022.

Jaffrelot, C. 2019. 'The Fate of Secularism in India.' In *The BJP in Power: Indian Democracy and Religious Nationalism*, edited by Milan Vaishnav. Washington, DC: Carnegie Endowment for International Peace. https://carnegieendowment.org/2019/04/04/bjp-in-power-indian-democracy-and-religious-nationalism-pub-78677 Accessed 15 March 2022.

Jain, C. and Prasad, N. 2018. *Quality of Secondary Education in India*. Singapore: Springer Nature.

Jain, S., Lall, M. and Singh, A. 2021. 'Teachers' voices on the impact of Covid-19 on school education: Are ed-tech companies really the panacea?' *Contemporary Education Dialogue*, 18 (1), 58–89.

Jeffery, R., Jeffery, P. and Jeffery, C. 2007. 'The privatisation of secondary schooling in Bijnor: A crumbling welfare state?' In Kumar, K. and Oesterheld, J. (eds) *Education and Social Change in South Asia*. New Delhi: Orient Longman.

Jena, A.K. 2015. 'Students' perception is the instrument to predict the quality of teachers in higher education: A regression analysis.' *Journal on Educational Psychology*, 9 (1), 25–37.

Jha, J. and Jhingran, D. 2005. *Elementary Education for the Poorest and Other Deprived Groups: The real challenge of universalization*. New Delhi: Manohar.

Jha, M. 2019. 'Delhi SCERT to expand online teacher training to more subjects, grades via the ChalkLit App.' *The Indian Wire*. https://www.theindianwire.com/education/delhi-scert-exp and-online-teacher-training-subjects-grades-via-chalklit-app-159495/ Accessed 15 March 2022.

Juneja, N. 2010. 'Access to What? Access, Diversity and Participation in India's schools.' Research Monograph No.32. *National University of Educational Planning and Administration.* https://www.academia.edu/1339328/Access_to_What_Access_Diversity_and_Participation_in_Indias_schools Accessed 15 March 2022.

Justice Verma Commission Report on Teacher Education. 2012. *Report of the high-powered commission on teacher education constituted by the Hon'ble supreme court of India.* (Vol. 1). New Delhi: Government of India MHRD.

Kalra, A. 2017. 'Why India's Richest State Cannot Hire Enough Teachers.' *Indiaspend.* https://www.indiaspend.com/why-indias-richest-state-cannot-hire-enough-teachers-47765 Accessed 15 March 2022.

Karunakaran, T. and Bhatta, T.R. 2013. 'Willing horses: There is no water. Primary teacher education in Nepal.' *The Dawn Journal,* 2 (2).

Kaur, N. 2019. 'Draft National Education Policy 2019. An Overview.' *Voices of Teachers and Teacher Educators,* VIII (I), 90–101. https://ncert.nic.in/pdf/publication/journalsandperiodicals/vtte/vtte_July_2019.pdf Accessed 15 March 2022.

Kauts, D.S. and Kaur, N. 2019. 'Effect of teacher's focused guidance on attainment of the lesson objectives in mathematics among secondary school students in relation to their intelligence and locus of control.' *International Journal of Research in Social Sciences,* 9 (2), 618–638.

Ketelaar, E., Beijaard, D., Boshuizen, H.P.A. and Den Brok, P.J. 2012. 'Teachers' positioning towards an educational innovation in the light of ownership, sense-making and agency.' *Teaching and Teacher Education,* 28 (2), 273–282.

Khan, F. and Lall, M. 2020. 'Covid-19, Child Labour and Education: Hidden gender issues in India.' UCL CEID Blog. https://blogs.ucl.ac.uk/ceid/2020/06/24/khan-lall/ Accessed 15 March 2022.

Khanna, R. 2020. 'Teachers' Education: The real need of Indian education system.' *BWEducation.* http://bweducation.businessworld.in/article/Teacher-Education-The-Real-Need-Of-Indian-Education-System/05-10-2020-327992/ Accessed 15 March 2022.

Khanna, R. and Kareem, J. 2021. 'Creating inclusive spaces in virtual classroom sessions during the Covid pandemic: An exploratory study of primary class teachers in India.' *International Journal of Educational Research Open,* 2, 100038.

Khatua, S. and Chaudhury, R.D. 2019. In Search of Quality: A study on Elementary Education in Rural India. https://doi.org/10.31219/osf.io/wyfap. Accessed 15 March 2022.

Khullar, M. 1991. 'In Search of Relevant Education'. Occasional Paper No.1. New Delhi: Centre for Women's Development Studies.

Kidwai, H., Burnette, D., Rao, S., Nath, S., Bajaj, M. and Bajpai, N. 2013. In-service teacher training for public primary schools in rural India findings from district Morigaon (Assam) and district Medak (Andhra Pradesh).

Kim, H., Talreja, V. and Ravindranath, S. 2019. 'How do you measure happiness? Exploring the happiness curriculum in Delhi schools.' *Education Plus Development. Brookings.* https://www.brookings.edu/blog/education-plus-development/2019/11/13/how-do-you-measure-happiness-exploring-the-happiness-curriculum-in-delhi-schools/ Accessed 15 March 2022.

Kingdon, G. 2007. 'The progress of school education in India.' *Oxford Review of Economic Policy,* 23 (2), 168–195.

Kingdon, G.G. 2017. *The Private Schooling Phenomenon in India: A Review. Centre for the Studies of African Economies.* Working paper – 2017/04.

Kingdon, G. and Muzammil, M. 2013. 'The school governance environment in Uttar Pradesh, India: implications for teacher accountability and effort.' *The Journal of Development Studies,* 49 (2), 251–269.

Kingdon, G.G. and Sipahimalani-Rao, V. 2010. 'Para-teachers in India: Status and impact.' *Economic and Political Weekly,* 59–67.

Kingdon, G.G. and Teal, F. 2007. 'Does Performance Related Pay for Teachers Improve Student Performance? Some Evidence from India.' *Economics of Education Review,* 26 (4), 473–486.

Koirala-Azad, S. and Fuentes, E. 2009. 'Introduction: Activist scholarship – possibilities and constraints of participatory action research.' *Social Justice,* 36 (4), (118), 1–5.

Kondalamahanty, A. 2019. 'An Entrepreneurial Mindset: For Delhi Kids, It's Never Too Early To Start.' *Inc42.* https://inc42.com/features/entrepreneurial-mindset-for-delhi-kids-its-never-too-early-to-start/ Accessed 15 March 2022.

Kremer, M. and Muralidharan, K. 2008. 'Public and private schools in rural India.' In Peterson, P. and Chakrabarti, R. (eds) *School Choice International.* Cambridge, MA: MIT Press.

Kremer, M., Muralidharan, K., Chaudhury, N., Hammer, J. and Rogers, F. 2005. 'Teacher Absence in India: a snapshot.' *Journal of the European Economic Association*, 3 (23), 658–667.

Kukreja, R.A. 2019. 'A political economy analysis of education in India.' *Global Policy Insights*. http://globalpolicyinsights.org/a-political-economy-analysis-of-education-in-india.php Accessed 15 March 2022.

Kumar, A. 2018. 'Innovating in Education: NGO Interventions in New Delhi Government Schools.' *Harvard Library*. http://nrs.harvard.edu/urn-3:HUL.InstRepos:40049977 Accessed 15 March 2022.

Kumar, K. 2005. *Political agenda of education: A study of colonialist and nationalist ideas*. New Delhi: SAGE Publications.

Kumar, K. 2019. 'Dilution of the right to education act.' *Economic & Political Weekly*, *54* (14), 14–15.

Kumar, K. and Sarangapani, P.M. 2004. 'History of the quality debate.' *Contemporary Education Dialogue*, 2 (1), 30–52.

Kundu, A. and Rice, M. 2019. 'Indian educators' perceptions of their inclusion implementation practices in secondary schools.' *British Journal of Special Education*, 46 (4), 398–422.

Kundu, A., Bej, T. and Rice, M. 2021. 'Time to engage: Implementing math and literacy blended learning routines in an Indian elementary classroom.' *Education and Information Technologies*, 26 (1), 1201–1220.

Kundu, P. 2019. 'Deteriorating quality of education in schools: Are teachers responsible.' *Economic & Political Weekly*, 54 (24), 34–41.

Kundu, P. 2020. 'Indian education can't go online – only 8% of homes with young members have computer with net link.' *Scroll India*. https://scroll.in/article/960939/indian-education-cant-go-online-only-8-of-homeswith-school-children-have-computer-with-net-link Accessed 15 March 2022.

Lall, M. 2008. 'Educate to hate: The use of education in the creation of antagonistic national identities in India and Pakistan.' *Compare*, 38 (1), 103–119.

Lall, M. 2011. 'Pushing the child centred approach in Myanmar: The role of cross national policy networks and the effects in the classroom.' *Critical Studies in Education*, 52 (3), 219–233.

Lall, M. 2013. 'National Identity, Citizenship and the Role of Education in India.' In Mitra, S. (ed.) *Citizenship as Cultural Flow, Structure, Agency and Power*, Springer, Berlin, 151–166.

Lall, M. and Anand, K. (Forthcoming) 2022. *How neoliberalism underpinned the rise of Hindu nationalism – the role of education in bringing about contemporary India*.

Lall, M. and Nambissan, G. (eds) 2011. *Education and Social Justice in the Era of Globalisation: Perspectives from India and the UK*. New Delhi: Routledge.

Lall, M., Anand, K., Bali, M., Banerji, A., Jain, S., Khan, F. and Singh, A. 2020. 'What works and why in Indian government schools – Teachers' voices in Delhi NCR.' *IRDSE*. https://www.irdse.org/front/Final-Report.pdf Accessed 15 March 2022.

Lasky, S. 2005. 'A sociocultural approach to understanding teacher identity, agency and professional vulnerability in a context of secondary school reform.' *Teaching and Teacher Education*, 21 (8), 899–916.

Lave, J. and Wenger, E. 1991. *Situated Learning: Legitimate peripheral participation*. Cambridge, UK: Cambridge University Press.

Leander, K.M. and Osborne, M.D. 2008. 'Complex positioning: Teachers as agents of curricular and pedagogical reform.' *Journal of Curriculum Studies*, 40 (1), 23–46.

Leder, G.C. 1992. 'Mathematics and gender: Changing perspectives.' In D.A. Grouws (ed.) *Handbook of research on mathematics teaching and learning (a project of the National Council of Teachers of Mathematics)*. 597–622. Macmillan.

Lederman, D. 2020. 'Will shift to remote teaching be boon or bane for online learning?' *Inside Higher Education*. https://www.insidehighered.com/digital-learning/article/2020/03/18/most-teaching-going-remote-will-help-or-hurt-online-learning Accessed 15 March 2022.

Lennert da Silva, A.L. and Mølstad, C.E. 2020. 'Teacher autonomy and teacher agency: a comparative study in Brazilian and Norwegian lower secondary education.' *The Curriculum Journal*, 31 (1), 115–131.

Lipponen, L. and Kumpulainen, K. 2011. 'Acting as accountable authors: Creating interactional spaces for agency work in teacher education.' *Teaching and Teacher Education*, 27 (5), 812–819.

Liu, S. and Meng, L. 2009. 'Perceptions of teachers, students and parents of the characteristics of good teachers: A cross-cultural comparison of China and the United States.' *Educational Assessment, Evaluation and Accountability*, 21 (4), 313–328.

London, J., McGuire, J.B. and Santos, F. 2019. 'We become what we talk about: How experimenting with dialogue can change an organisation's culture.' In J. Chlopczyk and C. Erlach (eds), *Transforming organisations. Management for Professionals* (155–175). Champagne: Springer.

The Logical Indian. 2018. 'Delhi: Govt Schools Reached A Record High Of 90.68% Pass Percentage, 2.37% Increase From Last Year.' *The Logical Indian*. https://thelogicalindian.com/news/delhi-govt-schools-pass-percentage/ Accessed 17 March 2022.

The Logical Indian. 2019. 'Delhi: For The First Time In 8 Yrs, Pass Percentage For Class XI Students Touch 80%.' *The Logical Indian*. https://thelogicalindian.com/news/students-pass-percentage Accessed 17 March 2022.

Magnússon, G. 2019. 'An amalgam of ideals: Images of inclusion in the Salamanca Statement.' *International Journal of Inclusive Education*, 23 (7–8), 677–690.

Maher, C., Hadfield, M., Hutchings, M. and de Eyto, A. 2018. 'Ensuring rigor in qualitative data analysis: A design research approach to coding combining NVivo with traditional material methods.' *International Journal of Qualitative Methods*, 17 (1), 1609406918786362.

Mahesh, S. 2020. A need now but no replacement. *The New Indian Express*. https://www.newindianexpress.com/education/2020/may/06/a-need-now-but-no-replacement-teachers-share-concerns-about-online-classes-during-Covid-19-2139605.html Accessed 15 March 2022

Mahoney, J. 2020. 'Remote learning for elementary students poses unique challenges.' *The Globe and Mail*. https://www.theglobeandmail.com/canada/article-remote-learning-for-primary-level-students-poses-unique-challenges/ Accessed 15 March 2022.

Maithreyi, R. 2021. *Educating Youth: Regulation Through Psychosocial Skilling in India*. SAGE Publishing India.

Majumdar, M. and Mooij, J. 2011. *Education and inequality in India: A classroom view*. Routledge Contemporary South Asia Series No. 46. London: Routledge.

Manjrekar, N. (ed.) 2021. *Gender and Education in India: A Reader*. London: Routledge.

Markee, N. 2002. 'Language in Development: Questions of theory, questions of Practice.' *TESOL Quarterly*. 36 (3), 265–274.

Marlena, A. 2017. Understanding Delhi's Education Revolution. *Aam Admi Party*. Accessed 16 March 2022. https://aamaadmiparty.org/understanding-delhis-education-revolution/

März, V. and Kelchtermans, G. 2013. 'Sense-making and structure in teachers' reception of educational reform. A case study on statistics in the mathematics curriculum.' *Teaching and Teacher Education*, 29, 13–24.

McCuaig, L. and Quennerstedt, M. 2018. 'Health by stealth – exploring the sociocultural dimensions of salutogenesis for sport, health and physical education research.' *Sport, Education and Society*, 23 (2), 111–122.

McTaggart, R. 1991. 'Principles for participatory action research.' *Adult Education Quarterly*, 41 (3), 168–187.

Medhi, T. 2020a. 'Meet the 6 Ed-tech start-ups that have seen record growth amid Covid-19 lockdown.' *Your Story*. https://yourstory.com/2020/06/edtech-startups-growth-coronavirus-byjus-unacademy-toppr-startups Accessed 16 March 2022.

Medhi, T. 2020b. 'Learning in quarantine: These Ed-tech start-ups raised funds amid the Covid-19 pandemic.' *Your Story*. https://yourstory.com/2020/05/edtech-startups-raised-coronavirus-funding Accessed 16 March 2022.

Mehendale, A. and Mukhopadhyay, R. 2020. 'School System and Education Policy in India: Charting the Contours.' In P.M. Sarangapani and R. Pappu (eds), *Handbook of Education Systems in South Asia*. Global Education Systems.

Mehrotra, S. and P.R. Panchamukhi. 2006. 'Private Provision of Elementary Education in India: Findings of a survey in eight States.' *Compare: A Journal of Comparative & International Education*, 36 (4), 421–442.

Menon, R. 2014. 'Caught Between "Neglect" and a Private "Makeover": Government Schools in Delhi', in Ravi Kumar (ed.), *Education, State and Market: Anatomy of Neoliberal Impact* (114–138). New Delhi: Aakar.

Menon, R. 2017. 'On the Margins of "Opportunity": Urbanisation and Education in Delhi's Metropolitan Fringe'. In William T. Pink and George W. Noblit (eds), *Second International Handbook of Urban Education* (445–467). Switzerland: Springer.

Menon, S. 2020. 'Coronavirus: How the lockdown has changed schooling in South Asia.' BBC. https://www.bbc.co.uk/news/world-south-asia-54009306 Accessed 16 March 2022.

MHRD. 2016. Projected Population in Different Age Group – 2016. https://www.education.gov.in/sites/upload_files/mhrd/files/statistics/PopulationProjection2016%20updated.pdf Accessed 21 April 2022.

Michael, S. 2005. 'The promise of appreciative inquiry as an interview tool for field research.' *Development in Practice*, 15 (2), 222–230.

Miller, S. 2005. 'Language in Education: Are we meeting the needs of linguistic minorities in cities?' In Banerji, R. and Surianarian, S. 2005. *City Children, City Schools: Challenges of universalising elementary education in urban India.* Pratham Resource Centre Working Paper (in collaboration with UNESCO).

Min, M. 2019. 'School culture, self-efficacy, outcome expectation, and teacher agency toward reform with curricular autonomy in South Korea: a social cognitive approach.' *Asia Pacific Journal of Education*, 1–17.

Ministry of Human Resource and Development, MHRD. 2009. Teacher Development and Management. Discussions and suggestions for policy and practice emerging from the International Conference on Teacher Development and Management, held at Vidya Bhavan Society, Udaipur 23–25 February 2009. New Delhi: MHRD.

Ministry of Human Resource Development. 2003. *A Manual for Planning and Implementation of Inclusive Education in SSA.* SSA India. https://tinyurl.com/2p85mexh Accessed 21 April 2022.

Ministry of Human Resource Development, MHRD. 2012. Vision of Teacher Education in India: Quality and Regulatory Perspective, Report of the High-Powered Commission on Teacher Education Constituted by the Hon'ble Supreme Court of India, Vol. 1.

Ministry of Law and Justice. 2016. The Rights of Persons with Disabilities Act, 2016. New Delhi: Ministry of Law and Justice, Government of India.

Mir, T.A. 2020. 'Building Capacities: National Initiative for School Heads and Teachers.' *Greater Kashmir.* https://www.greaterkashmir.com/news/opinion/building-capacities-2/ Accessed 16 March 2022.

Mishra, S. 2020. 'Covid-19 lock down: Schools innovate to remain connected.' *Odisha Bytes.* https://odishabytes.com/covid-19-lockdown-schools-innovate-to-remain-connected/ Accessed 16 March 2022.

Mitra, A. and Singh, J. 2019. 'Rising unemployment in India: A statewise analysis from 1993–94 to 2017–18'. *Economic and Political Weekly*, 54 (50), 12–16.

Mooij, J. 2008. 'Primary education, teachers' professionalism and social class about motivation and demotivation of government school teachers in India.' *International Journal of Educational Development*, 28 (5), 508–523.

Mooij, J. and Jalal, J. 2012. 'Primary education in Delhi, Hyderabad and Kolkata: Governance by resignation, privatisation by default.' In *Governing India's Metropolises,* 157–182. Routledge India.

Mudi, A. 2020. 'Teaching in the time of Coronavirus.' *The Wire.* https://livewire.thewire.in/personal/teaching-in-the-times-of-coronavirus/ Accessed 16 March 2022.

Mukerji, S. and Walton, M. 2016. 'Learning the right lessons: Measurement, experimentation and the need to turn India's right to education act upside-down.' In *India Infrastructure Report 2012* (147–164). Routledge India.

Mukhopadhyay, R. and Sarangapani, P.M. 2018. 'Introduction: Education in India between the state and market-concepts framing the new discourse: Quality, efficiency, accountability.' In *School education in India* (1–27). Routledge India.

Mukhopadhyay, S. and Mani, M.N.G. 2002. 'Education of Children with Special Needs.' In *India Education Report: A profile of basic education*, edited by R. Govinda, 96–108. New Delhi: Oxford University Press.

Munby, H. 1984. 'A qualitative approach to the study of a teacher's beliefs.' *Journal of Research in Science Teaching*, 21 (1), 27–38.

Munshi, K. and Rosenzweig, M. 2006. 'Traditional Institutions Meet the Modern World: Caste, Gender and Schooling Choice in a Globalizing Economy.' *American Economic Review*, 96 (4), 1225–1252.

Muralidharan, K. and Kremer, M. 2006. 'Public and Private Schools in Rural India.' Harvard University, Department of Economics. Cambridge, MA.

Muralidharan, K. and Sundararaman, V. 2013. *Contract teachers: experimental evidence from India.* (Working Paper 19440). National Bureau of Economic Research.

NDTV Education. 2021. 'Now, Delhi Government Schools Will Teach International Curriculum: Arvind Kejriwal.' *NDTV Education.* https://www.ndtv.com/education/delhi-government-ib-board-signs-mou-for-delhi-board-of-school-education/amp Accessed 16 March 2022.

Nambissan, G.B. 2003. 'Educational deprivation and primary school provision: a study of providers in the city of Calcutta.' https://opendocs.ids.ac.uk/opendocs/handle/20.500.12413/3982 Accessed 16 March 2022.

Nambissan, G.B. 2006. 'Terms of inclusion: Dalits and the Right to Education.' In *The Crisis of Elementary Education in India,* Ravi Kumar (ed.). New Delhi: Sage Publications.

Nambissan, G.B. 2021. 'The Changing Urban and Education in Delhi: Privilege and exclusion in a megacity.' *Education and the Urban in India Working Paper Series 9.* Max Weber Stiftung, India Branch, New Delhi.

Nambissan, G.B. and Ball, S.J. 2010. 'Advocacy networks, choice and private schooling of the poor in India.' *Global Networks,* 10 (3), 324–343.

Naik, J.P. 1979. 'Equality, quality and quantity: The elusive triangle in Indian education.' *International Review of Education,* 25 (2), 167–185.

Narula, A. and Kalra M.B. 2019. 'Exploring in-service teachers' beliefs about happiness.' *International E-Journal of Advances in Education.* Vol. V, Issue 14, August, 2019. http://ijaedu.ocerintjournals.org/tr/download/article-file/801585 Accessed 16 March 2022.

Naseem, M.A. and Stöber, G. 2014. 'Textbooks, identity politics, and lines of conflict in South Asia.' *Journal of Educational Media, Memory, and Society,* 6 (2), 1–9.

National Curriculum Framework for Teacher Education. 2009. *Towards preparing professional and humane teacher.* New Delhi: National Council for Teacher Education.

National Curriculum Framework. 2005. New Delhi: National Council for Educational Research and Training.

National Institute of Educational Planning and Administration (NIEPA). 2016. State Report card, Elementary Education in India: Where do we stand? http://udise.in/Downloads/Elementary-STRC-2016-17/07.pdf Accessed 16 March 2022.

National Policy of Education. 2020. Ministry of Human Resource Development, New Delhi, May 31, 2020. https://www.education.gov.in/sites/upload_files/mhrd/files/NEP_Final_English_0.pdf Accessed 16 March 2022.

Nawani, D. 2013. 'Continuously and comprehensively evaluating children.' *Economic and Political Weekly,* 33–40.

NCERT (National Curriculum of Educational Research and Training). 2006. National Curriculum Framework Position Paper: National Focus Group on Examination Reform.

NCERT. 2009. Towards Preparing Professional and Humane Teacher (NCFTE). New Delhi: National Council for Teacher Education.

NCERT. 2017. National Achievement Survey 2017, District Report Cards. http://nas.schooledunfo.in/dashboard/nas_ncert#/ Accessed 21 April 2022.

The New India Express. 2019. 'Delhi government's education reform scheme 'Chunauti' based on Abhijit Banerjee's model: Kejriwal.' *The New India Express.* https://www.newindianexpress.com/cities/delhi/2019/oct/14/delhi-governmentseducation-reformscheme-chunauti-based-on-abhijit-banerjees-model-kejriwal-2047518.html Accessed 17 March 2022.

The News Minute. 2020. 'BYJU'S sees 6 million new students' access free lessons on its platform in March.' *The News Minute.* https://www.thenewsminute.com/article/byju-s-sees-6-million-new-students-access-free-lessons-its-platform-march-122008 Accessed 17 March 2022.

Nilsson, P. 2003. *Education for All: teacher demand and supply in Africa.* Brussels: Education International.

NISHTHA Training Report. 2019. 'Integrated Teacher Training for Change – Samagra Shiksha.' *NISHTHA.* https://itpd.ncert.gov.in/mod/page/view.php?id=1473 Accessed 16 March 2022.

Norberg, A., Dziuban, C.D. and Moskal, P.D. 2011, 'A time-based blended learning model.' *On the Horizon,* 19 (3), 207–216.

Noronha, R. 2017. 'Jawahar Navodaya Vidyalayas: Taking education to rural homes.' *India Today.* https://www.indiatoday.in/magazine/cover-story/story/20170821-education-jawahar-navodaya-vidyalayas-rural-quality-education-1028894-2017-08-11 Accessed 16 March 2022.

NUEPA. 2010. Elementary Education in India: Progress towards UEE, Analytical Report (2007–08). New Delhi: National University of Education Planning and Administration.http://www.dise.in/Downloads/Publications/Publications%202008-09/Flash%20Statistics%202008-09.pdf Accessed 16 March 2022.

NUEPA. 2014. 'Elementary Education in India: Progress towards UEE. Flash Statistics.' *DISE* 201314. http://www.dise.in/downloads/publications/publication2013-14/flashbook2013-14.pdf Accessed 16 March 2022.

Ohara, Y. 2012. 'Examining the Legitimacy of Unrecognized Low-Fee Private Schools in India: Comparing different perspective.' *Compare: A Journal of Comparative & International Education*, 42 (1), 69–90.

O'Sullivan, M. 2006. 'Lesson observation and quality in primary education as contextual teaching and learning processes.' *International Journal of Educational Development*, 26 (3), 246–260.

Otter.ai. 2019. Help center: Frequently asked questions. https://otter.ai/help-center [Sign-in required]

Outlook. 2019. 'Delegation of teachers from US visits Delhi government's school of excellence.' *Outlook The News Scroll*. https://www.outlookindia.com/newsscroll/delegation-of-teachers-from-us-visitsdelhi-governments-school-of-excellence/1568189 [No longer available]

Pandey, S. 2020. 'Covid-19 set the ground for Ed-techs to shine.' *BW Education*. http://bweducation.businessworld.in/article/Covid-19-Set-The-Ground-For-EdTechs-To-Shine-/01-07-2020-292834/ Accessed 16 March 2022.

Passey, D., Shonfeld, M., Appleby, L., Judge, M., Saito, T. and Smits, A. 2018. 'Digital agency: Empowering equity in and through education.' *Technology, Knowledge and Learning*, 23 (3), 425–439.

Pathak, A. 2019. 'The threat to the idea of a public university.' *The Hindu*. https://www.thehindu.com/opinion/op-ed/the-threat-to-the-idea-of-a-public-university/article62108904.ece Accessed 16 March 2022.

Pathak, A. 2020. 'Patriotism need not be free from criticality or art of resistance.' *The Indian Express*. https://indianexpress.com/article/opinion/columns/aam-aadmi-party-arvind-kejriwal-deshbhakti-curriculum-in-delhi-schools-6305770/lite/ Accessed 16 March 2022.

Pearce, K.E. and Rice, R.E. 2017. 'Somewhat separate and unequal: Digital divides, social networking sites, and capital-enhancing activities.' *Social Media+ Society*, 3 (2).

Peercy, M.M. and Troyan, F.J. 2017. 'Making transparent the challenges of developing a practice-based pedagogy of teacher education.' *Teaching and Teacher Education*, 61, 26–36.

Perryman, L.A. 2013. 'Addressing a national crisis in learning: open educational resources, teacher-education in India and the role of online communities of practice.' In *Seventh Pan-Commonwealth Forum on Open Learning (PCF7)*, 2–6.

Peters, R.S. 1967. 'What is an educational process?' In R.S. Peters (ed.), *The Concept of Education* (1–23). London: Routledge and Kegan Paul.

Piattoeva, N. 2015. 'Elastic numbers: National examinations data as a technology of government.' *Journal of Education Policy*, 30 (3), 316–334.

Planning Commission, Government of India. 2009. Delhi Development Report. New Delhi: Academic Foundation.

Powell, A., Watson, J., Staley, P., Patrick, S., Horn, M., Fetzer, L. and Verma, S. 2015. 'Blending Learning: The Evolution of Online and Face-to-Face Education from 2008-2015.' *International association for K-12 online learning*. https://eric.ed.gov/?id=ED560788 Accessed 16 March 2022.

Praja Foundation report. 2019. State of Public (School) Education in Delhi. *Praja*. https://www.praja.org/praja_docs/praja_downloads/State%20of%20Public%20(School)%20Education%20March%202019.pdf Accessed 16 March 2022.

Prabhu, S. 2021. 'UP Polls: Arvind Kejriwal alleges Yogi govt 'copying' AAP's happiness curriculum project.' *Republic World*. https://www.republicworld.com/amp/elections/uttar-pradesh/up-polls-arvind-kejriwal-alleges-yogi-govt-copying-aaps-happiness-curriculum-project.html Accessed 16 March 2022.

Preskill, H. and Tzavaras Catsambas, T. 2006. *Reframing Evaluation Through Appreciative Inquiry*. Thousand Oaks, CA: Sage.

Press Trust of India. 2019. 'Delhi Govt issues notice to 151 schools for not having special educator.' *India Today*. https://www.indiatoday.in/education-today/news/story/delhi-govt-issues-notice-to-151-schools-for-not-having-special-educator-1593168-2019-08-29 Accessed 16 March 2022.

Priestley, M. and Biesta, G. (eds). 2013. *Reinventing the Curriculum: New trends in curriculum policy and practice*. A&C Black.

Priestley, M., Biesta, G.J.J., Philippou, S. and Robinson, S. 2015. 'The teacher and the curriculum: Exploring teacher agency.' *The SAGE Handbook of Curriculum, Pedagogy and Assessment*, 187–201.

Priyam, M. 2015. *Contested Politics of Educational Reform in India: Aligning opportunities with interests*. Oxford: Oxford University Press.

PROBE Team. 1999. *Public Report on Basic Education in India*. New Delhi: Oxford University Press.

PTI. 2020. 'From AAP's education master to Kejriwal's second-in-command – Manish Sisodia dons multiple hats.' *Outlook India*. https://timesofindia.indiatimes.com/city/delhi/from-aaps-education-master-to-kejriwals-second-in-command-manish-sisodia-dons-multiple-hats/articleshow/74160913.cms Accessed 21 April 2022.

PTI. April 2021. 'Entrepreneurship Mindset Curriculum helped students grow family biz during lockdown: Sisodia.' *Outlook India*. https://www.hindustantimes.com/education/news/entrepreneurship-curriculum-helped-students-grow-family-biz-in-lockdown-sisodia-101618123455783.html Accessed 21 April 2022.

Putnam, R. and Borko, H. 2000. 'What do new views of knowledge and thinking have to say about research on teacher learning?' *Educational Researcher*, 29 (1), 4e15.

Raghunath, P. 2020. 'Shiksha: my experiments as an education minister – book review.' *Learning Curve*, (6), 90–91.

Rajeshwari. 2020. 'The resurgence of Ed-Tech amid the coronavirus pandemic: Implications for an altered educational landscape.' *The New Leam*. https://www.thenewleam.com/2020/06/the-resurgence-of-ed-tech-amid-the-coronavirus-pandemic-implications-for-an-altered-educational-landscape/ Accessed 16 March 2022.

Ram, A. and Sharma, K.D. 1995. *National Policy on Education: An overview*. Delhi: Vikas Publishing House.

Ramachandran, V. 2005. 'Why School Teachers Are Demotivated and Disheartened.' *Economic and Political Weekly*, 40 (21), 2141–2144.

Ramachandran, V. 2018. '"The problem" are our children learning?' Seminar, 706.

Ramachandran, V. and Naorem, T. 2013. 'What it means to be a Dalit or tribal child in our schools: A synthesis of a six-state qualitative study.' *Economic and Political Weekly*, 43–52.

Ramachandran, V. and Pal, M. 2005. 'Teacher Motivation in India.' *Department for International Development Paper*. https://assets.publishing.service.gov.uk/media/57a08c5b40f0b64974001172/3888Teacher_motivation_India.pdf Accessed 16 March 2022.

Ramachandran, V., Bhattacharjea, S. and Sheshagiri, K. 2008. 'Primary School Teachers: the twist and turns of everyday practice.' Bangalore, New Delhi: Educational Resource Unit.

Ramberg, M.R. 2014. 'Teacher change in an era of neo-liberal policies: a neo-institutional analysis of teachers' perceptions of their professional change.' *European Educational Research Journal*, 13 (3), 360–379.

Rao, V. 2019. 'Blended Learning: A New Hybrid Teaching Methodology.' *Online Submission*, 3 (13).

Resch, K. and Schrittesser, I. 2021. 'Using the Service-Learning approach to bridge the gap between theory and practice in teacher education.' *International Journal of Inclusive Education*, 1–15.

Riddell, A.R. 1999. 'The need for a multidisciplinary framework for analysing educational reform in developing countries.' *International Journal of Educational Development*, 19 (3), 207–217.

The Right of Children to Free and Compulsory Education Act. (RTE Act). 2009. New Delhi: The Gazette of India.

Risbud, N. 2016. 'Delhi: City Profile – Poverty, Inequality and Violence in Urban India: Towards Inclusive Planning and Policies.' *Institute for Human Development*. https://idl-bnc-idrc.dspacedirect.org/bitstream/handle/10625/55690/IDL-55690.pdf Accessed 16 March 2022.

Robinson, N.R. 2012. 'Preservice music teachers' employment preferences: Consideration factors.' *Journal of Research in Music Education*, 60 (3), 294–309.

Robinson, N. and Gauri, V. 2010. 'Education, labor rights, and incentives: Contract teacher cases in the Indian courts.' *Policy Research Working Paper 5365*. World Bank.

Ross, M., Perkins, H., and Bodey, K. 2016. 'Academic motivation and information literacy self-efficacy: The importance of a simple desire to know.' *Library & Information Science Research*, 38 (1), 2–9.

Sachs, J. 2016. 'Teacher professionalism: Why are we still talking about it?' *Teachers and Teaching*, 22 (4), 413–425.

Sahoo, N. 2020. 'Here's the syllabus Kejriwal govt followed to change the fate of Delhi's public schools.' *The Print*. https://theprint.in/opinion/heres-thesyllabus-kejriwal-govt-followed-to-change-the-fate-of-delhis-public-schools/358777 Accessed 16 March 2022.

Sandhu, S. 2021. 'Teachers within neoliberal educational reforms: A case study of Delhi.' In *Building Teacher Quality in India: Examining policy frameworks and implementation outcomes*. Emerald Publishing Limited.

Sankar, D. 2007. 'Teacher's time on task: quantity and nature of task.' Paper presented at the conference on Quality Education for All in South Asia, New Delhi.

Sarfaraz, K. April 2021. 'Delhi schools shut, but no word yet on teachers' attendance.' *Hindustan Times*. https://www.hindustantimes.com/cities/delhi-news/delhi-schools-shut-but-no-word-yet-on-teachers-attendance-101618163668594.html Accessed 17 March 2022.

Sarangapani, P.M. 2010. 'Quality Concerns: national and extra-national dimensions.' *Contemporary Education Dialogue*, 7 (1), 41–57.

Sarangapani, P.M., Nawani, D., Latha, K., Banga, J. and Ullal, N. 2017. *Teacher Resource Centres in India: A sourcebook*. TISS. https://clix.tiss.edu/wp-content/uploads/2018/03/TEC-Sourcebook.pdf Accessed 17 March 2022.

Sargent, J. and Casey, A. 2021. 'Appreciative inquiry for physical education and sport pedagogy research: a methodological illustration through teachers' uses of digital technology.' *Sport, Education and Society*, 26 (1), 45–57.

Sarin, M.N. 2019. 'The Rights of Children to Free and Compulsory Education Act (RTE) in India: An exploration of its child centred policy.' PhD diss., University College London.

Sarkar, T. 2021. 'History as Patriotism: Lessons from India.' *Journal of Genocide Research*, 1–11.

Sarva Shiksha Abhiyaan. 2002. *Education for all: Guidelines of the Government of India*. New Delhi: Ministry of Human Resource Development (MHRD).

Sarva Shiksha Abhiyan. 2007. Inclusive Education in SSA. New Delhi: MHRD.

Saxena, S. 2013. 'Dilli ke Sarkaree Schoolon Kee Dasha: Ek Baangee' (in Hindi), *Shiksha Vimars*h, 15 (3), 37–42.

SCERT Delhi. 2018. *Happiness Curriculum, Grade 6-8*. New Delhi. SCERT and DoE.

Scott, J.T., and Armstrong, A.C. 2019. 'Disrupting the deficit discourse: Reframing metaphors for professional learning in the context of appreciative inquiry.' *Professional Development in Education*, 45 (1), 114–124.

Schweisfurth, M. 2015. 'Learner-centred pedagogy: Towards a post-2015 agenda for teaching and learning'. *International Journal of Educational Development*, 40, 259–266.

Scruggs, T.E. and Mastropieri, M.A. 1996. 'Teacher perceptions of mainstreaming/inclusion, 1958–1995: A research synthesis.' *Exceptional Children*, 63 (1), 59–74.

School Education Quality Index (SEQI). 2019. *Niti AAYOG*. https://www.niti.gov.in/sites/default/files/2019-09/seqi_document_0.pdf Accessed 17 March 2022.

Sen, A. and Dreze, J. 1995. 'Basic education as a political issue.' *Journal of Educational Planning and Administration*, 11 (1), 1–26.

Sengupta, M. 2012. 'Anna Hazare and the idea of Gandhi.' *The Journal of Asian Studies*, 71 (3), 593–601.

Sellar, S. 2015. 'Data infrastructure: A review of expanding accountability systems and large-scale assessments in education.' *Discourse: Studies in the Cultural Politics of Education*, 36 (5), 765–777.

Sellar, S. and Lingard, B. 2013. 'PISA and the expanding role of the OECD in global educational governance.' *PISA, power, and policy: The emergence of global educational governance*, 185–206.

Shah, P.J. and Veetil, V.P. 2006. *Private Education for the Poor in India*. Working Paper Series. Rochester, NY: SSRN.

Shahdeo, K. 2020. 'The Pathology of Online Education in a Hierarchical Society like India.' *The New Leam*. https://www.thenewleam.com/2020/06/the-pathology-of-online-education-in-a-hierarchical-society-like-india / [Page not found]

Sharma, A.K. 2020. 'Covid-19: Creating a paradigm shift in India's education system'. *The Economic Times*. https://economictimes.indiatimes.com/blogs/et-commentary/covid-19-creating-a-paradigm-shift-in-indias-education-system/ Accessed 17 March 2022.

Sharma, K. 2016. 'State and politicisation of education in India: A comparative study between NDA and UPA regime.' https://docplayer.net/64965625-State-and-politicisation-ofeducation-in-india-acomparative-study-between-nda-and-upa-regime-kangkana-sharma.html Accessed 17 March 2022.

Sharma, K. 2020. 'Peeping parents, sleeping students, bullying- online classes are a nightmare for teachers.' *The Print*. https://theprint.in/india/education/peeping-parents-sleeping-students-bullying-online-classes-are-a-nightmare-for-teachers/458522/ Accessed 17 March 2022.

Sharma, K. 2021. 'How govt portal Diksha with '3 cr hits/day' has become key tool for teachers during Covid.' *The Print*. https://theprint.in/india/education/how-govt-portal-diksha-with-3-cr-hits-day-has-become-key-tool-for-teachers-during-covid/591678/ Accessed 17 March 2022.

Sharma, M. 2018. 'Seeping deficit thinking assumptions maintain the neoliberal education agenda: Exploring three conceptual frameworks of deficit thinking in inner-city schools.' *Education and Urban Society*, 50 (2), 136–154.

Sharma, R.N. 2002. *Indian Education at the Crossroads*. Delhi: Shubhi Publications.

Sharma, R., Jain, A., Gupta, N., Garg, S., Batta, M., and Dhir, S.K. 2016. 'Impact of self-assessment by students on their learning.' *International Journal of Applied and Basic Medical Research*, 6 (3), 226.

Sherman, B. and Teemant, A. 2021. 'Agency, identity, power: An agentive triad model for teacher action.' *Educational Philosophy and Theory*, 1–25.

Shukla, P.D. 1988. *The New Education Policy*. Delhi: Sterling Publishers Private Ltd.

Siddarth, D., Shankar, R. and Pal, J. 2021. 'We do politics so we can change politics': communication strategies and practices in the Aam Aadmi Party's institutionalization process. *Information, Communication & Society*, 24 (10), 1–21.

Singal, N. 2006. 'Inclusive education in India: International concept, national interpretation.' *International Journal of Disability, Development and Education*, 53 (3), 351–369.

Singal, N. 2019. 'Challenges and opportunities in efforts towards inclusive education: reflections from India.' *International Journal of Inclusive Education*, 23 (7–8), 827–840.

Singal, N., Pedder, D., Malathy, D., Shanmugam, M., Manickavasagam, S. and Govindarasan, M. 2017. 'Insights from within activity based learning (ABL) classrooms in Tamil Nadu, India: Teachers perspectives and practices.' *International Journal of Educational Development*, 60 (C), 165–171.

Singal, N., Samson, M. and Sommerville, M. 2018. 'Educating Children with Disabilities in Government Schools in India: Classroom Based Insights.' Presentation made at Re-mapping Global Education, the Comparative and International Education Society annual conference, Mexico City, March 25–29.

Singh, A.K., Rind, I.A. and Sabur, Z. 2020. 'Continuous Professional Development of School Teachers: Experiences of Bangladesh, India, and Pakistan.' *Handbook of Education Systems in South Asia*, 1–27.

Singh, L. and Shakir, M. 2019. 'Teacher education: Issues and concerns in current scenario.' *International Journal of Research and Analytical Reviews*, 6 (2), 1082–1091.

Singh, R. and Sarkar, S. 2012. *Teaching Quality Counts: How student outcomes relate to quality of teaching in private and public schools in India*. Young Lives.

The Siasat Daily. 2021. 'AAP promises to provide free school education in Punjab.' *The Siasat Delhi*. https://www.siasat.com/aap-promises-to-provide-free-school-education-in-punjab-2234862/amp/ Accessed 17 March 2022.

Swamy, V.K. 2021. '10 NGOs rejuvenating education in India.' *Give India*. https://www.giveindia.org/blog/top-10-education-ngos-rejuvenating-education-in-india/ Accessed 17 March 2022.

Skrtic, T.M. 1991. *Behind Special Education: A critical analysis of professional culture and school organization*. Denver, CO: Love Publishing Company.

Smail, A. 2014. 'Rediscovering the teacher within Indian child-centred pedagogy: implications for the global Child-Centred Approach.' *Compare: A Journal of Comparative and International Education*, 44 (4), 613–633.

Soundararaj, G. 2019. 'Teacher perspectives on pedagogical changes: an ethnographic study in the rural primary schools of Tamil Nadu, India.' https://jyx.jyu.fi/handle/123456789/64266 Accessed 17 March 2022.

Spencer, C. 2007. 'Qualitative data analysis with NVivo.' *Journal of Emergency Primary Health Care*, 5 (3), 1–2.

Srinivasan, M. 2021. Fostering future entrepreneurs. *The Hindu*. https://www.thehindu.com/education/fostering-future-entrepreneurs/article34178962.ece Accessed 17 March 2022.

Sriprakash, A. 2010. 'Child centred education and the promise of democratic learning: Pedagogic message in rural Indian primary schools.' *International Journal of Educational Development*, 30 (3), 297–304.

Sriram, J. 2015. 'AAP expels Yogendra Yadav, Prashant Bhushan.' *The Hindu*. https://www.thehindu.com/news/cities/Delhi/aap-expels-four-rebel-leaders/article7123615.ece Accessed 17 March 2022.

Staker, H. and Horn, M. 2012. 'Classifying K-12 blended learning.' *Innosight Institute*. http://192.248.16.117:8080/research/bitstream/70130/5105/1/BLENDED_LEARNING_AND_FEATURES_OF_THE_USE_OF_THE_RO.pdf Accessed 17 March 2022.

Straubhaar, R. and Friedrich, D. 2015. 'Theorizing and documenting the spread of Teach For All and its impact on global education reform.' https://digital.library.txstate.edu/handle/10877/8338 Accessed 17 March 2022.

Subrahmaniam, F.V. 2015. 'Reaching for the stars: The incredible rise of Arvind Kejriwal.' *The Hindu Centre for Politics and Public Policy*, 25.

Subramanian, V.K. 2018. 'From Government to Governance: Teach for India and New Networks of Reform in School Education.' *Contemporary Education Dialogue*, 15 (1), 21–50.

Swaroop, S. 2001. 'Inclusion and beyond.' Paper presented at the North South Dialogue on Inclusive Education. Mumbai.

Tabulawa, R. 1998. 'Teachers' perspectives on classroom practice in Botswana: Implications for pedagogical change.' *International Journal of Qualitative Studies in Education*, 11(2), 249–268.

Taguchi, H.L. 2007. 'Deconstructing and transgressing the theory: Practice dichotomy in early childhood education.' *Educational Philosophy and Theory*, 39 (3), 275–290.

Talreja, V. and Bhat, S. 2020. 'The 4 Pillars of Delhi's School Education.' *The Bastion*. https://the bastion.co.in/politics-and/the-4-pillars-of-delhis-school-education-reforms/ Accessed 17 March 2022.

Tarmo, A. 2018. *Science Teachers' Beliefs and Teaching Practices in Tanzanian Secondary Schools*. PhD diss. University of Sussex.

Teacher Development Coordinator Handbook LIC-2. 2017. *Look for Understanding and Response*. State Council of Educational Research and Training.

Teacher Development Coordinator Handbook LIC-3. 2018. *Lesson Planning*. State Council of Educational Research and Training.

Teacher Development Coordinator Handbook LIC-4. 2018. *Teaching Learning Strategies*. State Council of Educational Research and Training.

Thamarasseri, I. 2008. *Education in the Emerging Indian Society*. New Delhi: Kanishka Publishers.

Tilak, J.B. 2004. 'Public subsidies in education in India.' *Economic and Political Weekly*, 343–359.

Tilak, J. 2016. 'Rejuvenation of Government Schools in India.' National University of Educational Planning and Administration. https://www.researchgate.net/publication/305995470_Rejuvenation_of_Government_SchoolsinIndia Accessed 17 March 2022.

Tilak, J.B. 2018. 'Education poverty in India.' In *Education and Development in India* (87–162). Singapore: Palgrave Macmillan.

The Times of India. 2019. 'Delhi private schools improve student count, corporations lag.' *Times of India*. http://timesofindia.indiatimes.com/articleshow/70595376.cms?utm_source=conten tofinterest&utm_medium=text&utm_campaign=cppst Accessed 17 March 2022.

Tiwari, A., Das, A. and Sharma, M. 2015. 'Inclusive education a "rhetoric" or "reality"? Teachers' perspectives and beliefs.' *Teaching and Teacher Education*, 52, 128–136.

Tiwary, M.K., Kumāra, S. and Mishra, A.K. (eds). 2017. *Dynamics of Inclusive Classroom: Social diversity, inequality and school education in India*. Orient Blackswan.

Tooley, J. and Dixon, P. 2003. *Private Schools for the Poor: A case study from India* (1–27). Reading: CfBt.

Tooley, J. and Dixon, P. 2006. '"De Facto" Privatization of Education and the Poor: Implications of a Study from Sub-Saharan Africa and India.' *Compare: A Journal of Comparative & International Education*, 36 (4): 443–462.

Tooley, J., Dixon, P., Shamsan, Y. and Schagen, I. 2010. 'The relative quality and cost-effectiveness of private and public schools for low-income families: A case study in a developing country.' *School Effectiveness and School Improvement*, 21 (2), 117–144.

Tyagi, A. 2017. 'Can AAP Claim Credit for Delhi Govt Schools Outperforming Private?' *The Quint*. https://www.thequint.com/voices/blogs/delhi-public-school-exam-results-better-than-priv ate Accessed 17 March 2022.

UNESCO. 1994. 'The Salamanca Statement and framework for action on special needs education.' Adopted by the World Conference on Special Needs Education; Access and Quality. Salamanca, Spain, 7–10 June. Unesco.

UNESCO. 2008. 'The Global Monitoring Report: Regional overview of South and West Asia.' http://www.ungei.org/154743e.pdf [Page not found]

UNESCO. 2010. 'Education for all, global monitoring report.' https://unesdoc.unesco.org/ark:/48223/pf0000186525 Accessed 17 March 2022.

UNESCO. 2014. 'Joint Proposal of the EFA Steering Committee on Education Post 2015.' Paris: Education for All Steering Committee.

UNESCO. 2015. 'Education 2030. Incheon Declaration and Framework for Action.' Paris: UNESCO.

UNESCO. 2020. 'Global Education Monitoring Report 2020. Inclusion and Education: All means all.'

UNESCO MGIEP. (n.d.). 'Govt of Delhi organises workshop for Special Educators in Screening Different Learners.' UNESCO. https://mgiep.unesco.org/article/govt-of-delhi-organises-workshop-for-special-educators-in-screening-different-learners Accessed 17 March 2022.

United Nations. 2006. *United Nations Convention on the Rights of Persons with Disabilities.* www.un.org/development/desa/disabilities/convention-on-the-rights-of-persons-with-disabilities.html Accessed 17 March 2022.

United Nations. 2015. 'Transforming Our World: The 2030 agenda for sustainable development'. New York: United Nations. https://sustainabledevelopment.un.org/post2015/transformingourworld Accessed 17 March 2022.

Unterhalter, E. 2019. 'The many meanings of quality education: Politics of targets and indicators in SDG 4.' *Global Policy*, 10, 39–51.

van der Haar, D. and Hosking, D.M. 2004. 'Evaluating appreciative inquiry: A relational constructionist perspective.' *Human Relations,* 57 (8), 1017–1036.

Vasavi, A.R. 2019. 'School differentiation in India reinforces social inequalities.' In *The India Forum* (Vol. 3).

Vaughan, N. 2014. 'Student engagement and blended learning: Making the assessment connection.' *Education Sciences*, 4 (4), 247–264.

Venkatanarayanan, S. 2015. 'Economic liberalization in 1991 and its impact on elementary education in India.' *SAGE Open*, 5 (2).

Verma, P. 2020. 'Covid-19 impact: Ed-tech companies reap dividend as school, universities go online.' *The Economic Times.* https://economictimes.indiatimes.com/industry/services/education/ed-tech-cos-reap-dividend-as-schools-univs-go-online/articleshow/74782879.cms?from=mdr Accessed 17 March 2022.

Verma, R. and Gupta, P. 2020. 'We analysed BJP voters who voted AAP in Delhi but Modi in Lok Sabha. This is what we found.' *ThePrint.* https://theprint.in/opinion/we-analysed-bjp-voters-who-voted-aap-in-delhi-modi-in-lok-sabha/360480/ Accessed 17 March 2022.

Wadia, L.C. 2020. 'Online school education in India during and beyond the pandemic.' *Observer Research Foundation.* https://www.orfonline.org/expert-speak/online-school-education-india-during-beyond-pandemic-69317/ Accessed 17 March 2022.

Wermke, W. and Höstfält, G. 2014. 'Contextualizing teacher autonomy in time and space: A model for comparing various forms of governing the teaching profession.' *Journal of Curriculum Studies*, 46 (1), 58–80.

Wermke, W. and Forsberg, E. 2017. 'The changing nature of autonomy: Transformations of the late Swedish teaching profession.' *Scandinavian Journal of Educational Research*, 61 (2), 155–168.

Wermke, W., Olason Rick, S. and Salokangas, M. 2019. 'Decision-making and control: Perceived autonomy of teachers in Germany and Sweden.' *Journal of Curriculum Studies*, 51 (3), 306–325.

Wheatley, K. F. 2002. 'The potential benefits of teacher efficacy doubts for educational reform.' *Teaching and Teacher Education*, 18 (1), 5–22.

Williamson, B. 2020. 'New pandemic edtech power networks.' *Code Acts in Education.* https://codeactsineducation.wordpress.com/2020/04/01/new-pandemic-edtech-power-networks/ Accessed 17 March 2022.

Williamson, B. and Piattoeva, N. 2019. 'Objectivity as standardization in data-scientific education policy, technology and governance.' *Learning, Media and Technology*, 44 (1), 64–76.

Williamson, B., Eynon, R. and Potter, J. 2020. 'Pandemic politics, pedagogies and practices: digital technologies and distance education during the coronavirus emergency.' *Learning, Media and Technology*, 45 (2), 107–114.

Woelfel, J. and Haller, A.O. 1971. 'Significant others, the self-reflexive act and the attitude formation process.' *American Sociological Review*, 74–87.

Wolfenden, F. 2015. 'TESS-India OER: Collaborative practices to improve teacher education.' *Indian Journal of Teacher Education*, 01 (03), 33–48.

Wood, A., Nusser, T., Di Folco, M., Tatlow, H., Simon-Kumar, N., Phillips, T. and Buklijas, T. 2021. 'Online education for schoolchildren during Covid-19: a scan of policies and initiatives around the world.' *Covid and Society.* https://covidandsociety.com/online-education-schoolchildren-covid-19-scan-policies-initiatives-around-world/ Accessed 17 March 2022.

Woodhead, M., Frost, M. and James, Z. 2013. 'Does growth in private schooling contribute to Education for All? Evidence from a longitudinal, two cohort study in Andhra Pradesh, India.' *International Journal of Educational Development*, 33 (1), 65–73.

Woods, P. 1979. *Divided School.* London: Routledge.

World Bank. 2018. *Learning to Realize Education's Promise. World Development Report*. Washington DC: World Bank

World Education Forum. 2015. *Education 2030. Incheon Declaration and Framework for Action*. Paris: UNESCO

Yadav, S.K. 2012. 'Impact of in-service teacher training on classroom transaction. SSA INSET packages in States: An assessment.' New Delhi: NCERT.

Yagnamurthy, S. 2017. 'Continuous and comprehensive evaluation (CCE): policy and practice at the national level.' *The Curriculum Journal*, 28 (3), 421–441.

Yan, Y. 2019. 'Governance of government middle schools in Beijing and Delhi: Supportive accountability, incentives and capacity.' PhD diss. National University of Singapore.

Yan, Y. 2020. 'Governance of government middle schools in Beijing and Delhi: Teacher training, career advancement and stakeholder communication.'

Yeatman, A. 2014. *Postmodern Revisionings of the Political*. London: Routledge.

Index

virtual schools, 157
Vishwas, 51
vocational education, 21, 40, 42, 91, 102

water, 7, 11, 12, 28, 34, 49
weak students, 25, 35, 51, 123–7, 132
WebEx, 141
West Bengal, 34, 113, 161 n.7
WhatsApp, 141, 145, 152
WiFi, 12, 139
women, 28, 121–3, 165
    enrolment/retention, 34

household labour, 122
    public transport, safety on, 11, 12
World Bank, 4, 24, 38
World Education Forum, 4, 24
World Happiness Report, 50
writing, 125

YUKTI, 142, 161 n.5

zero-rejection policy, 109
Zoom, 16, 17, 141, 149, 150, 151, 152

Lightning Source UK Ltd.
Milton Keynes UK
UKHW021756300922
409653UK00002B/9

9 781800 081390